The Statebuilder's Dilemma

The Statebuilder's Dilemma

On the Limits of Foreign Intervention

David A. Lake

Cornell University Press
Ithaca and London

First published 2016 by Cornell University Press

First printing, Cornell Paperbacks, 2016

Printed in the United States of America

Library of Congress Cataloging-in-Publication Data

Names: Lake, David A., 1956– author.
Title: The statebuilder's dilemma : on the limits of foreign intervention / David A. Lake.
Description: Ithaca ; London : Cornell University Press, 2016. | ©2016 | Includes bibliographical references and index.
Identifiers: LCCN 2016003464 | ISBN 9781501700309 (cloth : alk. paper) | ISBN 9781501704468 (paperback)
Subjects: LCSH: Nation-building. | International relations. | Iraq—Politics and government—2003– | Somalia—Politics and government—1960–1991. | Somalia—Politics and government—1991– | United States—Foreign relations—21st century.
Classification: LCC JZ6300 .L355 2016 | DDC 327.1/17—dc23
LC record available at http://lccn.loc.gov/2016003464

Cloth printing   10 9 8 7 6 5 4 3 2 1

Paperback printing   10 9 8 7 6 5 4 3 2 1

To my students,
from whom I have learned much

Contents

Preface

This is my second book prompted by the Iraq War. Watching my country waste trillions of dollars and throw away the lives of thousands of its young men and women in uniform on an unnecessary and ultimately fruitless war was intellectually and emotionally searing. Opposed by most of the international community and many of our otherwise stalwart allies, this ill-conceived war greatly undermined the international authority of the United States that has sustained the Pax Americana for over seven decades. The occupation that followed was based on hubris and naïve hopes. In turn, it failed to build a new state that can defend its borders, police its society, and ensure a modicum of political stability. Rather than promote a shining example of democracy in action in the Middle East, the United States left a house of cards that collapsed in the first wind. These mistakes were, at best, criminally stupid, if not criminal. We, as a people, are better than this. Yet no one has been prosecuted nor, indeed, have any systemic reforms of the policymaking process been undertaken in the years since the war began. With many ungoverned spaces in the world today, and persistent fears of transnational terrorism, we are poised to repeat the mistakes of the past.

Both my book *Hierarchy in International Relations* (2009) and now this one have been written in the hope that we might avoid similar errors of ignorance and judgment. Though prompted by the Iraq War, both go beyond that conflict to embed the problems of sustaining authority and building states into broader theories of international relations. The ultimate aim is to understand better world politics, not just the war and its consequences. That the dissipating of authority and the statebuilder's dilemma explored here are not unique to the United States does not excuse our leaders. Choices matter, even if the range is sometimes more limited than we might desire. Explaining why mistakes are made is the first and necessary step toward avoiding them in the future.

The lessons of this book are admittedly pessimistic. Statebuilding rests on a fundamental dilemma that cannot be obviated—it is, in fact, a true dilemma. In various presentations I have made over the past several years, nearly every audience has through its questions searched for some path to statebuilding success. Unfortunately, they look in vain, as will readers of this book. At best, the international community or its great powers can create incentives for factions and political entrepreneurs in failed states to build new states on their own. But, for reasons explained here, we cannot do it for them, however much we might want to speed them on their way. This is an unhappy truth, but a truth that we must face.

The Statebuilder's Dilemma

Introduction

Statebuilding remains the largest social project of the modern world. In Europe, North America, East Asia, and other regions where states are now generally regarded as consolidated, statebuilding was an organic, incremental, and evolutionary process that unfolded over centuries. Although propelled by competition with other political units, statebuilding was historically a largely internal development.[1] Today, in regions where unconsolidated states predominate, current practice reveals great faith in externally led social engineering, reflected in efforts by the international community and individual states to rebuild failed states. Yet, as in the past, there is no state-in-a-box that can be designed abroad and shipped to a foreign, often war-torn land for assembly with easy-to-follow instructions printed in multiple languages. After three decades of greatly increased international statebuilding activity, this much is obvious. With expectations now tempered by experience, there is no doubt that the process is difficult, demanding, dangerous, and, unfortunately, prone to failure.

The central task of all statebuilding is to create a state that is regarded as legitimate by the people over whom it exercises authority.[2] This is a necessary condition for stable, effective governance over the long run. In recent decades, statebuilders have gained new appreciation of the critical importance of legitimacy and have elevated this goal in their planning. A key problem in all international statebuilding attempts, however, is that states sufficiently motivated to bear the costs of building a state in some distant land are likely to

---

1. On statebuilding in Europe, see Tilly 1990; Downing 1992; Spruyt 1994; Ertman 1997. On statebuilding in modern Africa, see Herbst 2000; Boone 2003, 2014.
2. Unless otherwise noted, "statebuilding" throughout this text refers to international or external statebuilding, in which at least one other state intervenes in the domestic politics of a target state with the intention of improving internal governance. This is explained more fully below.

have interests in the future policies of that country, and will therefore seek to promote leaders who share or are at least sympathetic to their interests and willing to implement their preferred policies. Except in rare cases where the policy preferences of the statebuilder and the population of the country whose state is to be built coincide, promoting a leader "loyal" to the statebuilder undermines that leader's legitimacy at home. This trade-off between legitimacy and loyalty is the statebuilder's dilemma. The greater the interests of the statebuilder in the target state, the more likely it is to intervene; the greater the costs it is willing to bear, the more likely it is to install a loyal leader, and the less likely that leader will be to govern legitimately. Ironically, as seen in the case of the United States in Iraq since 2003, the greater the interests of the statebuilder in the target country, the less likely statebuilding is to succeed in building a legitimate state that can survive on its own into the indefinite future.

The Argument in Brief

Ungoverned spaces are, today, one of the most important threats to international order.[3] In early 2015 alone, Boko Haram, originating in the northeast periphery of Nigeria, wrought havoc not only at home but also in neighboring Chad and Niger. Founded in Somalia, al-Shabab carried out major attacks in Kenya, including one in which 147 college students were killed. Forged in the chaos of the Syrian civil war, the Islamic State of Iraq and Syria (ISIS) not only conquered up to one-third of neighboring Iraq but also recruited affiliates in Algeria, Egypt, Jordan, Libya, Pakistan, the Philippines, and possibly the West Bank and Gaza.[4] Operating out of several failed states, especially Yemen, al-Qaeda remains a potent force. On a single day in 2015, June 26, al-Shabab attacked a base of African Union peacekeepers in Somalia, killing up to fifty soldiers, and ISIS or ISIS-inspired terrorists destroyed a chemical plant in France, decapitating one person in the process; launched a suicide bombing in Kuwait that killed twenty-seven worshippers at a mosque; and killed thirty-eight tourists at a beach resort in Tunisia.

Not only do insurgent groups hiding within failed states inflict enormous damage on local populations and fuel further chaos but they also pose significant existential threats to states in North America, Europe, and elsewhere around the globe. Attracted by extremist ideologies, disaffected citizens may travel abroad for training, only to return home to carry out atrocities, as in the *Charlie Hebdo* and November 2015 attacks in Paris. "Lone-wolf" terrorists, propelled by extremist messages from abroad, may attack in the name of ji-

3. On ungoverned spaces, see Clunan and Trinkunas 2010. For more skeptical views of the importance of ungoverned spaces, see Patrick 2006, 2007; Mazarr 2014.
4. ISIS is also known as the Islamic State of Iraq and the Levant (ISIL) or, simply, the Islamic State (IS). On ISIS affiliates, see Moore 2015. For a depiction of ISIS affiliates and attacks, see Yourish, Giratikanon, and Watkins 2015.

had, as suspected in the Boston Marathon bombing in April 2013 and the attack in San Bernardino, California in 2015 in which fourteen died and twenty-one were injured. Groups may also attack the "far enemy" that supports their repressive states at home, expanding conflicts far beyond their original borders.[5]

The threat from individuals and groups hiding in the interstices of the international system remains real. Whether we like it or not, states and the international community more generally are forced to respond to these attacks. In what is an essentially conservative response that aims to sustain the decentralized system of violence control embedded in autonomous sovereign states, a key strategy has been to try to build more capable states that can govern their own territories effectively. Statebuilding has emerged as the central pillar of a global counterinsurgency strategy.

Yet statebuilding fails more often than it succeeds.[6] Haiti, Rwanda, Somalia, and now Afghanistan and Iraq are all generally regarded not only as failed states but as statebuilding failures.[7] The list could easily be extended. In each of these post–Cold War interventions, externally authorized statebuilders, typically the United Nations or a "coalition of the willing" led by the United States, have sought to rehabilitate a state that has fallen into anarchy and the flames of communal violence. In only a handful of recent cases, arguably Cambodia, East Timor, and possibly Liberia, has statebuilding succeeded in creating a legitimate government, but even in these instances success was short-lived. Afghanistan remains a statebuilding work in progress, though with dubious prospects of long-term success. Even historically, only West Germany and Japan appear to be success stories—"shadow" cases against which more recent efforts are judged in this book.[8] The record of statebuilding is grim and offers few reasons for optimism.

Any individual statebuilding effort can fail for a variety of reasons. Good strategies may be poorly implemented, a common refrain from optimists who remain wedded to contemporary theories and practices of statebuilding. Strategies themselves may be flawed, as was the case in many liberal statebuilding attempts in the post–Cold War period.[9] Underlying all failures, however, is the statebuilder's dilemma. States willing to bear the high costs of major statebuilding efforts always attempt to install leaders who share their interests rather than those of the citizens of the target states. In today's era, where the policy preferences of those willing to build states for others and those in need of new states diverge substantially, emplacing loyal leaders in power fatally undermines the legitimacy of the new state.

5. Gerges 2009.
6. For a primer on statebuilding, see Sisk 2013. For other literature reviews with an emphasis on evaluation, see Heathershaw and Lambach 2008; Whaites 2008; Tschirgi 2010; Marquette and Beswick 2011; Gravingholt, Leininger, and von Haldenwang 2012.
7. See P. Miller 2013, 16.
8. Dobbins, McGinn, et al. 2003.
9. Paris 2004.

To understand why statebuilding so often fails, it is important to explain why states themselves collapse. States fail for a reason—or perhaps reasons. Each failure is, of course, unique. To paraphrase Leo Tolstoy, every unhappy state is unhappy in its own way.[10] But states that fail today often do so because they are faced with societies that are deeply and perhaps irretrievably fractured. In some, state predation under the hand of an economic elite causes grave inequality and deep rifts in society. As in many states disrupted by the Arab Spring, exploited classes and groups rise up in revolt to build a better future, though continuing instability is more often the result. On this path to failure, the state itself is a partisan and wars against its own people. In other cases, traditional prestate social formations such as clans, tribes, or sectarian groups parallel, challenge, and ultimately undermine the state.[11] Here, the state is not necessarily weak, but society is "too strong" and prevents political consolidation. Political entrepreneurs can then assemble the kindling of past resentments and, in the shadow of state weakness, set the spark of violence. Once the fire takes hold, even cosmopolitan individuals who cannot be protected by the state are forced into their traditional communal groupings for safety against the flames. The most toxic cases are where horizontal class cleavages overlap with vertical communal cleavages to form a volatile mix that is easily ignited. In deeply fractured societies, it is all too easy to burn down the house.

Following Max Weber, states are "compulsory organizations" that successfully uphold "the claim to be a monopoly of the legitimate use of physical force" within a given territory.[12] Failed states lose their monopoly and legitimacy as they are pulled apart by societal conflicts. Statebuilding is a process of restoring—or in some instances creating for the first time—that monopoly of violence and especially its legitimacy. Yet legitimacy is neither something that is conferred by the international community on a state nor a principle that inheres in particular institutions that can be exported to fragmented societies. Rather, legitimacy can be conferred on a state only by its own people. Statebuilding is not just a matter of getting the institutions "right," as I explain below, but a process of social transformation that, to be successful, must realign the internal cleavages that caused the state to fail in the first place and then, paradoxically, were typically deepened by the conflict itself.

The most effective role for a statebuilder is as a catalyst for social order. In the political chaos of a failed state, prior authority has evaporated, and groups threaten to cycle between different sets of institutions and laws and, thus, produce continuing instability. Usually bringing greater coercive force to bear than any of the parties in the failed state, the statebuilder can declare that a particular social order with a specific set of rules and institutions will be the "law of the land" now and into the future. If that declaration is sufficiently

10. Tolstoy, *Anna Karenina*, first line (any edition).
11. Weiner 2013.
12. Weber 1978, 54, 56.

credible, social groups will accommodate the new social order, become vested in the institutions, and thus legitimate the state. This is the promise of state-building.

The statebuilder's dilemma, in turn, is rooted in the modern concept of sovereignty. First and foremost, the international system is a decentralized mechanism for controlling private violence. As a collection of sovereign polities, states are responsible for controlling the projection of force across their borders; in turn, any violence emanating from within their territories is assumed to be purposeful or permitted by the state. If one state is, thus, the target of violence originating from another, the second state is held responsible, and the violence is considered an act of war, subject to retaliation. In this way, Westphalian sovereignty limits interstate violence and inhibits trans-border conflicts potentially started by extremists within societies from escalating. Through statebuilding, in turn, the international community seeks to bolster the principle of sovereignty on which the system is based and to extend and strengthen it in those areas where it is fragile. Yet statebuilding also fundamentally challenges the logic of Westphalia. To shore up states so that they can fulfill their responsibilities to govern otherwise ungoverned spaces, other states must intervene directly in the internal affairs of failed states. To save the principle of sovereignty, paradoxically, states must break that very same principle.

In seeking to resolve this paradox, the international community limits and constrains statebuilding efforts in ways that render commitments noncredible, undermining the catalytic role that statebuilders might otherwise play. Though sovereignty in practice is quite permissive, statebuilders and the international community both seek to limit interventions into the internal affairs of other states. On the one hand, today, in our postcolonial world, statebuilders do not want to assume permanent responsibility for governing failed states. To limit their responsibility, statebuilders seek to return the failed state to sovereignty as quickly as possible, as the United States certainly intended in the case of Iraq after 2003. On the other hand, the international community (and especially other weak states) also seeks to bolster the principle of sovereignty as a bulwark against external meddling into the domestic politics of its members. Together, constrained by the principle of sovereignty, statebuilders arrive on the scene with limited mandates, limited powers, and limited time. Under severe restrictions, statebuilders do not seek and are not authorized to transform society but only to restore peace and security in ways that do not infringe on the ultimate authority of the failed state. Statebuilders have an incentive, therefore, to create a system of *indirect* rule, and to do so as quickly as possible.

Second, and equally important, sovereignty does not permit, and the system of states has not developed, any higher authorities with responsibility for rebuilding failed states. The decentralized system of violence control is itself dependent on the willingness of individual states to support their weakest members. Even when approved by some multilateral body, statebuilding remains a purely voluntary undertaking by coalitions of the willing. Since statebuilding can be enormously costly, and good governance creates positive externalities that encourage free riding, only states with interests in the failed state are likely to volunteer for this service. This is the root of the statebuilder's dilemma. Although statebuilders can be catalysts for social order, only self-interested states take on this responsibility. The greater their interests in a failed state, the more likely they are to support a loyal leader who, as a result, is likely to lack legitimacy.

States have sought to manage the statebuilder's dilemma in different ways at different times. As practiced by many states prior to 1990 and exemplified by the role of the United States in Central America in the early twentieth century, some statebuilders evince little concern for the legitimacy of the states they support. Even in their informal empires, statebuilders privileged their own interests and policies by supporting loyal leaders willing to do their bidding.[13] For the United States, this led to support for pro-American autocratic and even despotic rulers, including Rafael Leonidas Trujillo in the Dominican Republic (1930–1961), Anastasio Somoza Garcia and his sons in Nicaragua (1937–1979, though with several intermissions), and François and Jean-Claude Duvalier in Haiti (1957–1986).[14] The cost of this support, however, was that the political opposition inevitably became anti-American. This pattern of informal empire through the promotion of loyal leaders, now often recoded as instances of statebuilding, has been quite common.[15]

Current practice increasingly recognizes the importance of building legitimate states but in doing so makes the statebuilder's dilemma more acute. Liberal statebuilding, beginning with the end of the Cold War, elevated the goal of building legitimate states and premised strategy on the belief that democracy and free markets would be sufficient to legitimate a government in the eyes of its people. Pursued in both Iraq, as described in chapter 4, and Somalia, discussed in chapter 5, this assumption turned out to be tragically wrong and was eventually abandoned, although not before shocking levels of human suffering resulted. Replacing liberal theory in Iraq and Afghanistan after 2007, a new theory of statebuilding based on counterinsurgency warfare (COIN) also highlights the need for state legitimacy. Rather than relying on popular participation to legitimate the state, COIN focuses on providing security and other public goods to win the "hearts and minds" of the people. In my view, and as experience in Iraq and Afghanistan suggests, this is an important step in the right direction, though it does not resolve the fundamental dilemma.

Regardless of strategy, the statebuilder's dilemma is a true dilemma. The trade-off between the legitimacy and loyalty of newly installed leaders cannot be obviated simply by reforms or improved practice. Rather, the dilemma is

---

13. On informal empire, see Doyle 1986; Lake 2013b.
14. Kinzer 2006; Loveman 2010.
15. See Pei, Amin, and Garz 2006; P. Miller 2013.

inherent in all external statebuilding and cannot be wished away. The larger the statebuilding effort required, the more acute the dilemma becomes. States are not altruists. They do not engage in statebuilding haphazardly or from the goodness of their hearts. Especially in the industrialized democracies most capable of the effort today, voters demand a return on the blood and treasure expended. The greater the costs of statebuilding, therefore, the more the statebuilder will insist on the installation of a leader likely to be loyal to its interests—as defined by its own constituents.

The statebuilder's dilemma, in turn, implies that international statebuilding efforts will tend to fail to build legitimate states. Deeply divided societies that lack effective legal institutions must overcome the cleavages which have often been exacerbated by state breakdown and violence. In this unpropitious setting, venal, self-interested politicians must build new support coalitions to sustain themselves in office. Those anointed by the statebuilder and who share its interests will find this task proportionately harder than "nationalist" politicians closer to the median citizen in their societies. Faced with limited mandates and time, statebuilders will channel support and resources to their selected leader, who will then divert those resources to his own narrow political coalition with the acquiescence if not the active support of the statebuilder.[16] Ruling with a narrow base of support, in turn, the leader will be less legitimate and may be less effective in sustaining himself in office.[17] The great irony of the dilemma is that, however much statebuilders may worry about threats from ungoverned spaces or claim to desire legitimacy for the states they seek to construct, they continue to undermine their own efforts by the offsetting desire to ensure that loyal leaders are in power. The result is states that remain fragile and at risk of failure but that pursue policies favored by the statebuilders. In short, through the statebuilder's dilemma, statebuilding as the reconstitution of the *legitimate* monopoly of violence will likely fail, the more so as the interests of the statebuilder and the median member of the target society diverge.

This prediction, however pessimistic, is borne out by case studies of Somalia and Iraq, bookends to the post–Cold War era of statebuilding. In Somalia, the United Nations and the United States entered under nearly ideal conditions as, first, humanitarians and, then, relatively neutral statebuilders. Attempting to rebuild the country according to liberal statebuilding theory, however, the United Nations soon provoked the opposition of the local warlords, who attacked the United States and led it to withdraw—reflecting the near-truism that states without strong interests in the failed state will refuse to bear high costs. Subsequent interventions in Somalia by regional states, principally

16. For similar conclusions that follow from the strategic incentives of external powers and, especially, local elites, see Barnett and Zurcher 2009; Barnett, Fang, and Zurcher 2014. For a related approach focusing on foreign aid, see Girod 2015. For a similar argument on U.S.–client state relations in the Middle East, see Jamal 2012.

17. For suggestive empirical evidence, see Lake and Fariss 2014; Pickering and Kisangani 2014.

Ethiopia, have been directed at preventing an irredentist regime from coming to power. In this case, Ethiopia's efforts to secure its borders have produced only continuing anarchy and violence. In Iraq, the United States implemented liberal statebuilding, switched to COIN, and throughout backed a relatively loyal leader—Prime Minister Nouri al-Maliki—who then undermined statebuilding efforts by his sectarian behavior. In both cases, statebuilding failed to create legitimacy for reasons entirely predictable given the statebuilder's dilemma.

Ultimately, statebuilding must be an indigenous process. The ability of foreign powers to build states is limited. External statebuilding that ignores legitimacy can still produce autocratic, repressive, and, most important, illegitimate states—much as the United States did in Central America in the twentieth century. This is also the implicit rationale behind the argument for "good enough" governance in fragile states, discussed in the conclusion.[18] If the international community cannot have it all, at least some rule, no matter how fragile and illegitimate, may be better than none at all. The dilemma can also be moderated at the margin by multilateral statebuilding efforts, though under current international institutions it can never be eliminated entirely.

Legitimate states can be built best by creating international incentives for societies to settle their internal conflicts and construct effective governance structures on their own. The most powerful incentives available to the industrialized democracies—the states now most capable and likely to engage in external statebuilding—are the promise of integration into the Western political and economic order constructed since 1945. Such integration has the potential to reshape the domestic politics of failed states in directions more compatible with the interests of would-be statebuilders, alleviating somewhat the trade-off between legitimacy and loyalty. This is, however, a strategy likely to pay dividends only over the long term. In the short run, statebuilders will still be trapped by the statebuilder's dilemma.

Defining Success

Any evaluation of statebuilding must begin from a conception of success—or at least progress—and failure. Many assessments leave this standard implicit. Somewhat more pernicious, advocates of a particular theory of statebuilding often measure success by the theory itself. Liberals, for instance, believe that democracy and free markets are necessary to create a legitimate state, and then measure success by the degree of democracy and the extent to which markets are competitive.[19] If the theory is flawed, as I shall argue that liberalism and

18. Krasner 2013.
19. This is common, though often implicit, in the institutionalist literature discussed below. For a more explicit measure of success in terms of democracy, see P. Miller 2013, 227–234.

others are, then the achieving of goals or benchmarks implied by the approach will not necessarily indicate real progress.

As noted above and explained in chapter 1, the state is an organization with a monopoly on the legitimate use of physical force in a given territory. The problem of failed states today, in turn, is the ungoverned spaces that create hiding places for transnational insurgents, terrorists, criminals, and those who would challenge the global order. Statebuilding is, then, a process of consolidating the monopoly of legitimate force in all corners of a country's territorially defined realm. A successful state is one that can sustain this monopoly without outside assistance against potential challengers. This implies a continuum. The most successful states are those in which systematic and organized challengers to the monopoly of legitimate violence are rare; this is characteristic of the advanced industrialized democracies in North America and Europe, where threats to the regime are typically tiny and ephemeral, one-off attacks at worst by lone-wolf terrorists. Even unusual attacks, such as that perpetrated by al-Qaeda on September 11, 2001, do not disrupt consolidated states but serve only to heighten their resolve. Less successful states face more frequent challengers but also retain sufficient public support for the monopoly of force—otherwise known as legitimacy—that the latter are easily repulsed; or, if attacks occur, they do not result in a loss of control or territory. This includes a range of unconsolidated democracies and autocracies that govern with relatively high levels of repression. Unsuccessful states confront active challengers to their monopoly, becoming ever more unsuccessful in direct proportion to the size of the challenge and the extent of their territory they do not control, or can deter challengers only with the substantial and continued assistance of some outside power—most likely the statebuilder. Theorists and practitioners may disagree on the best way to achieve success, but the legitimacy of the monopoly on physical force is the standard by which statebuilding ought to be assessed. Though legitimacy may be difficult to measure precisely at any moment in time, it is the sustained ability of the state to deter challengers to its authority or to cope with those challengers that do arise over time that indicates success or a "consolidated" state.

In this volume, I am primarily concerned with armed or militarized statebuilding, cases in which the external party—the foreign statebuilder—employs coercive force with the intent to reconstruct another state's monopoly of legitimate violence.[20] Statebuilding efforts, of course, come in many forms, ranging from foreign aid to advisers for disarmament, demobilization, and reintegration (DDR) or security sector reform (SSR), military advisers and

20. Focusing on military occupations (which are close analogies to statebuilding efforts), Edelstein (2008) defines success by whether the target state poses threats to the occupier or its interests in the future. This would be equivalent, in my analysis of statebuilding, to sustaining a loyal leader in power. He finds that a strong majority of military occupations since 1815 have failed.

trainers, peacekeepers, and the deployment of troops for potential combat operations. At what point along this range efforts are transformed from humanitarian assistance to armed statebuilding is ambiguous, and depends in part on the intentions of the statebuilder. Buying influence over a poor but nonetheless stable government through foreign aid may be more intrusive than, say, assisting a state to professionalize its police force; but the latter would constitute statebuilding, as it intends to expand the state's coercive capacity, whereas the former does not. Armed statebuilding crosses another threshold represented by the deployment of peacekeepers or combat troops intended to provide stability directly and assist in the reconstruction of a state's own coercive apparatus. Such deployments are often combined with nonmilitarized forms of statebuilding, such as DDR and SSR, but constitute the most significant statebuilding efforts and are used only in the most problematic cases.[21] It is in such instances that the statebuilder's dilemma is most intense. Unless otherwise noted, when used in this volume the term "statebuilding" refers to armed statebuilding by some foreign state or international organization.

There is no definitive list of cases of armed statebuilding, even for the most studied statebuilder, the United States. Minxin Pei, Samia Amin, and Seth Garz define statebuilding by three criteria: (1) the goal of intervention must be regime change or the survival of a regime that would otherwise fail, (2) large numbers of ground troops must be deployed, and (3) military and civilian personnel must subsequently participate in the political administration of the target country. By these criteria, they characterize seventeen of more than two hundred U.S. military interventions abroad since 1900 as statebuilding episodes, or roughly 8 percent of the total number.[22] This does not include multilateral statebuilding efforts, such as in Somalia (see chapter 5) in which the United States nonetheless played a lead role. Of these statebuilding cases, all those before 1945 occurred in Central America and the Caribbean, with four postwar cases in this region as well. They also include West Germany and Japan after 1945, now standard cases of "successful" statebuilding, as well as South Vietnam and Cambodia.[23] Similarly, Paul Miller provides a comprehensive and somewhat more systematic list of United States and United Nations statebuilding cases, defined by (1) the deployment of international military forces and (2) the absence of annexation or imperialism with (3) the intent to improve a failed state's governance. By these criteria, he identifies forty instances of armed statebuilding since 1898, overlapping substantially with Pei

---

21. Since I select only cases of armed statebuilding, and thus failed states likely in the most dire circumstances, one must be careful in generalizing any conclusions about the statebuilder's dilemma to nonmilitarized statebuilding efforts. I expect the same dilemma to recur in less severely "failed" states in attenuated form—states participating in DDR or SSR efforts will still be those with the strongest interests in the future of the failed state, and thus still incline to support leaders who share their interests—but with lower costs of effort, the trade-off between legitimacy and loyalty will be less acute.

22. Pei, Amin, and Garz 2006, 64–66.

23. Dobbins, McGinn, et al. 2003; Dobbins, Poole, et al. 2008.

et al.'s list, including the Central American and post-1945 cases.[24] I do not attempt to produce a definitive inventory of armed statebuilding attempts in this study but rely on the efforts of others. The Central American and West German and Japanese cases, accepted as armed statebuilding efforts in nearly all studies, form a running backdrop in the rest of this volume to the two in-depth case studies of Iraq and Somalia.

The Prevailing Wisdom

The focus here on state legitimacy differs from current understandings of state failure and, in turn, statebuilding. The existing literature emphasizes getting national political institutions "right." This emphasis recurs both at the deep level of politics, where observers and practitioners identify predatory institutions as the root evil, and at the surface, where analysts debate the proper strategy and tactics of statebuilding. This concentration on institutions implicitly accepts and is premised on a particular theory of state legitimation, one grounded in liberalism. Institutions are, no doubt, important. But in this focus the underlying social cleavages that undermine institutions and ultimately bring down states are ignored.[25] Statebuilding requires not just new institutions that channel politics in more productive directions, but deep and long-lasting social transformations that permit groups embittered by violence to accord legitimacy to a new state in ways that previously proved elusive.

The Institutional Origins of State Failure

A near-consensus has emerged in the academy and policy community that limited government is optimal for economic growth and prosperity.[26] It is almost a truism, but rich, prosperous states do not fail.[27] The corollary—one that has motivated statebuilders since the end of the Cold War—is that institutions that limit predation by the government are necessary for economic and political stability and long-term success.

Although history has obviously not ended, liberalism remains triumphant.[28] Within the liberal consensus, some government is necessary to limit violence and appropriation and to provide public goods, such as security, but too much government leads to state rent seeking and other directly unproductive activities

---

24. P. Miller 2013, 205–227.
25. For exceptions, see Coyne 2008; Ghani and Lockhart 2008; Barnett and Zurcher 2009.
26. As a reflection of this consensus, see World Bank 1997.
27. Across a variety of theories and empirical studies, we know that coups, revolutions, and democratic reversals drop off dramatically once average GDP per capita crosses some threshold. Przeworski et al. (2000, 98) place the threshold at approximately $6,000 in 1975 dollars, the level reached in Argentina in that year.
28. Fukuyama 1992.

that inhibit investment and growth.[29] In their widely acclaimed book *Why Nations Fail*, for instance, Daron Acemoglu and James Robinson draw a distinction between exclusive or "predatory" regimes that distort property rights and growth and inclusive or "pluralistic" governments that permit markets to function within socially accepted limits.[30] Similarly, Douglass North, John Wallis, and Barry Weingast distinguish between "limited access orders," where personal ties between elites who control the instruments of power limit competition and the circulation of new ideas and people, and "open access orders," where political participation is broad, transactions are governed by impersonal rules, and there are many routes to political power.[31] Bruce Bueno de Mesquita and his colleagues posit a continuum of regimes along two dimensions: the size of the selectorate (S), those who have a say over who is in power, and the minimum winning coalition (W), the group within the selectorate upon whom the leader is dependent for support. Small W/S regimes tend to produce private goods for the politically important and influential few, whereas large W/S regimes provide public goods of benefit to all or most members of their societies.[32] Reflecting the liberal consensus, the core idea behind these and many other works is that political institutions determine and reflect the distribution of political power within society, and that politically privileged groups manipulate the law and the economy to their advantage. Governments dominated by small elites will be predatory, and the "grabbing hand" of states will distort economic incentives and undermine long-term growth by rendering property rights insecure and discouraging investment.[33] Although extensive growth may be possible by shifting resources from agriculture to industry, intensive growth that depends on innovation and what Joseph Schumpeter originally called creative destruction is greatly reduced, if not impossible.[34] Limited governments, on the other hand, are responsive to their societies, provide public goods, and ensure a rule of law that treats everyone equally. Most important, governments have only limited authority over the economy and society and facilitate or at least do not impede innovation, change, and growth. Such dynamic and prosperous states, in turn, do not fail.

How and why limited governments arise only in some places at some times remains poorly explained. For Acemoglu and Robinson, limited government is an accident of history, driven by small initial differences that become self-reinforcing and send a society down the vicious or virtuous path. On the first, a predatory ruler seizes power and provides policies that benefit his political allies, who become even more politically powerful over time. Large rents gen-

29. On directly unproductive activities, see Bhagwati 1982.
30. Acemoglu and Robinson 2012.
31. North, Wallis, and Weingast 2009.
32. Bueno de Mesquita et al. 2003; Bueno de Mesquita and Smith 2011.
33. Shleifer and Vishny 1998.
34. Schumpeter 1942/1994.

erated by the government, in turn, stimulate competition between elites to seize the state, creating a revolving door of predators. On the second, a more inclusive regime arises, prosperity is shared more broadly, inequality declines, and liberalism comes to prevail.[35] North, Wallis, and Weingast see a similar process in the historical record, with the limited-access orders being the "natural state" that is overcome only when the rule of law and more inclusive political and social organizations are promoted by elites for their own interests.[36] Bueno de Mesquita et al. argue that small W/S regimes are stable because existing elites fear being left out of any alternative coalition, and large W/S regimes emerge only when elites attempt to displace one another by appealing to new groups in society and thereby enlarging the selectorate.[37]

Pulling together existing strands of theory, Weingast poses a model of limited government as a coordination problem between a large number of citizens. If all citizens act in concert, they can prevent state aggrandizement against their freedoms, but the more likely equilibrium is for citizens to free ride on one another and for the state to transgress the rule of law. When the state can share its gains with particular groups in society, successful coordination is even more difficult. Securing limited government is difficult and unlikely. Constitutional rules, however, can serve as a focal point around which citizens coordinate to limit the state. When the state violates clearly established constitutional limits—"red lines" in common parlance—it can provoke citizens to rally and demand a return to the status quo ante. Even this, however, appears to be a fragile equilibrium. Rule violations by the state are seldom unambiguous and thus are unlikely to trigger broad-based opposition, especially when the government can buy off opponents through redistribution.[38] States that do not get on the virtuous path or do not possess clear constitutional rules to solve their coordination problems are, in turn, more likely to fail.

The implication of this liberal consensus is that statebuilding is largely a process of designing and creating the "right" institutions. States must be capable enough to provide public goods but not so capable that they can appropriate the wealth of their societies. This is the same problem identified by James Madison in formulating the Constitution of the United States. "In framing a government," he wrote, "you must first enable the government to control the governed, and in the next place oblige it to control itself."[39] And for many analysts and observers, the solution is the same as Madison's: a system of institutional checks and balances that prevents the tyranny of faction over the will of the people. However, statebuilding de novo, as enjoyed in the United States in Madison's time, may be easier than statebuilding after civil war. Institutions aggregate social forces in different ways and, thus, matter for policy and politics.

35. Acemoglu and Robinson 2012.
36. North, Wallis, and Weingast 2009.
37. Bueno de Mesquita et al. 2003.
38. Weingast 1997.
39. Hamilton, Jay, and Madison 1961, 322.

But institutions do not, by themselves, alter the underlying cleavages in society that cause state failure in the first place. Unless social groups buy into these new institutions, conflicting social pressures will still threaten the state and undermine its legitimacy.

Institutional Solutions to State Failure

Since the end of the Cold War and the triumph of liberalism, statebuilding practice has been to seek democratic, inclusive, and limited governmental institutions tailored to the specifics of the country in question. The general strategy, found in nearly pure form in the case of Iraq after 2003 (see chapters 3 and 4), has been to convene a constitutional convention with all major stakeholders represented and move rapidly to elections, often beginning at the local level and moving up to the national level. Greater democracy is assumed to be the path to peace, not only between but also within countries.[40] But within this emphasis on more democratic institutions, considerable debate remains about strategy and tactics, especially the optimal type of institution and the sequencing of democratization. My purpose here is not to resolve the debate over which institutions are preferred under what circumstances, but simply to highlight the focus of current statebuilding strategy on institutions as proximate solutions for social conflict.

The academic literature has long focused on the relative efficacy of power-sharing versus power-dividing institutions for resolving deep-seated social conflicts. Power-sharing institutions are designed to be both inclusive, guaranteeing all major social groups a role in government decision making, and proportional, often setting fixed allocations of appointments to government positions (presidents, vice presidents, ministerial positions, and so on) or shares of state resources (for example, oil revenues in the case of Iraq after 2003). Within a power-sharing system, groups are intended to be more or less autonomous and self-governing, managing their own affairs and possibly their own regions within the state as much as possible. Intergroup cooperation then occurs—in principle—at the highest levels between elite representatives of each group, who hopefully can see the big picture and moderate the demands of their perhaps more extreme members. In horizontally divided societies, this occurs along class lines through a form of corporatism.[41] In vertically divided societies, elite bargaining forms a type of consociationalism.[42] Regardless of group structure and type of institution, with all groups represented at the center they are expected to check and balance one another and prevent a tyranny of the majority or even any minority from emerging. As two of their more prominent critics note, power-sharing institutions are now "the

---

40. Paris 2004.
41. Adam 1998. On corporatism more generally, see Schmitter 1974; Katzenstein 1985.
42. Lijphart 1968.

international community's preferred remedy for building peace and democracy after civil wars."[43] Nonetheless, though potentially important in the short run in inducing groups to give up violence, power-sharing institutions also reinforce and possibly reify social cleavages, thereby making peace more difficult over the long term.[44]

Power-dividing institutions, on the other hand, are intended to diffuse any central political fissure in society and organize politics along many countervailing cleavages. Power-dividing institutions begin with extensive civil rights that empower all citizens equally and then separate powers so that different branches of government can check and balance one another, making the state itself or policy more difficult for any single group or coalition of groups to capture permanently. By driving political wedges between groups in society and requiring coalitions that cut across major lines of cleavage, the ambition is to diffuse social conflict. Empirical results appear to indicate that power-dividing institutions reduce the probability of ethnopolitical crises and armed violence that may be associated with state failure, but it is less clear how effective they are in rebuilding states after large-scale violence.[45] Given that power-dividing institutions require social groups to give up some measure of control over their own identities, those states willing to adopt power-dividing institutions after internal war may be those in which social peace would likely have prevailed under other institutions just as well.

A second theme in the institutionalist literature is the timing of democratic reforms. In all post–Cold War instances in which the United States served as the primary statebuilder, democratic elections were held on average within two years after the intervention and in all cases within three years.[46] Similar strategies are followed by other states and international organizations. Critics of this rapid move to elections argue that emotions are often too raw after internal conflict, under acute time constraints political parties will form along previous internal cleavages, and therefore competition will likely exacerbate tensions rather than lead to legitimacy for the new government. As in Egypt after the fall of President Hosni Mubarak, "early" elections, such as those that brought the Muslim Brotherhood to power, can lead to renewed group-based animosity and continuing conflict. Though the weight of evidence favors the critics, the important point here is that this key issue and debate is yet again a largely institutional solution to the problem of social conflict.[47]

43. Roeder and Rothchild 2005, 5.
44. Ibid., 6.
45. Roeder 2005. Hoddie and Hartzell (2005) find that power-sharing institutions per se are not effective but that offers to create power-sharing institutions do serve as credible signals of majority group willingness to accommodate minority group concerns.
46. Lake 2010a, 260, 266.
47. Snyder 2000; Hegre et al. 2001; Reilly 2002, 2008; Paris 2004; Diamond 2006; Collier, Hoeffler, and Soderbom 2008; Collier 2009; Brancati and Snyder 2011, 2013; Matanock 2013.

Critics of institutional solutions, while supporting democratization, focus largely on problems of tactics. Strategy was not aligned with local conflict ecologies; institutionalization should precede liberalization; the political, military, and humanitarian missions were poorly integrated, and more.[48] Most advise ways of improving the current model rather than eschewing statebuilding completely or recommending a fundamentally new approach. Although skeptical of current theory and practice, the majority of these critics accept the central importance of institutions as solutions to state failure and as the main levers of statebuilding. Missing from the discussion, but central to the questions of legitimacy that drive this book, are the underlying social cleavages that can doom states and statebuilding to fail.

Moreover, these institutional solutions do not, by themselves, mitigate the statebuilder's dilemma. Even if a perfect institution is designed—whatever that might entail—and the sequencing of steps is implemented optimally, if the statebuilder still intervenes to promote a favored leader who represents its interests rather than those of the target society, that leader will still lack legitimacy. Without broad social support, the leader will be forced to govern undemocratically—perhaps subverting the institutions under which he or she assumed power, however well designed—and will divert resources from improving social welfare to building a support coalition to sustain himself or herself in office.

The fact is that the failure of statebuilding is overdetermined.[49] We do not know what institutions are optimal in war torn countries. Nor do we know the proper sequencing of institutional reforms. Since nearly all statebuilding efforts have failed, and so many things could be done wrong, it is hard to identify the cause or causes of those failures. But given some variation in practice and policies, the near-universal trend of failure suggests a more systematic cause. Underlying all of these problems of institutional design and implementation is the fundamental trade-off between legitimacy, a prerequisite for statebuilding success, and loyalty, the desire to promote a leader at least sympathetic to the interests of the statebuilder. When this dilemma is acute and the trade-off is steep, no matter which institutions are chosen or which strategies are implemented, the state will likely fail in attaining legitimacy. The limits of external statebuilding are reached precisely when the statebuilder cares the most about the future policies of the failed state.

---

48. Von Hippel 2000, esp. 78–79; Paris 2004, esp. chap. 10; Doyle and Sambanis 2006, 334–342; Ghani and Lockhart 2008. This critical literature is large and growing. Among those with a focus on "lessons learned," see Chesterman 2004; Rotberg 2004; Fukuyama 2006b. For a nuanced critique that argues against "one size fits all" sequencing and for an approach that tailors tactics to the specifics of a failed state, see P. Miller 2013. On the need to incorporate local context, see Richmond and Mitchell 2012; Richmond 2014. On the pathologies of peacekeepers themselves, see Autesserre 2014.
49. Tansey 2013.

Society, Legitimacy, and Statebuilding

My approach differs from the prevailing institutionalist view in two ways. First, institutionalists are fundamentally liberals, in the classic sense of this term, who believe the legitimacy of the state follows from democracy and free markets. As already highlighted and as discussed in more detail in later chapters, this liberal model of statebuilding is itself deeply flawed and has repeatedly failed to provide the legitimacy necessary for successful statebuilding. Throughout this book, in turn, I build on a relational view of authority which posits that legitimacy follows from an exchange in which the ruler—whether this be the statebuilder or the new state—provides essential public services to the population, which reciprocates with support and compliance with its rules. In this relational view, legitimacy derives from a mutually beneficial exchange in which the state provides a social order of benefit to society, and society in turn complies with the extractions (for example, taxes) and constraints on its behavior (for example, law) that are necessary to the production of that order. The contract becomes self-enforcing—or legitimate—when individuals and groups become vested in that social order by undertaking investments specific to the particular authority relationship. In this way, legitimacy follows from social order, not the other way around as in the prevailing model. In the exchange of services for support, in other words, it is not democracy or markets but society itself that confers legitimacy on the state. This approach to authority is central to the COIN strategy adopted by the United States in Iraq and Afghanistan after 2007. Most important, it envisions authority and legitimacy as negotiated and dynamic attributes of political systems that produce rather than rest on institutions.

Second, and following from this relational approach to authority, attention shifts from institutions to social formations within the country that support (or not) the state.[50] All politics is at the same time a mix of cooperation among individuals and groups that aims to improve social welfare and bargaining by those same individuals and groups over the division of the gains. Cooperation is necessary to create a social order that encourages specialization, exchange, and productive investment and to produce public goods that support these activities. Faced with collective-action problems in large-scale societies that thwart voluntary cooperation, the state possesses a comparative advantage in providing order and public goods due to its monopoly on the legitimate use of force. At the same time, individuals and groups bargain over the division of the gains from cooperation, even those produced or facilitated by the state. In horizontally segmented societies, classes struggle over the distribution of wealth between elites and masses. In vertically segmented societies, communal groups wrestle over how wealth is divided between social factions. When bargaining gets especially intense and difficult, social forces tear apart

---

50. For a somewhat similar approach, see Ghani and Lockhart 2008; Fukuyama 2011, 2014.

the state and undermine its ability to provide the cooperation that makes wealth and economic growth possible. At the extreme, states fail when the struggle over distribution destroys the social order that sustains cooperation. The fight over the golden eggs kills the goose that lays them.

Statebuilding is an externally led process that aims to recreate a state sufficiently strong to weather distributional conflict so that it can provide the social order and public goods necessary to expand wealth and social well-being. To earn legitimacy from its society, the state must produce enough cooperation and ensure that everyone gets a sufficient share to induce groups to accept its authority and, in turn, to work within rather than challenge its rules. Statebuilders can in principle facilitate indigenous statebuilding efforts by helping establish a social order and setting expectations that the order so created will endure into the future. In short, through their significantly greater resources and coercive capabilities, statebuilders can lend credibility to a newly formed state. By creating expectations of stability, the statebuilder encourages specific investments and the vesting of interests in the new social order. Stability and, in turn, legitimacy follow from the expectations of many individuals. Statebuilders have a comparative advantage, as it were, in resetting expectations in more positive directions. This is how international statebuilders can play a positive role in rehabilitating failed states.

Attention to legitimacy and the social foundations of state authority, however, reveals more clearly the statebuilder's dilemma, ignored by the institutionalist approach. Statebuilding is difficult and unlikely to succeed under the best of circumstances. Large-scale social engineering to ameliorate deep social factionalization is more art than science—a high-wire act without a net—that nonetheless has potentially devastating effects on the daily lives of millions. It is not something that should be undertaken lightly. Yet all of the strategic and tactical problems of statebuilding identified by others are dramatically worsened by the statebuilder's dilemma. In the end, it is the high costs of statebuilding that limit states willing to take up the challenge to those with deep interests in failed states, and it is the corresponding desire of such countries to support leaders who will assist in realizing those interests that dooms statebuilding efforts to failure.

Outline of the Book

The chapters below follow the outline of the argument summarized earlier. Chapter 1 examines why states fail and the challenges of statebuilding that follow from deep social cleavages exacerbated by prolonged violence. Chapter 2 focuses on Westphalian sovereignty and its importance as a decentralized institution to control violence between states. This creates the context in which the statebuilder's dilemma becomes both necessary and inescapable. Chapter 3 explains the statebuilder's dilemma in more detail, suggesting when it will be more or less acute. That chapter also examines several prominent theories of state legitimation and argues that none resolves the dilemma.

The statebuilder's dilemma is then explored in the cases of Iraq (chapter 4) and Somalia (chapter 5), selected to illustrate the trade-off between legitimacy and loyalty and its pernicious effects.[51] U.S. statebuilding efforts in Central America in the early twentieth century and similar efforts in West Germany and Japan after World War II are used as "shadow" cases against which Iraq and Somalia are compared. Although not developed in any detail, these other statebuilding efforts run as a thread through all the chapters. As already explained above, in Central America the United States did not place any priority on legitimacy, thus partially obviating the dilemma but also creating long-term instability in the region. In West Germany and Japan, the policy preferences of the United States and the target societies did not differ dramatically, and in any event could be bridged relatively easily through economic aid and the promise of integration into the Pax Americana. In these rare cases of statebuilding success, the dilemma was not acute. In both Iraq and Somalia, however, the statebuilder's dilemma ultimately led to a lack of legitimacy and failed statebuilding efforts.

Somalia and Iraq also possess extreme values on several key variables, which help shed light on the arguments developed in this book. First, Somalia is a case in which the United States had relatively few interests but where, in a humanitarian gesture by a lame-duck president, it nonetheless intervened militarily in 1992 to provide aid. As the United States was eventually drawn into a statebuilding mission and the costs became evident, it quickly withdrew, demonstrating one horn of the statebuilder's dilemma: that states without significant interests in the future of a failed state are unwilling to bear the burden. The other horn is then exposed by Ethiopia's intervention in Somalia, starting in 2006 after an irredentist regime finally came to power in Mogadishu. Iraq represents the other end of the continuum of U.S. interests, standing out as the most important foreign policy undertaking of the George W. Bush presidency. Seen as critical to the future of the Middle East and the U.S. role in that region, Iraq was the centerpiece of the administration's policy of transformation. With broad and deep U.S. interests in the country, Iraq demanded not only success but, more important, a leader who was at least sympathetic to U.S. demands. Here, the statebuilder's dilemma is revealed in extreme form. Because U.S. interests were so intense in Iraq—or at least were believed to be—the case throws the statebuilder's dilemma into sharp relief and clearly demonstrates its core logic.

51. Plagued by the same trade-off, Afghanistan could easily have been chosen in lieu of Iraq, but only one such case could be included for reasons of length. Iraq was chosen simply on the nonscientific principle of personal interest; it is the case that motivated my investigation of the statebuilder's dilemma and one about which I have written extensively before. See Lake 2010–2011, 2013a.

Second, Somalia and Iraq were also chosen to illustrate how indigenous statebuilding can, in fact, succeed. Overall, both countries are failed statebuilding attempts and thus cannot serve as a test of why statebuilding fails. Thus, I am cautious throughout in claiming that the statebuilder's dilemma is the cause of statebuilding failure, though I do argue that analytically it is prior to most of the reasons for failure examined by others. However, both countries also contain autonomous regions that, cut off from international assistance and intervention, have evolved relatively stable and effective de facto state structures. Insulating itself from the chaos that followed the breakdown of the Somali state, and isolated from international involvement and aid because it lacks recognition as a sovereign state, Somaliland has emerged as a striking example of indigenous statebuilding success, becoming one of the most stable and, surprisingly, democratic states in the region. Long opposed to rule from Baghdad, and gaining new autonomy as a result of the no-fly zone instituted by the United States after the 1991 Persian Gulf War, Iraqi Kurdistan is also a successful example of indigenous statebuilding. These within-case examples demonstrate how statebuilding can succeed in the absence of significant international involvement. Together, they help illustrate the malign effects of the statebuilder's dilemma and bolster its importance as a cause of statebuilding failure.

The argument of this book is, quite frankly, highly pessimistic and critical of all statebuilding efforts. The statebuilder's dilemma is always present, though it can vary in degree. To counter this essential pessimism, the conclusion probes feasible alternatives. One possible route is that statebuilders might aim only for "good enough" governance.[52] This entails giving up some measure of legitimacy and countenancing a measure—perhaps a large measure—of authoritarianism and repression in return. This is, in essence, a return to the realpolitik that characterized U.S. statebuilding efforts in Central America in the first half of the twentieth century. This strategy, at best, creates short-term stability in policy, as adopted by the loyal leader, at the expense of long-term instability for the leader himself. As policies favored by the statebuilder are foisted on an unwilling society, resentment expands against both the leader and the external patron, eventually undermining both.

An alternative is multilateral statebuilding. With more countries involved with and overseeing any operation, the hope is that the statebuilder will be more neutral or focused on legitimacy. Yet under existing international institutions, which are still dependent on voluntary assessments and the political and economic support of the great powers, it remains the case that only states with interests in the failed state will step forward with either resources or troops. The multilateral nature of the effort in Somalia in the early 1990s, for instance, did not succeed in securing U.S. aid absent strong interests in the future of that state. Conversely, the African Union operation in Somalia since

52. See Krasner 2013.

2007 remains dominated by Ethiopia and Kenya, two interested parties. Multilateralism may soften the dilemma, but it cannot eliminate the trade-off between legitimacy and loyalty.

The most viable approach to statebuilding is for the international community and its leading states to recognize the limits on their ability imposed by the statebuilder's dilemma and to focus instead on creating an international environment conducive to indigenous state formation. Through the use of carrots and sticks, states might shape incentives for fragile states by making access to the security and economic benefits of the Pax Americana, in general, or the European Union, in particular, contingent on domestic groups settling their differences, agreeing on a social order, and governing themselves effectively. This is best done by enlarging the possible gains from international cooperation, which can help mitigate some of the distributional concerns within otherwise failed states, and by making access to those gains dependent on effective governance. Through integration into the Pax Americana and global economic institutions, moreover, the domestic political economies of fragile states may be reshaped in ways that make their domestic interests more compatible with those of the United States and its European partners. This was the logic behind the largely successful attempt by the European Union after 1989 to leverage access to the single market to promote effective rule of law in the former communist states of Eastern Europe that might have otherwise fallen into domestic instability and violence, ultimately producing stable, economically open, capitalist, and, most importantly, "loyal" regimes that are also legitimate. In the end, failed states will have to fix themselves—but other states can help shape their futures, albeit only at the margins.

1

Building Legitimate States

Any theory of statebuilding must begin with a conception of state failure. One cannot prescribe effective treatments for sick patients before diagnosing what brought them to death's door. Similarly, states cannot be rebuilt until we know what led them to fail. Central to the concept of the state is the notion of legitimacy, which is what evaporates when states disintegrate. Scholars and practitioners alike avoid discussing legitimacy because the concept is squishy, vague, and impossible to define precisely or to operationalize in any neat fashion. Yet reconstructing this elusive quality is central to all statebuilding.

This chapter focuses on the challenge of rebuilding legitimacy in the aftermath of state failure. I begin with the nature of the state, probe the two principal pathways through which states fail, and then consider the role of external statebuilders. The key problem leading to failure is deep factionalization within society. The promise of statebuilding is to catalyze and then guarantee a new social order into the indefinite future, prompting social interests to become vested in that order and transforming it into a set of self-enforcing institutions.

How States Succeed

As noted in the introduction, Weber famously defined the state as a compulsory organization that successfully claims a monopoly of the legitimate use of physical force within a given territory.[1] This definition highlights two essential features of what it means to be a state.[2] First, the *monopoly* on the legiti-

---

1. Weber 1978, 54, 56.
2. Some augment this basic definition by restricting legitimacy to the existence of at least a modicum of democracy, but if legitimacy is a quality of states, we should be open to the

mate use of physical violence gives the state a comparative advantage in solving collective action problems that would otherwise plague society, allowing it to produce a social order that generates incentives for investment and improved well-being. Cooperation within any society is always problematic, requiring, at a minimum, the coordination of actions by many autonomous actors and, at a maximum, hard bargaining between those actors over the division of the gains from cooperation. The state is not necessary for cooperation, of course. In strategic settings characterized only by the need for coordination, such as in fixing standards for consumer products, self-enforcing agreements among large numbers of participants are possible. Even in strategic settings requiring collaboration—the adjustment of behavior between actors when each retains an incentive to defect—even large social collectivities can successfully organize voluntarily and spontaneously for social action under favorable conditions.[3] Nonetheless, the state's monopoly on physical violence gives it a unique advantage in reducing free riding by extracting contributions to public goods and punishing those who would defect from agreed practices. Threats of violence can induce and sustain cooperation when it is not otherwise an equilibrium. The state's monopoly on physical coercion ensures that economies of scale in violence and public goods are realized and that conflicts between overlapping and inconsistent rules potentially set by other private authorities are minimized. This same monopoly, however, creates the potential that the state will abuse its powers for the self-aggrandizement of its leaders or groups that capture its powers for themselves. The temptation to engage in predatory behavior, however, is tempered by the need for legitimacy by the state.

Second, the *legitimacy* of the state's monopoly of physical violence reinforces its comparative advantage in solving collective action problems. As long recognized by political philosophers, "pure" coercive power cannot govern a society, at least not for long.[4] Keeping soldiers and tanks on every street corner and spies in every coffeehouse and living room is not only costly but ultimately ineffective. Any regime that desires to endure must find some mechanism for inducing what Margaret Levi calls "quasi-voluntary compliance"—behavior that is voluntary because subjects choose to comply, but quasi-voluntary

---

question of whether democracy is necessary for legitimacy or even enhances legitimacy. By assuming that democracy is necessary for legitimacy, a theory of state failure and statebuilding is introduced by the backdoor. A normative standard is also imposed on what should be an analytic concept. I discuss this point at greater length below. Similarly, some add that states must provide a minimum level of public goods. But, again, how effective and responsive the state is to the demands of its citizens ought to be considered as a possible cause of state failure rather than an inherent part of the concept. A good definition is minimalist in that it isolates a category for analysis without prejudging the causes of the phenomenon or building in unnecessary normative restrictions.

3. Ostrom 1990; Lansing 2006.
4. See Tyler 2001; Zelditch 2001.

because noncompliance can in principle be sanctioned.[5] Legitimacy is the bridge between choice and compulsion.

Legitimacy

Legitimacy is constituted by the collective acceptance of a ruler's right to rule. That is, a state is legitimate when citizens recognize that it has the right to issue certain commands and, in turn, that they have an obligation or duty to comply. Thus, a ruler is legitimate—possesses authority—when directives and laws are understood by subordinates as binding on the members of the relevant community, even if they fail to comply in practice at all times. Legitimacy does not require that subordinates acknowledge or accept the moral goodness of a ruler or her laws, although that sometimes occurs.[6] Rather, since legitimacy is a social rather than an individual attribute, its normative status follows rather than precedes its social acceptance, especially in fragile or failed states.

Legitimate rules are obligatory. That is, obligation arises from the collective's belief in the rightfulness of rule. Even though I might occasionally defect from the law (for example, exceed the speed limit) or even reject that the state has the right to enact certain laws (for example, monitoring phone calls and e-mail, restricting a woman's reproductive freedom), if enough others accept this law or right, the state is thereby empowered to make binding decrees regardless of my personal beliefs or motivations and to punish me for violating such laws. Alternatively, no matter how fervently I might believe in the rightness of a ruler, if everyone around me denies that authority and defies the law, the ruler cannot be regarded as legitimate. It is this collective belief that legitimates (and limits) a state and gives it authority over its members.[7]

Legitimacy exists when the constraints on individual action are produced not only by the coercive power of the ruler but also by the collectivity of subordinates itself. It is this double-faced conception of legitimacy that reconciles the seeming paradox that while consent to authority is collectively voluntary, authority is individually binding and obligatory. As Peter Blau clarifies, from the perspective of the collectivity of subordinates, compliance with legitimate

---

5. Levi 1988, 48–70.
6. This definition of legitimacy differs from many others in not requiring a normative basis. I do not insist on normative beliefs because I am interested in how legitimacy arises from within anarchy after large-scale violence, which has typically had the effect of undermining whatever legitimating beliefs might have previously existed. If we require that legitimacy be normatively acceptable, it is hard to see how it could emerge from such an environment, except under some form of charismatic leadership—which is, for reasons explained below, itself a weak reed for effective statebuilding. The same positive theory of legitimacy employed here is used in studying the emergence of hierarchy in international relations—a similarly anarchic environment in which prevailing norms of sovereignty and equality explicitly conflict with the existence of authority by one state over another. See Lake 2009.
7. Bernard 1962, 169; Lasswell and Kaplan 1950, 133.

rule is the product of free will, as subjects consent to and affirm the authority of the ruler through practice. But from the standpoint of any individual subordinate, compliance is the result of "compelling social pressures" rooted in collective consent. In a pithy phrase, he concludes that "the compliance of subordinates in authority relationships is as voluntary as our custom of wearing clothes."[8]

The obligation to comply implies a further correlative right by the ruler to enforce commands in the event of noncompliance by subordinates. As John Day notes, "those who possess authority in political life, the rulers, are authorized not only to make laws and take decisions but to use coercive power when necessary to ensure obedience to those laws and acquiescence in those decisions."[9] Individuals still choose whether or not to comply with a ruler's demands, just as we individually decide whether to comply with the rules of the road, but those who violate authoritative commands are bound by the right of the ruler to punish their noncompliance. Many drivers fail to stop at posted signs, for instance, but if caught they accept the right of the state to issue fines or other punishments for breaking the law.

Thus, not only the power to command but the power to punish noncompliance legitimately ultimately rest on the *collective* acceptance of the ruler's right to rule. As Richard Flathman writes, "sustained coercion is impossible without substantial agreement among the members of the association about those very propositions whose rejection commonly brings coercion into play."[10] If recognized as legitimate, the ruler acquires the ability to coerce individuals because of the broad backing of others. Thus, rulers can enforce individual edicts even in the face of opposition if the general body of commands is accepted as legitimate by a sufficiently large body of the ruled.[11] Because a sufficient number of the ruled accept the ruler and his edicts as legitimate, the ruler can employ force against individual free riders and even dissidents. Knowing that a sufficient number of others support the ruler, in turn, potential free riders and dissidents are deterred from violating the rules, and overt force is rendered unnecessary or, at least, relatively rare.

Legitimacy, then, is the alchemist's dross through which a monopoly on violence is transformed into political authority. Legitimate rule, simply put, is

8. Blau 1963, 312–313.
9. Day 1963, 260.
10. Flathman 1980, 29.
11. I recognize the ambiguity in the phrase "sufficiently large." The smaller the proportion of the population that accepts the ruler as rightful, the more the ruler must rely on repression; but even repression, following Flathman, requires some minimal social support. Just where to draw the border between a tyranny and a minimally legitimate state is unclear. Legitimacy is also likely to be subject to "tipping points," as individual beliefs about the rightfulness of rule will interact with perceptions of the beliefs of others. This suggests that states that appear legitimate at one moment in time may lose legitimacy quite suddenly. For suggestive ways of thinking about this problem, see Kuran 1991 and Lohmann 1994.

the right to use physical force with the at least tacit assent of the relevant community to whom it may be applied. Successful statebuilding, in turn, requires not only the (re-)creation of a monopoly of violence but also the (re)establishment of the legitimacy of rule, or the collective acceptance by the people of that monopoly. Collective assent is a variable, not an absolute. The larger the proportion of the community that accepts its authority, the stronger or more legitimate is the state. In turn, the larger the territorial or policy domain over which the community accepts the state's right to regulate behavior authoritatively, the stronger the state. There is no threshold of legitimacy or state strength over which we would necessarily agree that statebuilding has been successful or under which it has clearly failed. As explained in the introduction, success is a relative term.

Interests and Legitimacy

The most basic but too often ignored question of politics is, Why are some states legitimate while others are not? Why and when does some group of individuals agree to live within a particular structure of authority, recognizing a potentially unique bundle of rights and duties, and other groups of individuals fail to reach sufficient agreement? There are many specific theories of legitimation, several of which are discussed in chapter 3. All theories and processes of legitimation, however, require that the authority relationship be self-enforcing.[12] That is, it must be in the self-interests of all actors—ruler and ruled—to abide by its terms. This section focuses on the especially thorny problem of self-interest and the collective recognition of the right to rule—or legitimacy.

Much has been written on how to limit the authority of the state—how to tie its hands, so to speak, so that it will live within the rights conferred on it by society. This is central to the institutionalist models reviewed in the introduction. Less discussed and, in my view, more important is how society binds itself to support the authority of the state and to police the boundaries of this authority. While checks and balances and other institutional solutions can limit the state, these solutions are ultimately endogenous, themselves the product of politics. The role of society in both supporting state authority—granting it legitimacy—and enforcing limits on that authority is too often overlooked.

As a self-enforcing relationship, the interests of society in the social order created by the state are of crucial importance in understanding its authority and, in turn, its legitimacy. Following Hedley Bull, a social order is "a pattern of human activity that sustains elementary, primary, or universal goals of social life," including security against violence resulting in death or bodily harm; an assurance that property will not be subject to challenges that are constant or

12. Weingast 1997.

without limit; and an expectation that promises and agreements, once made, will be kept. As a shorthand, we can think of social order as the protection of persons, property, and promises.[13] Although generic, social orders differ in their content, including the forms of violence permitted; the types of property protected and under what conditions; and the kinds of promises that must be kept and under what circumstances. Social order is both produced by and embodied in particular sets of rules and laws enacted by the state. It typically reflects, more or less, the preferences of the politically powerful individuals and groups in society: rules and laws, and in turn social orders, are always made by someone for some purpose and are rarely neutral in their political, social, and economic effects.

Individuals possess many and varied interests in social order. Political science and cognate disciplines currently lack complete theories of interests, often treating this core concept inductively or by assumption.[14] Nonetheless, as a useful simplification, individuals can be said to possess at least two kinds of interests.[15] The first, which for want of a better term I call ideological interests, captures a range of fundamental values and general attitudes toward politics, the economy, and society. Ideological interests are intuitive theories, sometimes codified in explicit philosophies or philosophical tracts, about preferred social orders and how best to realize them. In Western societies, attitudes are typically understood to vary along a left-right continuum, with a progressive orientation toward social life and concerns with care and fairness clustering on the Left and a more traditional or status quo orientation and concerns with loyalty, authority, and sanctity clustering on the Right.[16] In other societies with different cultural backgrounds, a single ideological dimension also appears to exist, but with different content.[17] This is an area where far more research is clearly necessary. These ideologies, in turn, may be rooted in genetics, psychology, socialization, or most likely some complex combination.[18] Potentially dynamic and evolving over an individual's lifetime, these ideological interests also appear rather "sticky" and resistant to change. Most important for my purposes here, they are context-independent sets of individual beliefs about social order that guide fundamental interests over policy.

Second, individuals also possess circumstantial interests, reflecting the existing social order in which they must function and the incentives it creates for or against different policies. Capitalists and workers, at least according

---

13. Bull 1977, 5.
14. Frieden 1999.
15. The two types of interests are, of course, analytic categories rather than actual differences. Whether any particular interest is found in one or the other category, or whether there are numerous intermediate types, is less important to the argument here than that some interests are context-independent and some are context-dependent.
16. See Haidt 2012.
17. Although work in this area is thin, on China see Pan and Xu 2015.
18. On genetics and political attitudes, see Hatemi and McDermott 2012; Benjamin et al. 2012. On psychology, see Haidt 2012; Gerber et al. 2011.

to Marxist theory, have diametrically opposed circumstantial interests. The theory of open economy politics posits that individuals in export- and import-competing industries will have different interests on trade policy, the first favoring free trade and the second protection.[19] Bureaucrats famously derive their interests from "where they sit." That interests vary by circumstance or context is nearly universally recognized, though theories of interests differ widely. Circumstantial interests need not be material in origin but may be socially constructed. In contrast to ideological interests, however, circumstantial interests change in response to the social order in which the individual is embedded.

Ideological and circumstantial interests are likely synergistic, leading individuals with particular ideological beliefs into certain occupations, for instance, or the demands of particular occupations forcing individuals to interpret their ideologies in creative ways. Those with particular ideological interests, in turn, may aim to codify those interests into law, thereby creating penalties for infractions that change circumstantial interests, and vice versa.[20] On the other hand, these sets of interests need not always reinforce one another. One can be a conservative who opposes government intervention in the economy but work in an import-competing industry and lobby for trade protection. Or as an example that may be familiar to some readers, one can be a political radical or libertarian who rails against the establishment from within the safety of a tenured professorship at a state university. Though there may be a tendency to resolve cognitive dissonance created by opposed ideological and circumstantial interests, humans appear remarkably flexible and able to sustain inconsistent ideas.

Ideological interests are a foundation for the legitimacy of the state, especially at the level of broadly shared beliefs. Divine right underpinned monarchies in the Middle Ages, reinforced by the authority of the established Church, just as religion today supports theocracies like Iran's. Liberalism, particularly the rights of personal freedom and free markets, legitimates, in part, the democracies now found in North America and Europe. At the very least, it is difficult for a state to create and sustain a social order that conflicts with widely shared ideological beliefs of a substantial majority of its society. Yet precisely because individuals often hold varying beliefs, as suggested by the left-right spectrum, ideology alone is typically insufficient to legitimate a state. Indeed, ideological differences can exacerbate underlying horizontal or vertical stratifications in society and make state failure more likely (see the next section in this chapter).

Critical to the self-enforcement of authority relationships are, ironically, circumstantial interests dependent on a specific social order. Though they vary as the environment changes, circumstantial interests can become vested in a

19. Frieden and Rogowski 1996.
20. Lake 2015.

social order, providing the glue that holds society together and legitimates the state. Typically a term of opprobrium decried by political reformers and radicals everywhere, vested interests—or, more politely, compliance constituencies—are individuals and groups who have acquired assets that are specific to or have more value in a particular relationship than in others.[21] Such vested interests are the second foundation of legitimacy, essential to any individual's or group's interest in supporting a specific authority relationship.

Actors acquire a wide variety of assets in everyday life. Individuals buy property, pursue an education, develop specialized knowledge and skills suited to particular occupations, and save for old age. Some assets will be generic, easily switched with little loss in value from one use or regime to another. Other assets will be highly specific to a particular social order and the policies on which it depends, and can be deployed to other uses or used under alternative policy regimes only with substantial loss in value.[22] At all levels, as actors invest in relationally specific assets they become dependent on the authority that produces that particular social order. In turn, they acquire incentives to support the ruler and suppress possible dissidents who would overturn that order. In this way, the group—as a community of actors vested in a particular order and relationship—legitimates the ruler's authority. Authority becomes more robust—more legitimate—as subordinates acquire more assets that are dependent on that particular form of authority.

As authoritative rules create incentives for actors, the parties respond by making investments premised, in part, on those rules and their attendant outcomes. Individuals acquire property on the expectation that the state will protect the current set of rights. They enter into contracts with one another with some confidence that prescribed actors and rules will help enforce those private agreements. The same holds for policies that follow from those authoritative rules. Americans condition their retirement savings on Social Security, Medicare, and other programs that assist the elderly. Firms invest in plants and equipment on the expectation that property protections and perhaps specific investment incentives will continue.

As they make order- and policy-specific investments, actors acquire new interests in preserving the authority that produces that order and those policies. In short, they become vested in the authority relationship and can be expected to devote political effort to defending it. American farmers, whose

21. On compliance constituencies, see Kahler 2001. Hurd (1999, 387) has criticized self-interest conceptions of legitimacy as inadequate because they imply that the ruled will be continually calculating their actions, contesting their bonds, and engaging in resistance. That we do not observe authority contracts being continually renegotiated, he suggests, indicates the need for and role of a more normative conception of legitimacy. This criticism, however, comes from an overly narrow understanding of self-interest. With vested interests, political orders get locked in and are not continually challenged or reevaluated.
22. On asset specificity, see Williamson 1975, 1985. On the role of specific assets in international hierarchy, see Lake 1999.

broad geographic dispersion gives them considerable clout within Congress and the ability to lobby effectively, are dependent on public agricultural subsidies. If these socially inefficient subsidies were withdrawn, crop prices would fall, land values would decline, and some now poorer farmers would be forced to shift to new occupations and acquire new skills. To forestall the decline in the values of their assets—both land and skills—farmers fight hard to maintain their current subsidies and would fight even harder to preserve their disproportionate representation in Congress were it ever challenged.[23] More generally, as President George W. Bush's failed attempt at reform again demonstrates, Social Security remains the "third rail" of U.S. politics. Because it affects so many people and conditions so deeply their lifetime consumption and savings habits, Americans as a whole are acutely dependent on the program, and politicians can change it only at their peril. The elderly, who cannot alter a lifetime of consumption and savings retroactively or redeploy their assets and start saving for a future under a different policy regime, are particularly vigorous advocates of the status quo. The same calculus occurs in developing countries as well, whether it is rural farmers adjusting practice to the incentives created by state marketing boards or cronies who are dependent on an autocratic leader for privileged access to government contracts and resources.[24] The greater the rule- or policy-induced investments, and the more specific those investments are to particular rules or policies, the greater the coalition in favor of preserving the extant authority and its policy outputs even when the results may be "suboptimal" relative to those enacted by an ideal social planner.

Vesting may also, over time, alter the composition of groups affected by rules and policies. In this way, circumstantial interests are themselves endogenous to policy. As the "winners" win, some fraction of their gains will be devoted to protecting their investments. Conversely, as the "losers" lose, they have less to fight with and may, at an extreme, be eliminated from the political arena.[25] As recent changes in tax law have contributed to increased income inequality in the United States, for instance, the wealthiest individuals have enjoyed even higher incomes and greater opportunity to use their disproportionate gains to pursue policies beneficial to themselves, while the poorest Americans have lost both economically and politically. Even groups initially harmed by a policy may, over time, redeploy their assets, make new investments, and eventually come to support what they initially opposed. For instance, renters in the United States are disadvantaged by the mortgage interest tax deduction. This creates incentives for people who might otherwise prefer renting to

---

23. On agricultural malapportionment, see Monroe 1994; Samuels and Snyder 2001; Broz and Maliniak 2010.
24. Bates 1981; Fisman 2001.
25. See Becker 1983; Rogowski 1989; Hathaway 1998.

purchase homes. Once they become homeowners, these erstwhile renters will be fervent advocates of the mortgage interest deduction. Again, the political decimation of the losers from policy occurs in developing countries as well. Agricultural policies biased against rural farmers and favoring urban dwellers lead to increased migration to the cities, swelling the ranks and political power of the latter at the expense of the former.[26] By favoring groups or realigning incentives, rules and policies strengthen defenders and weaken opponents and, thus, become harder to challenge or overturn. By creating winners, authority and its derived rules and policies create their own supporters who have stakes in the existing social order and who will act politically to protect their interests.

As relationally specific assets accumulate and the parties become vested in a particular social order, this self-interest legitimates the ruler's authority. The ruled accept the authority of the ruler and, indeed, empower the ruler to preserve and enforce the rules under which they benefit. It is precisely this effect that reformers rue; vested interests render the status quo and institutions hard to change. Yet it is these same vested interests that form the glue that holds society together and, more important, legitimate a state, ultimately allowing a social order to endure.

That the examples above are largely drawn from consolidated states is not a coincidence. Given some ideological diversity, it is precisely the vesting of interests in the state that make it strong and effective. The more social groups there are committed to defending the state's current authority, the stronger and more resilient the state is to possible challenges. Conversely, it is the absence of vested interests in the state that produces weak and ultimately failed states. Without institutionally specific assets, one constitution is as good as any other, and without a commitment to one set of rules, groups will be prone to cycle through alternative institutions (see below). Without constituencies dependent on a particular social order and authority structure, challenges to the state cannot be answered, and any particular ruler will be overwhelmed; increased coercion to hold onto office will only alienate even more social groups, and eventually the ruler will fall, only to be replaced by another ephemeral leader. When specific assets are destroyed by war or internal violence, as in failed states, this creates periods of openness, flux, or political plasticity during which society is "unmoored" and potentially subject to political chaos.[27] As explained in more detail later in this chapter, the challenge to statebuilders is not simply to create new institutions but to legitimate those institutions by creating social orders consistent with the ideological interests of a majority of society and vesting individuals and groups in their preservation.

26. Bates 1981.
27. On political plasticity, see Gourevitch 1986. Although cast in slightly different terms, on the effects of war on vested interests, see Olson 1982.

The task is to create self-enforcing authority that is recognized as legitimate and enduring by all.

How States Fail

There is no consensus definition of state "failure" or "fragility" (states at risk of failing).[28] Many scholars avoid defining these concepts at all, preferring instead to simply compile a list of failed states, typically based on instances of external interventions sanctioned by the United Nations. Others restrict failure to cases of large-scale internal violence. Yet not all "failed states" collapse into civil war. In my accounting, the communist states of Eastern Europe clearly failed in 1989—they were rejected by significant portions of their populations and fell—but in most the transition was peaceful (for example, Czechoslovakia, including the "velvet divorce"), although some, like Yugoslavia, did decline into horrific violence. Rather, we want a definition of failure that does not build into the concept particular causes or effects but allows us to isolate cases and then study their causes and consequences.[29]

Inverting Weber's definition, states fail or lose their "stateness" in one of two ways: a state can lose its *monopoly* on violence or it may lose its *legitimacy*—and sometimes losing one increases the odds of losing the other. Dichotomizing each variable creates four ideal types, as Weber himself would have appreciated, although there are in reality many intermediate combinations, as suggested by the continuous dimensions of figure 1.1.

Consolidated states possess a monopoly of violence and legitimacy. They are the only actors within their domains that can use physical force with the broad support of their societies. This characterizes, to a greater or lesser degree, most states in the developed world and many in the developing world.[30] It is the ideological compatibility of the social order and vesting of interests in the current state that render these entities consolidated. As explained above, and contrary to the institutionalist approach summarized in chapter 1, consolidated states possess vibrant, robust political institutions because groups within society have strong ideological and especially vested interests in preserving and defending those institutions.

Failed states, by contrast, possess neither a monopoly of violence nor legitimacy. The political center is not regarded as authoritative by the people residing

28. Von Einsiedel 2005, 15. On states of limited statehood, see Risse 2011. Limited statehood is, in many ways, a better definition, as it makes clear what is varying (state authority over issues and territory) and that statehood is continuous. Fragility, however, connotes the potential to fail, and for that reason I prefer the term in this context.
29. Although useful in many ways, Rotberg's (2004, 5–10) discussion of failure exemplifies these problems.
30. Even in strong states there are private authorities that may discipline members by nonviolent means legitimately, typically through some form of exclusion from the group and its benefits. See Lake 2010b.

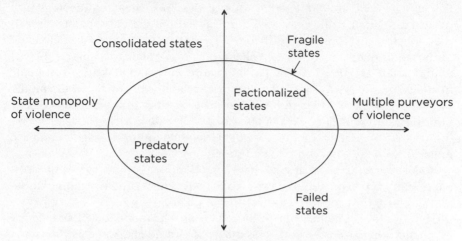

State legitimate purveyor of violence

Consolidated states

Fragile
states

State monopoly
of violence

Factionalized
states

Multiple purveyors
of violence

Predatory
states

Failed
states

State illegitimate purveyor of violence

Figure 1.1. A typology of states.
Following Weber, states can be disaggregated into whether they possess a monopoly on violence (horizontal dimension) and whether they are legitimate in the use of violence (vertical
dimension). Consolidated states fit the classic definition of units with a monopoly of the legitimate use of violence. Failed states lack both. Fragile states take two primary forms. Predatory states lack legitimacy but retain a monopoly on violence. Factionalized states possess a
measure of legitimacy but face other private authorities who can also wield violence with at
least a degree of legitimacy.

within the territory, and multiple groups are authorized by different fragments of the society to use force on their behalf. Iraq after the U.S. invasion
(see chapter 4) or Somalia during the 1990s (see chapter 5) clearly failed along
both dimensions. In such cases, in Weber's terms, there is effectively no state.
In failed states, ideology has typically lost its legitimating role. As explained
below, failure is both driven by and exacerbates social cleavages, undermining whatever unifying ability even shared ideological beliefs might have previously possessed. In turn, failed states have few if any vested interests. Theory
suggests that such interests were already thin on the ground or the state
would otherwise not have failed. Through failure and often violence, groups
that previously defended the state have either had their assets destroyed (or
greatly depreciated) or fled the country with whatever they could carry. In
the instability that ensues, individuals have few incentives to acquire new assets dependent on any particular authority. In consolidated states, authority
is embedded into society through vested interests. In failed states, by contrast,
authority is weakened through their absence.

Fragile states, in turn, are found in two forms, with two paths to possible
failure. Not all fragile states, of course, fail. Some may be sufficiently repressive
to preserve their monopoly of force for long periods, despite weak legitimacy.

Others may have multiple coercive forces within their territory but retain sufficient legitimacy to hold together for decades. In such states, ideology may sustain a ruler, or sufficient vested interests exist at least at the elite level so that overthrowing the state is difficult. Threats to the state provoke defenders of the status quo, deterring challengers. But fragile states all possess the potential to fail, and thus individuals and groups will avoid making investments in assets specific to any particular authority relationship. Society will emphasize mobile, generic assets that will likely be of value in any social order or portable assets that can be taken abroad. This creates a vicious circle and reinforces the potential for failure. With fewer vested interests, fragile states are more likely to fail than consolidated states.

Predatory or authoritarian states have limited or weak legitimacy but possess a monopoly on physical force. More accurately, the regime is regarded as legitimate by only a small fraction of the population—usually but not always the political or economic elite—which then uses its monopoly of violence to exploit its own citizens and suppress those who would challenge its continued rule. These are the states described in the introduction associated with "bad" institutions that favor the rich or limited political constituencies that typically become rich if they are not already so. Predatory states can be stable for long periods of time. Although biasing laws and outcomes in favor of the elite, predatory rulers will, in equilibrium, provide sufficient private goods to key members of their coalitions to prevent coups from within and limit predation against the public to levels not likely to stimulate active rebellion or revolution.[31] With assets concentrated in the elite, moreover, this group has very strong interests in defending the current authority structure.

Without broad legitimacy, predatory states are also more reliant than consolidated states on domestic coercion. Political repression not only deters direct challenges to the ruler but also increases the risk of honest political discussions, thereby making it difficult for potential revolutionaries to know the level of their own support within society and, thus, the prospects for successful rebellion. Without accurate information on the political preferences of their fellow citizens, and fearful of informants turning them in to the regime, individuals engage in widespread preference falsification, making organizing for collective action difficult.[32] Predatory states also commonly adopt strategies of divide and conquer. When the state pits group against group, socially isolated communities become sufficiently fearful of one another that they rely on the ruler to keep the peace, even though all might be better off under a more open political system more representative of their interests. This has been the strategy used by the Assad family and their regime in Syria for decades. This strategy, however, deepens rifts between groups and increases the potential for fragmentation, the second path to failure (see below).

31. Olson 2000; Bueno de Mesquita et al. 2003.
32. Kuran 1995.

With only limited legitimacy, predatory states may ultimately fail by losing their monopoly of violence. Repression by the state and the exclusion of significant groups from power may eventually produce a violent counterreaction in the form of civil unrest or revolution. When rebellion is observed, the state is likely to have overstepped its bounds, extracted too much from society, and killed the golden goose. Robert Mugabe of Zimbabwe appears on the verge of this revolutionary threshold. Although national income has fallen by roughly 40 percent since 2000, largely as a result of his predatory policies, he remains in power only by redistributing land to the poorest members of his society. Under extreme predation, if the opposition gains enough support and legitimacy from the population, the state's monopoly of violence can then erode, and the state can fail. Examples here include the classic revolutions in France, Russia, and China, as well as the Arab Spring revolutions that drove autocrats from power.[33] In other cases, exogenous shocks provide information and allow individuals to gain more accurate insights into their fellow citizens. In the collapse of communism, for instance, widespread opposition to the regimes, long suppressed and hidden, eventually rose to the surface.[34] Once it was clear that the Soviet Union under President Mikhail Gorbachev had repealed the Brezhnev Doctrine and would not intervene in support of Eastern European communist regimes, small demonstrations grew progressively larger until the illegitimacy of the regimes could no longer be disguised. The communist elites that had previously supported their states then refused to approve the violence necessary to retain control: in short, the elites themselves withdrew their consent and doomed their regimes in the face of newly revealed but widespread popular opposition.[35] A similar process appears to have been set in motion during the Arab Spring, when a self-immolation catalyzed demonstrations against the regime in Tunisia, which then spread rapidly to Libya and Egypt. The Arab Spring also illustrates, however, how a process of change, though similar at the beginning, can take different trajectories: Tunisia appears on the path to political stability under a new, more representative regime; after a period of instability, the old Egyptian military regime has resurfaced under the leadership of Abdel Fattah el-Sisi; and Libya has declined into chaos. Political change in fragile societies does not always lead to state failure.

In *factionalized* states, the state is rendered weak as a result of parallel private authorities that are regarded as legitimate by significant fractions of the

33. Skocpol 1979.
34. Kuran 1991; Lohmann 1994.
35. If a new regime emerges quickly and consolidates its control, analysts tend not to count revolutionary change as a state "failure," although I think these cases should be classified as failures as well. But if a new regime is not consolidated, and prolonged instability or civil war results, we do count this as a case of state failure, if only from the uncertainty and recurring low-level violence. Exactly when regime change is large enough to indicate that the previous government "failed" remains ambiguous.

population. Many such authorities are traditional groups such as tribes, clans, or sectarian organizations that exercise significant authority over their members.[36] These traditional groups then limit the authority of the state so that it does not compete with or infringe on their own. In portions of Africa, for instance, traditional land tenure practices were codified under colonialism and often privileged tribal chieftains, who then secured their authority by adjudicating land disputes and manipulating holdings to the advantage of their supporters. The role of the chiefs and their land practices were incorporated into decentralized and limited states on independence, preserving the power of the chiefs and their positions in society. Today, the chiefs remain potent political players with authority independent from and parallel to the state, and indeed compete with the state for authority over tribal members.[37] Private authorities, however, may also be of more recent origin. Mafias, criminal organizations, and the like often build authority for themselves by providing services to communities when the state cannot.[38] Insurgents do so as well, with ISIS being a prime example in the areas it has seized in Syria and Iraq.[39] Once in place, such authorities also act to limit state authority over those same communities. Regardless of whether the private authorities are of ancient or contemporary provenance, social groups can be "too strong" and prevent the state from consolidating its authority over those who are both their members and citizens.[40] Paradoxically, in relying on parallel private authorities, groups within factionalized states become vested in these same authorities and have interests in defending their rights. Those favored by land tenure practices, for instance, have interests in preserving the authority of the local chiefs. It is the strength of such private authorities that weakens the state.

Like predatory states, factionalized states can be stable for long periods. Though private authorities undercut the state by competing for the loyalty of

36. On clans, see Weiner 2013. On private authorities more generally, see Lake 2010b.
37. Boone 2014.
38. Gambetta 1993.
39. On insurgent provision of public goods, see Keister 2011. On the case of ISIS, see Hubbard 2015.
40. Whether traditional or new, private authorities matter politically because they are more effective actors than are "the masses" in general. Precisely because they possess some authority over their members, a degree of internal hierarchy, and leaders with at least some measure of legitimacy of their own, private authorities can mobilize members more effectively within the political system than ad hoc movements. Leaders can call members into action, whether simply to pressure government officials who may be more or less responsive to citizen demands or to participate in street demonstrations or even rebellions. In turn, dissatisfied citizens, perhaps blocked from communicating demands effectively to local representatives, can send complaints up the private authority's hierarchy and demand that their group leaders take action on their behalf. Indeed, it is their effectiveness in providing for members, representing them to the state and other groups, and mobilizing them for politics that secures the authority of the leaders themselves.

citizen-members, they may also constrain state predation, lessening revolutionary pressures.[41] In some societies, however, private authorities are sufficiently strong and entrenched that they challenge and undermine the authority of the state. Clans in Afghanistan and elsewhere continue to authorize blood feuds that are explicitly prohibited under public law. Sharia law is likewise regarded as superior to public law by sectarian groups in Muslim countries, and the object of many fundamentalists is to instill this belief into public law itself. Where private authority competes directly with public authority, the potential for state failure is greater.

The number of factionalized states in the world today remains substantial. Most African states, as suggested, suffer from parallel private authorities and unconsolidated states,[42] as do Afghanistan, Pakistan, Iraq, Syria, and many other political hot spots that are the objects of continuing international attention. Many more, such as Turkey or Iran, which have large Kurdish populations, are relatively consolidated states but also have significant minority communities that retain considerable private authority over their members.

Though factionalization may restrain state predation and lessen internal pressures for regime change, the danger is that private authorities provide ready raw material for extremists to mobilize communities against the state. Political entrepreneurs can choose to compete for power and office within the state or within their communities. For individuals with strong community ties and loyalties, options in the national political arena may be few. The more closely such entrepreneurs are associated with particular communities, the less likely they are to gain support from other groups. Thus, partisans will often choose to seek power and office within their communities and their private authorities. Extremists, in turn, may attempt to pull the state apart and rally members to their cause. Inciting violence along communal lines and activating memories of past abuse, extremists aim to provoke fear among all groups, especially their own. In the face of a weak state that cannot guarantee the safety of individuals, all are then driven into their communities for protection, further dividing society and weakening the state.[43] As the dependence of threatened individuals on their communities increases, the authority of the leadership expands and likely becomes more radical. It is all too easy in highly factionalized states for extremists to mobilize fear to bolster their own political agendas and seize authority for themselves. As they do so, however, the state separates at the seams and falls into a vicious downward spiral that results in failure. Although there is a lack of systematic evidence, it appears

---

41. Indeed, some range of private authorities may be essential in limiting state power even in effective developed or developing states. See Lake 2014.
42. Herbst 2000; Boone 2003.
43. Lake and Rothchild 1996.

that once the mobilization of fear begins, factionalized states are more likely than their predatory counterparts to fail.

These two paths to state failure are not inconsistent and can even reinforce one another, especially when one group within society captures the state and uses its coercive power to exploit other communities. As explained in chapter 5, this was the path taken by Somalia under Mohamed Siad Barre, who became increasingly predatory and exclusionist in his later years, exacerbating bitter clan rivalries that ultimately led to state failure. Indeed, it is often the fear that one group will capture the state and abuse others that rallies communities around their private authorities and strengthens extremists. This was the principal blockage to consolidating authority in the Afghan government under President Hamid Karzai, often accused of using the instruments of state power to favor his Pashtun tribe and relatives. Predation and factionalization form an especially toxic mix, with horizontal and vertical cleavages reinforcing each other and tearing society and the state apart.

The Challenge of Statebuilding

Statebuilding requires the construction or reconstruction of both the state's monopoly of violence and the legitimacy of that monopoly. As we know from the literature on civil war termination, in the absence of total victory, rebuilding the monopoly of force can be quite difficult. Barbara Walter describes this as "the critical barrier to civil war settlement."[44] The disarming of one or more groups or the merging of forces can leave groups vulnerable, hesitant to enter negotiations, and reluctant to implement agreements once reached. Most important, with coercion being their primary political instrument, disarming or merging forces implies changing the balance of power between the groups that existed at the time of agreement. This fatally undermines the credibility of any peace agreement. If one or the other party is weakened by its agreement to disarm, then the stronger party will have an incentive to violate the agreement in the future; fearing this, the weaker party will refuse to make or implement the agreement. Without denying its importance, this problem of rebuilding the state's monopoly of coercive violence is now relatively well understood—if still difficult to resolve.

Perhaps even tougher is rebuilding the legitimacy of the state after it is lost. Even in peaceful transitions, as in Eastern Europe after 1989, historical animosities, ideological differences, and preference heterogeneity can combine to create lasting political instability—as in Ukraine after the "Orange Revolution," eventually creating the opening through which Russia mobilized ethnic Russians to seize Crimea—or even separation, as in the velvet divorce between

44. Walter 1997.

the Czech Republic and Slovakia in 1993. After widespread violence, regardless of the perpetrators, the problem of reconstructing legitimacy can be overwhelming. Typically, the old political community has been torn apart by the fighting. Loyalty to the state, especially one controlled or dominated by the other group, has collapsed. Short of total victory by one side, the political differences that led to war must be accommodated by changing the prewar institutions and rules, but there is no foundation on which to build new institutions. I focus on rebuilding legitimacy because of its difficulty and importance and because we understand this process so poorly.[45]

Failed states face four core problems that thwart recovery and follow from the paths to failure described above. States that have failed and need to be rebuilt face, first, a lack of vested interests in any authority and, second, ineffective legal systems and political institutions, creating blank political slates; this might seem helpful, but it leaves societies without any means of avoiding political chaos. Third, the social cleavages that existed before failure have typically been deepened by violence, and fourth, potential leaders do not possess an obvious support coalition large enough to secure power. Statebuilders, either internal or external, must solve all four problems simultaneously.

Vesting Interests in the State

As noted above, fragile states possess few vested interests. Fearing that the state may fail, citizens will not invest in relationally specific assets. With few such assets, these same citizens have little incentive to defend the existing regime. With few defenders, the regime is fragile. Failed states, in turn, usually lack any vested interests. Some resources are destroyed in the fighting. Indeed, opponents may target each other's assets precisely to weaken their will to fight for the regime. Other assets flee the country if possible. Already thinly vested to begin with, failed states lack the glue to bind society together and to the new state.

Without significant vested interests in society, in turn, individuals are less likely to have stable expectations about future authority relationships and social orders. With fewer expectations of stability, they have less incentive to invest in any relationally specific assets. Failed states suffer from a chicken-and-egg problem: stable expectations are necessary to catalyze investments in specific assets, but such investments are necessary for stable expectations of the future. At best, individuals and groups in failed states invest in generic and highly mobile assets that are likely to possess some value no matter what happens in the future. Any statebuilder must "fix" expectations around a particular form of authority or state in order for new vesting to occur.

45. Von Einsiedel 2005, 19–20.

Law and Political Institutions

The lack of vested interests, in turn, implies that society and the state will lack stable institutions. Along with the lack of centralized political authority, state failure also implies the failure of the legal system, including both the national constitution on which the failed state rested and the laws passed by that state prior to its demise. Although in some cases existing law may be preserved in a transition period for lack of an alternative, neither the now defunct constitution nor previous state laws can be used to legitimize or justify new laws. Likewise, ideological interests proved insufficient to forestall failure, and thus form a weak foundation on which to rebuild legitimacy. These are, obviously, states in which the old institutions and interests proved insufficient to sustain social order.

The weak legal system of failed states has two important consequences. First, any new state is at least potentially subject to "cycling," in the formal sense of this term, in which policies preferred by one majority coalition are displaced by those preferred by a different majority, ad infinitum. This phenomenon was identified by the Marquis de Condorcet in 1785 in the wake of the French Revolution, and proven by Kenneth Arrow. Even under relatively simple and broadly accepted rules of preference aggregation, there may not be a stable political equilibrium.[46] Richard McKelvey generalized this insight in his "chaos theorem," which demonstrates that in any two-dimensional policy space any policy pair is possible under majority rule.[47] Such a situation is illustrated in figure 1.2. Assuming three actors (A, B, and C), equivalent to groups in the analysis here, and two issues, each actor has an ideal point denoted A, B, or C, with circular indifference curves (Euclidean preferences) around those ideal points. Starting from any arbitrarily chosen point x, such as the intersection of medians explained below, the intersections of the indifference curves define "win sets" in which alternatives within each "petal" are preferred by two actors to x. With pairwise comparisons and majority rule, A and B would vote for policy pair ab, but this can be defeated by a coalition of B and C who vote for pair bc, and then by a coalition of C and A who prefer ca, and so on. Although this is an analytic result rather than a prediction or an actual observation of voting outcomes, it nonetheless reveals the potential, at least, for political instability as fluctuating majorities churn through alternatives.[48] Political outcomes are, in this case, inherently unpredictable or "chaotic."

46. On the voting paradoxes, see Schwartz 1987. On social choice problems and legitimacy, see Patty and Penn 2014.
47. McKelvey 1976, 1979. For a nontechnical review of McKelvey's theorem and extensions, see Cox and Shepsle 2007.
48. The most telling critiques of social choice are that (1) in the real world, the assumptions of the theory are violated when real humans make decisions, and (2) in practice, the sets of preferences conducive to cycling are either nonexistent or, at most, rare. The examples of the latter, however, are mostly drawn from established democracies, not states that have failed. See Mackie 2003.

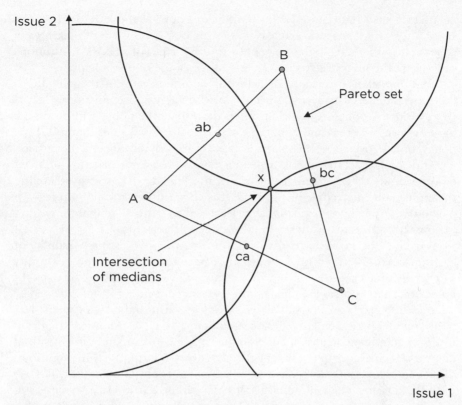

Figure 1.2. The problem of political cycling and statebuilding.
Policy preferences vary along two dimensions. Three actors with ideal points, denoted as A, B, and C, and Euclidean preferences can cycle through alternatives under pairwise comparisons and majority rule, with policy pair ab, supported by a coalition of AB, being defeated by bc by coalition BC, being defeated by ca by coalition AC, being defeated by ab by coalition AB, and so on. For all policy pairs within the Pareto set, no further improvements in welfare for any two actors are possible without reducing the welfare of the third. The intersection of medians, denoted *x*, is the product of majority voting on each dimension individually.

Kenneth Shepsle subsequently showed that political rules and especially agenda-setting rules (a choice function) can nonetheless create an equilibrium and a degree of predictability; that is, institutions can induce an equilibrium by determining the rules by which choices are made.[49] By controlling the agenda or the order and way in which alternatives are considered, institutions can eliminate cycling. For better or worse, however, this power also gives agenda setters the ability to determine the policy outcome. Sophisticated

49. Shepsle 1979. In essence, agenda control allows an agenda setter to determine which policy pairs are considered in which order. By exercising its power to restrict the range and order of alternatives, the agenda setter can typically realize its ideal policy. See Romer and Rosenthal 1978. For a review of agenda-setting models, see Cox 2005.

agenda setters can even move the equilibrium outside the Pareto set, or the set of alternatives that leave at least one actor better off without making any other actor worse off. In this view, by setting the rules of politics, institutions determine the policy selected from the entire range of possible policies.[50]

In an important extension, William Riker demonstrates further that instability over policy will be transformed into instability over institutions.[51] If rules induce a policy equilibrium, then the fight over policy will become a fight over rules. States may adopt one set of institutional rules that induces a policy, only to overturn those rules for another set that induces a second policy, and so on. Lacking established rules as required for a structure-induced equilibrium, politics within failed states may fall into the trap of cycling through many alternative institutions. It is the vesting of social interests in particular authority structures that at least reduces this potential for cycling in consolidated states by increasing the value of the status quo for all parties. Conversely, it is the absence of vested interests that makes the possibility of cycling so worrisome in failed states and, paradoxically, it is the possibility of cycling that makes acquiring new relationally specific assets so risky. In failed states, the possibility of instability breeds continuing instability.

To escape cycles and potential cycles, actors within failed states must rely either on ideological interests that can structure their decision making or on traditional, nonlegal rules of decision making.[52] Unfortunately, as a result of deep social cleavages magnified by the process of failure, the third condition discussed below, both agreement on ideology and communal trust will likely have broken down as well, limiting the effectiveness of these alternatives to political institutions for solving problems of collective decision making. Political instability remains a real threat to new states without robust institutions and, in turn, deeply vested interests. The failure to recognize this intense relationship is, perhaps, the most serious error of the institutionalist approach outlined in the introduction and of the related liberal theory of legitimation discussed in chapter 3.

Distributional Concerns

In fragile states, groups typically struggle over the gains from social cooperation. At the same time as these gains are the glue that holds societies together, hard bargaining over their distribution threatens to tear society apart. Horizontal class cleavages pit elites against the masses. Vertical communal cleavages set traditional social groups against one another. In predatory states, one class or group succeeds in capturing the state and repressing others, possibly increasing its rate of exploitation. Factionalized states with multiple purveyors of

---

50. For an application to the U.S. House of Representatives, see Cox and McCubbins 2005.
51. Riker 1980; also Gourevitch 1999.
52. Riker 1984; Gourevitch 1999.

violence may escape high levels of repression, as the state itself remains weak, but may also become more violent.

Failed states retain these lines of cleavage and the distributional struggles that both create and reinforce them. More important, failure itself exacerbates these cleavages in four critical ways. First, the breakdown of social order reduces the gains from cooperation: internal exchange becomes more precarious, and specialization is mitigated, infrastructure erodes, and investment declines. As the gains from cooperation shrink, there is less to fight over. At the same time, however, each group fighting for survival in more desperate circumstances is motivated to compete ever harder over its share of the now smaller pie. In very poor, violence-ridden states, the latter effect appears to dominate as economic decline exacerbates class and communal conflict.

Second, and more important, state failure strengthens group allegiances, especially for traditional communal groups with strong ascriptive traits. As the state fails, individuals are driven to narrower identity groups for protection. In Yugoslavia, for instance, it did not much matter how cosmopolitan one's self-identity was; once the violence broke out, one became a Serb, Croat, or Muslim in the eyes of others, and a potential target. Fear and the need for self-help drove everyone into their socially constructed but nonetheless real ethnic containers. As the conflict deepened, the identities of many former Yugoslavs hardened and have remained so after the violence has ended. Intergroup cleavages are almost always worsened, not mitigated, in the process of state failure, especially so as the level of violence increases.

Third, the outbreak of conflict in failed states worsens distrust between groups, making cooperation even more difficult. It is rare that groups that were trying desperately to slaughter one another can sit down together in a new legislature or other body and work out effective ways to restart the economy and divide its benefits fairly. Nelson Mandela is widely credited with leading such a reconciliation process in South Africa but for this reason is also regarded as an exceptional individual and admired as a leader. Transitional justice efforts may help mitigate distrust, but old wounds are hard to heal entirely.[53] Far more commonly, former combatants are not good negotiating partners and need even tougher commitment mechanisms to make deals viable.

Finally, failure typically deepens ideological cleavages, especially if they overlap with class or sectarian divisions. Even though vested interests may have depreciated or been destroyed altogether in the process of failure, individuals will retain their ideological interests. Shared beliefs may help legitimate new states, or at least their form as divinely supported monarchies, religiously backed theocracies, or liberal states that back individual freedoms and free markets. Yet failure and the ensuing violence often weaken these

---

53. Chesterman 2004; Boraine 2005.

shared beliefs, leaving individuals and groups more polarized or at least more politically alienated than before. Rather than provide a foundation on which to restore the legitimacy of the state, ideological differences may now inhibit state consolidation.

For these reasons, rebuilding failed states is especially hard. There is no "original position" in which institutions can be designed and resources distributed under a veil of ignorance, as John Rawls termed it.[54] Rather, not only are the groups and the unfairness of the prior regime manifest, but the hostility and animosity between groups has worsened. This has two further implications.

To transfer legitimacy from the group to the state, a necessary process in the consolidation of state authority, individuals must be convinced that the state can provide a more secure social order that leaves them better off than the group with which they are associated by tradition or ascription. The state cannot just provide any order and gain the support of its citizens. It must provide a better order and a larger social product than can the groups acting autonomously. In the state of nature, perhaps the state can beat nothing with something. But in the hardened environment of a postconflict failed state, the new state must beat something with something even better. This has been a continuing problem in Somalia. As discussed in chapter 5, as the clans and even warlords have acquired a larger role in providing public services to members and have produced a measure of social order, even the business community, which has learned to live with instability, is reluctant to support a new but potentially predatory state.

In addition, groups reinforced by war will possess internal leaders with some measure of authority. At a minimum, leaders of groups successful enough to organize and participate in the political process will have earned the ability to speak for the group and represent it to others. With this authority comes the opportunity for leaders to act in their own interests rather than in those of the group as a whole. Just as state leaders may thwart democracy by acting in their self-interest rather than the national interest, group leaders may pursue their own standing and political gains rather than those of their followers. Importantly, leaders may develop a vested interest in their positions as leaders—and the privileges and rents that follow from that status—that would not carry over into a new state either because they might be excluded from power or because they might simply become one of several group leaders in the new central government.[55] To the extent that leaders are vested in privileged positions within their groups and have autonomy in conducting affairs, they may also undercut efforts to forge new political orders and states.

54. Rawls 1999.
55. This calculus is central to the stability of federal institutions. See Filippov, Ordeshook, and Shvetsova 2004.

Problematic Leadership

Finally, an essential task for new leaders in failed states is to build political support coalitions to sustain themselves in office. Current statebuilding efforts are typically premised on a fundamentally naïve model of politics in which leaders are assumed to be "true democrats" or sincerely interested only in stabilizing their failed states. Practice implicitly assumes that all parties involved in the process possess largely if not entirely selfless motives in enhancing statehood, political stability, and economic prosperity. National political leaders put "country first" over their narrow partisan or coalitional needs—even over their political or personal survival. Most important, it is assumed that they will accept and live within new, more participatory political institutions rather than subvert them for their own political ends. Although I do not doubt that there are some "true democrats" in the world today, it is certainly not the case that all leaders are of this type.[56] Rather, in nearly all positive theories of politics, we assume that political leaders seek their own political survival and, contingent on retaining office, to redistribute wealth and other benefits to themselves and their political coalition.[57]

In failed states, "natural" political leaders able to unite the country are rare. Indeed, were such charismatic leaders readily identifiable, they would have already risen to power with broad-based support or, more likely, been killed by rivals during the violence. In the chaos of a failed state, leaders will almost certainly lack a strong, independent, and broad base of political support. Contenders with their own committed supporters will likely be blocked by rivals. Strong barons always prefer a weak monarch. With the acquiescence of all critical parties but the fervent support of none, new leaders will need to build their own coalitions from scratch to sustain themselves in office. Being the least objectionable candidate is a fragile position, stable only so long as renewed fighting or anarchy is worse. Given these inherent weaknesses, we can expect new leaders to use their positions as intermediaries with external statebuilders to direct the flow of foreign aid or other resources to their newly formed political coalitions.

Despite frequent calls for "leadership" in failed states to surmount the difficulties that caused the state to fail in the first place, selfless leaders who are willing and able to play a role as neutral statebuilder are rare. We cannot expect a George Washington or even a Nelson Mandela to arise whenever they are needed. Indeed, the greater the need for leadership, the more likely such effective leaders will have been assassinated during conflict or blocked by more partisan rivals. Rather, statebuilders must work with the imperfect, egoistic, and partisan leaders that are likely available.

56. On election monitoring as a way of screening for true democrats, see Hyde 2011. The phrase is hers.
57. Bueno de Mesquita et al. 2003.

The Promise of Statebuilding

Statebuilders face daunting challenges in failed states. Few in early modern Europe likely understood statebuilding as a conscious, designed process. Rather, it was an organic, incremental practice that unfolded over centuries without a clearly specified end. It is, perhaps, the hubris of modern society that we believe that strong, effective states can be intentionally created within a matter of months or years.

Absolute victory by one party to a civil war may allow the victor to impose a solution to the problems of cycling and the absence of institutions and law, igniting the process of vesting critical to long-term stability and the consolidation of the state.[58] This is likely the path followed by today's modern states, especially in Europe; in earlier days, a warlord conquered a territory, proclaimed himself king, established a dynasty with a spouse usually drawn from the defeated but local elite, and then—if his position was sufficiently secure and credible—society accommodated itself to the new regime. Today, when the parties to a conflict are stalemated or the international community is unwilling to tolerate the casualties and suffering of a drawn-out civil war, the four problems identified above become acute: the lack of social interests vested in a regime prompts cycling through alternative institutions; those institutions are unable to induce an equilibrium; social fissures deepened by the failure of the state create continued fear that invigorates traditional social forces that themselves have vested interests opposed to state consolidation; and national leaders will be rare.

Picking a Social Order

The promise of statebuilding is that, like domestic victors, external powers can impose a solution that sticks. By creating and guaranteeing a new regime that is sufficiently credible, the statebuilder can catalyze social groups to become vested in the new state, despite their enduring antagonisms and fears of possible exploitation. The statebuilder, in other words, can "plant a stake" in the ground that announces that the new social order will be "this," not "that," with "this" set of institutions, rules, and policy outcomes. In imposing an order and a set of attendant policies, the statebuilder acts in ways similar to an agenda setter in a structure-induced equilibrium. If the statebuilder's claim is sufficiently credible, social interests will then accommodate themselves to the new order, investing in assets premised on "this" set of institutions and policies. Once invested, these same social forces will develop an interest in defending the new state against challenges. In short, the state will be consolidated. This, at any rate, is the promise.

---

58. On absolute victory and post–civil war peace, see Walter 2002.

At the moment of failure, when interests vested in the prior state have faded away, the statebuilder may have some leeway in terms of which social order it can impose and guarantee. In the occupations of West Germany and Japan, for example, the United States dominated societies that were devastated by the war and whose economies were in ruins. The fascist and militarist ideologies that had taken hold during the 1930s rapidly lost support as the consequences of war became clear to all. The fighting destroyed many assets specific to the prior social order. In the wake of war, no new order was readily apparent, but few had significant interests in defending the old one. Neither society was a tabula rasa—a blank slate on which the United States could write anything it chose. Nonetheless, the flattened political landscape did give Washington freedom to insist on a new social order that was capitalist, not socialist, based on competitive market principles, not the prewar and wartime cartels that had dominated the economy, and that reflected moderate "Christian" democratic principles. The former fascist, authoritarian, and internationally aggressive states were, in this way, redirected into the capitalist, democratic, and liberal states that they are today. Other failed states, however, continue to possess vestiges of the prior vested interests or, more likely, reinvigorated and reified traditional social forces that limit the range of social orders the statebuilder can sustain. Statebuilders usually do not have the same ability to shift the political trajectories of failed states that the United States did in the exceptional cases of West Germany and Japan. Yet failure does usually create a measure of plasticity in politics.

With a degree of latitude in selecting a new social order, a statebuilder can most easily legitimate a new state when the social order it imposes—the stake it plants in the ground and guarantees to defend—is close to that preferred by all (or many) members of society. When there is a social order with its attendant policies that is preferred by a stable majority of citizens (a "Condorcet winner," in the language of social choice theory), however unlikely that might be in a state that has failed, a statebuilder concerned only with legitimacy should pick that order. When social preferences are such that cycling is possible, the statebuilder should, at a minimum, select an order within the Pareto set, the triangle connecting the ideal points of actors A, B, and C in figure 1.2. Although the status quo has likely deteriorated significantly through the failure of the state, and a wide variety of improvements are likely possible, the most preferred social orders will be those associated with policies within this area. At any point within the Pareto set, no further improvements are possible without reducing the welfare of at least one party. At a maximum, the statebuilder should select the intersection of medians, illustrated in figure 1.2 by the point x. If the policy dimensions are separable or independent from one another, a decision rule that considered each dimension individually would produce this result.[59]

59. Mackie 2003, 176–178. If the dimensions are nonseparable, dimension-by-dimension voting will necessarily select the intersection of medians unless voters are sophisticated. A

Cycling may still occur anywhere within the Pareto set, of course, including at the intersection of medians. It is for this reason that the statebuilder must credibly commit to defend the order it has chosen, as it is not necessarily a unique equilibrium.[60] Yet the more closely the new order reflects the policy preferences of the largest number of individuals, the more readily it will gain support. Thus, a statebuilder concerned only with legitimacy should aim at this "central" tendency within society.[61] It was not a coincidence, in this view, that the United States selected a social order that both fulfilled its interests in the defeated states and appealed to the moderate-to-conservative democratic forces in both West Germany and Japan, the great silent majorities who were at best ambivalent about the fascists and who sometimes suffered under their rule. This strategy for legitimating states is important for the larger argument of this book. If a statebuilder cares only about the legitimacy of the new state it is promoting, it will create a social order and attendant policies that aim to make as many individuals within the target population as well off as possible. By doing so, statebuilders have the best chance for catalyzing social support for new states.

Planting a stake near the political center need not require democracy or representative institutions—though these may help the statebuilder identify where that center lies.[62] Rather, the more the new social order conforms to what some or, better, most citizens want of their government, the more easily the policies it produces will be accepted by the population and the more legitimate the new state will become. Such a social order will not prevent cycling or deep distributional conflicts from overwhelming the new state—thus the need for an external guarantor. But such a social order, perhaps preferred by none but closest to the policy preferences of many, has the best chance of becoming legitimate.

Guaranteeing a Social Order

Regardless of the precise social order imposed, however, the statebuilder must have two essential qualities to sustain it. First, it must be potentially stronger and more powerful than any of the domestic factions that might resist or defect from the new social order and state. Strength does not require

---

statebuilder concerned only with the legitimacy of the target state could also choose the social order in the minmax set, if it exists, the set of points toward which a set of winning political platforms will tend to converge over a sequence of winning elections. See Kramer 1977.

60. As explained above, even if the intersection of the medians is selected, x can be defeated under majority rule by any alternative in the win sets.

61. In American politics, this is equivalent to assessing institutions by their responsiveness to public opinion. See Sabl 2015.

62. Indeed, if cycling is possible, democracy is not guaranteed to "settle" at the intersection of the medians or even within the Pareto set. This is the essence of the social choice critique of democracy.

that the statebuilder have more troops on the ground than the largest faction, only that it have the capacity and will to mobilize greater force than any faction should it be necessary. If it is able to punish challengers to the new state in principle, such challengers will be deterred, and even small deployments by the statebuilder may be sufficient. Indeed, the most important role of troops on the ground is not their ability to fight but their presence as a costly signal of the statebuilder's commitment to the new state.[63]

Second, the statebuilder must also commit to defend the new state into the indefinite future. Any timeline or "date certain" for the termination of its support raises the possibility of future political instability, which in turn discourages investments in assets specific to the new state. Without such regime-specific investments, future instability becomes more likely, causing individuals to sustain their ties to private authorities and groupings that, in turn, prevent further state consolidation. The commitment of the statebuilder must last longer than the process of vesting interests in the new state. This commitment need not require boots on the ground indefinitely. Once the process of vesting ignites, the direct role of the statebuilder can be rolled back. But it is the commitment of the statebuilder to return and defend the state against challengers that remains important until the latter is consolidated. Ironically, the larger and more ironclad the commitment of the statebuilder, the quicker the process of vesting interests will be, and the sooner the statebuilder will be able to reduce its role and withdraw. Conversely, the more the statebuilder tries to force the process of vesting by announcing its withdrawal—attempting to encourage local partners to step up and take charge of their own fate, as tried by the Bush administration in Iraq (see chapter 4)—the less vesting will occur and the longer its presence will be necessary to achieve stability.

Without advocating a return to imperialism, objectionable on other grounds, it was nonetheless the greater strength and perceived commitment of the European countries to govern their colonies in perpetuity that promoted the accommodation of local social forces to their new governance structures, which then allowed the empires to endure so long with such minimal military forces. It was this same combination of strength and seeming permanence that facilitated the successful U.S. statebuilding efforts in West Germany and Japan after 1945, where the victor of World War II retained hundreds of thousands of troops in each country and proclaimed its commitment to stay for decades, or more, if necessary.[64] Even after the start of the Cold War reoriented the mission of the occupation troops, and efforts were made to rehabilitate the defeated countries and return them to full sovereignty quickly so as to maximize their contributions to the new containment effort, there was little doubt

---

63. On troop deployments as signals of commitment, see Schelling 1966, chap. 2.
64. The most common estimate of the expected length of the U.S. occupation of Germany was forty years. See Lake 1999, 176–178.

about the commitment of the United States to stay in Europe and East Asia and maintain its worldwide network of bases anchored in West Germany and Japan. Having staked new social orders in these countries, the United States then successfully guaranteed them, setting off the process of vesting that produced two of the stronger and more consolidated states in the world today. This is a goal of all statebuilding attempts.

States fail for many reasons, but deep social cleavages that leave the state unconsolidated or pull it apart are a fundamental cause. The challenge for statebuilders is to create or re-create a *legitimate* monopoly of the use of violence. This is a demanding task, thwarted by the conditions that led to failure in the first place and aggravated by destruction of specific assets and ideological divisions widened during the conflict. The great promise of statebuilding is to establish and credibly guarantee a new social order around which social interests can become vested. This is most easily done by "staking" the social order where it can gain the greatest support within the country.

Yet the promise of statebuilding is often unfulfilled. As discussed in chapter 2, seeking to preserve the principle of sovereignty necessary to sustain the system of decentralized violence control, statebuilders are restricted to limited and temporary interventions that fail to encourage the vesting of social interests in the new state. More important, statebuilding is a costly undertaking that, to succeed, should be of indefinite duration. Any state willing to bear high costs over an unlimited time horizon will likely have interests of its own in the state that failed. When the interests of the statebuilder and the average citizen in the failed state differ, as they do in most cases today, the statebuilder will not be a neutral arbiter that prefers legitimacy to all other goals but rather a self-interested partisan that will support new leaders favorable to its interests. This desire for a "loyal" leader pulls policy away from the center and undermines the new leader's legitimacy. This is the statebuilder's dilemma, discussed at length in chapter 3.

2

Problems of Sovereignty

Sovereignty is the basic constitutional principle of modern international politics and a defining aspiration of contemporary states.[1] As such, the principle sets the context in which statebuilding succeeds or fails. Indeed, the statebuilder's dilemma would not exist were it not for the pervasive hold of this principle, which divides the globe into territorially distinct units with "ultimate" authorities within each. As background to the larger dilemma, this chapter examines the concept of sovereignty and how it conditions contemporary practices of statebuilding. I develop four central arguments in consecutive sections of this chapter.

First, the international system is a decentralized mechanism for controlling violence. In essence, each state as a sovereign entity is charged with responsibility for violence emanating from its territory. Failed states are problematic, as they create gaps in this system that threaten to unravel the whole. Statebuilding, in turn, is a fundamentally conservative attempt by other states to shore up weak or failed members of the international community so that they can fulfill their responsibilities.

Second, sovereignty itself contains a paradox. Although states must support the principle of sovereignty to bolster and sustain the decentralized system of violence control, they must also accept in practice a right or at least the need to intervene in fragile or failed states. The principle of sovereignty is frequently violated in practice. But the deeper problem is that such violations not only occur but are actually inherent and even required when states are not fully capable of controlling violence themselves. This is the paradox of sovereignty: to protect the principle of sovereignty, states must in practice violate or be prepared to violate that principle.

1. On constitutional structures of international relations, see Reus-Smit 1999.

Third, since practice must allow for some interventions into the internal affairs of others, opportunistic interventions may arise that go beyond restoring the ability of states to govern their ungoverned spaces. Indeed, the international community is well aware that states, under the guise of statebuilding, may intervene in others to promote favored leaders and policies—which then creates the statebuilder's dilemma. In response, and especially in light of the historic abuses by the Europeans during the era of overseas empires, the international community today attempts to regulate the practice of statebuilding by requiring some form of multilateral authorization and oversight and by restricting the size, duration, and resources of such missions. As a consequence, statebuilding today must be conducted in a limited fashion with the goal of withdrawing and returning the failed state to full sovereignty as soon as possible. This undermines the credibility of the statebuilder so necessary to the process of vesting interests in the state, explained in the previous chapter.

Fourth, and most important, though a multilateral approach might be expected to mitigate the role of self-interest, statebuilding efforts are still dependent on the willingness of states to assist voluntarily their fragile or failed brethren. Lacking independent coercive forces that might build states in ungoverned spaces, or autonomous taxation powers that would allow some multinational entity to hire coercive forces on an ad hoc basis for such missions, the international community is limited to "coalitions of the willing"—sometimes of one state, sometimes more, but in all cases composed only of those willing to pay the costs of building a state outside their own jurisdictions. By implication, states with significant interests in the failed state will be most likely to volunteer for statebuilding efforts. Some states may volunteer from a sense of altruism or participate for the larger collective good of shoring up the system of violence control itself, but these efforts are typically limited to increasing foreign aid or providing advisers in the processes of disarmament or security sector reform. As the costs of statebuilding increase, only the self-interested typically step forward for the most dangerous duty. Despite attempts to control the statebuilder's dilemma by limiting the powers of statebuilders, the international community is ultimately dependent on the voluntary efforts of what will inevitably be self-interested states. This is the foundation of the statebuilder's dilemma.

The Principle of Sovereignty

Although often misunderstood and sometimes believed to possess mystical qualities, sovereignty is merely a statement about how political authority should be organized within and between states. As now understood, the principle asserts that public authority is indivisible and culminates in a single apex in each territorially defined state and simultaneously prohibits intervention by other similarly sovereign units.

The modern concept of sovereignty is said to have been established in the Peace of Westphalia (1648), composed of the Treaties of Münster and Osnabrück, classically described by Leo Gross as the "majestic portal" through which the age of modern, sovereign states supposedly arrived.[2] In actuality, the emergence of the principle of sovereignty was far more gradual and less linear than in the orthodox version, with at least four major "signposts" along the way. Important for the story of international statebuilding, however, the early phases of sovereignty's emergence were struggles over the division of authority between kings and the pope. Only in the latter phases did interstate relations become the focus of attention.

The deep origins of sovereignty date from the investiture controversy of the eleventh and twelfth centuries, begun when Catholic officials revoked the right of the Holy Roman emperor, then the child Henry IV, to appoint the pope and created the College of Cardinals.[3] In 1075, now grown, Henry withdrew his support from Pope Gregory VII, declaring him a "false monk," and began once again appointing his own bishops. Gregory then excommunicated Henry, deposing him as German king and setting off an internal struggle within the empire for control. One year later, Henry capitulated, appearing before the pope in a hair shirt at Canossa, only to then invade Italy to depose Gregory. Although the pope's Norman allies defeated Henry's German forces, they then sacked Rome and set off a popular uprising that overthrew Gregory anyway. Successive popes continued to stimulate rebellions and wars within the Holy Roman Empire, leading to a dramatic decline in its political centralization. This first stage of the controversy eventually ended with the Concordat of Worms, signed in September 1122, through which some rights of investiture were returned to the pope. A similar controversy played out in England during this same period. The investiture controversy hardly settled the issue, however, and monarchs and popes continued to struggle over the division of authority in Christendom, with the pope still claiming the more limited power to depose rulers.[4]

The second major signpost was the Peace of Augsburg in 1555. Following the Reformation, the Holy Roman Empire once again fell into near chaos, with the Catholic emperor, Charles V, now facing off against Lutheran monarchs resisting his authority, resulting in the Schmalkaldic War (1546–1547). Although Charles won on the battlefield, instability continued, and Protestantism eventually became too deeply entrenched to eradicate. A compromise was finally reached at Augsburg based on the now famous principle of *cuius regio, eius*

2. Gross 1948.
3. One could, of course, begin the story of sovereignty in ancient Greece and Rome, but the notion was sufficiently different in those periods that most accounts start with the investiture controversy. On earlier conceptions, see Reus-Smit 1999. On the struggle over authority during the eleventh and twelfth centuries, see Bisson 2009.
4. Havercroft 2012, 124.

religio (whose realm, his religion), granting princes within the empire the right to choose the official religion within the domains they controlled.[5]

The third signpost is, of course, the Peace of Westphalia. Following a period of relative quiet in the religious wars, the Thirty Years' War broke out in 1618 as a local dispute over the appointment of a new king in Bohemia. Once again setting the Catholic emperor against Protestant princes struggling for greater autonomy, it soon became a "world war" pitting the "universalist" Habsburg dynasty, in league with the pope in Rome, against the nascent "particularistic" states seeking to escape from imperial hcgemony.[6] The war ended with the Treaties of Münster and Osnabrück. Westphalia was a general settlement that sought to address the range of political and religious issues that had been scouring Europe for centuries. Affirming the principle of *cuius regio, eius religio*, Westphalia went further in claiming *rex est imperator in regno suo* (each king is an emperor in his own realm), effectively ending the Holy Roman Empire's claim to be a trans-European polity and, more important, asserting that ultimate or final authority in a territory was vested in each monarch.[7] Although none of the princes at Westphalia anticipated anything like the contemporary concept of sovereignty, by the end of the Thirty Years' War the seeds had certainly been planted.

With Westphalia, two major principles of sovereignty were fairly clearly established, though practice continued to differ. First, the sovereign possesses ultimate or final authority over the people and territory of a given realm. As articulated by Jean Bodin in his *Six Books of the Commonwealth* (1576), the first major treatise on the subject, "persons who are sovereign must not be subject in any way to the commands of someone else and must be able to give law to subjects, and to suppress or repeal disadvantageous laws and replace them with others—which cannot be done by someone who is subject to the laws or to persons having power of command over him."[8] Second, this ultimate authority was indivisible, a unity that could not be divided between different authorities. This idea of indivisibility also originates with Bodin, who concluded that if sovereignty was absolute, the sovereign's authority could not be divided between branches or levels of government or between different actors. Sovereignty by its very nature, he claimed, could be vested only in a single person within a political community.[9] This view was echoed by other jurists, including Hugo Grotius, the Dutch legal theorist whose classic *De Jure Belli ac Pacis* (1625) was the first major work of international law; he wrote that "sovereignty is a unity, in itself indivisible."[10] Along with the first principle, the as-

---

5. This right, however, was limited to Lutherans, excluding the rapidly growing Calvinist sect and sowing the seeds of future instability.
6. Osiander 2001.
7. Havercroft 2012, 120.
8. Brown, Nardin, and Rengger 2002, 273.
9. Keene 2002, 43.
10. Quoted in ibid., 44.

sumption of indivisibility implies that authority must culminate in a single apex at the level of the state—indeed, it is this apex that defines the state.

The consolidation of ultimate and indivisible authority in the state implied a third principle of nonintervention, but this was not made explicit for another century.[11] This has led revisionists to move the date at which the principle of sovereignty emerged to the late eighteenth century, which can serve as the fourth and final signpost, but even then there was no radical break point, only the slow, incremental elaboration of philosophical principles in the context of continuing political struggle. If to be sovereign meant that the monarch is the ultimate authority in a single, hierarchically ordered domain, it necessarily implied that no one else could exercise authority in that same area or over the same people. By extension, no other power could intervene legitimately in the "internal" affairs of a sovereign state. The first explicit statement of the principle of nonintervention was by Christian von Wolff, writing in 1748 that "to interfere in the government of another, in whatever way indeed that may be done is opposed to the natural liberty of nations, by virtue of which one is altogether independent of the will of other nations in its action."[12] Writing a decade later and seeking to popularize Wolff's more philosophical view for international lawyers, Emmerich de Vattel agreed that no state had a right to intervene in the internal affairs of any other. Since nations were "free and independent of each other, in the same manner as men are naturally free and independent," he wrote, "each nation should be left in the peaceable enjoyment of that liberty which she inherits from nature."[13]

Although established as a principle by the late eighteenth century, the practice of intervention continued unabated, prompting efforts to codify the notion into international law in the nineteenth and twentieth centuries. The first serious attempts originated in Latin America in the Calvo and Drago doctrines, articulated in 1868 and 1902, respectively. The first doctrine, posed by Carlos Calvo, an Argentine jurist, holds that jurisdiction in international investment disputes lies with the country in which the investment is located. Proclaimed by the then Argentine foreign minister Luis Maria Drago, the second doctrine declared that no foreign power could use force against a Latin American country to collect debt. Both doctrines have subsequently become recognized claims under customary international law as well as being embodied in several national constitutions and treaties.

Nonetheless, the principle of nonintervention remained a topic of constant agitation. At the Sixth International Conference of American States, convened in Havana in 1928, the Commission of Jurists recommended the adoption of the principle "No state has a right to interfere in the internal affairs of another."[14]

---

11. On the gradual emergence of the principle of nonintervention, see Glanville 2014.
12. Quoted in Krasner 1999, 21.
13. Vattel 1758/2008, preliminaries, §15.
14. Krasner 1999, 21.

The proposal was rejected by the United States on the grounds that it had a right to intervene to protect the lives of its nationals should internal order break down. Under the new Good Neighbor policy, however, the United States finally relented in 1933 at the Seventh International Conference and agreed to the Convention on Rights and Duties of States, which included the language that "no state has the right to intervene in the internal or external affairs of another." Elaborating further, the Charter of the Organization of American States, signed in 1948, declares: "No State or group of States has the right to intervene, directly or indirectly, for any reason whatever, in the internal or external affairs of any other State. The foregoing principle prohibits not only armed force but also any other form of interference or attempted threat against the personality of the State or against its political, economic, and cultural elements." The principle was universalized in article 2 (7) of the United Nations Charter, which states that "nothing contained in the present Charter shall authorize the United Nations to intervene in matters which are essentially within the domestic jurisdiction of any state or shall require the Members to submit such matters to settlement under the present Charter." Although the principle is stated in very general terms, there is now a large corpus of General Assembly resolutions, meeting records, reports, letters, and official documents clarifying its meaning and specific applications.[15]

Stephen Krasner describes this principle of nonintervention or exclusion as the primary trait of "Westphalian" sovereignty, though it actually followed that conclave by at least a century and was not universally acclaimed in law until after World War II.[16] Luke Glanville, in a detailed analysis of the concept of sovereignty and the responsibility to protect, argues persuasively that "the supposed 'traditional' rights of sovereignty were firmly and unambiguously established by the society of states for the first time only in 1945," meaning that sovereignty as we understand it today is actually of comparatively recent origin.[17] Nonetheless, this principle structures international relations in deep ways.

Controlling Transnational Violence

As the principle of sovereignty evolved, a necessary corollary formed that states are responsible for all violence that originates from their territories.[18] If states were the ultimate authorities within their realms, it followed that they were and could be held responsible for all violence emanating from within

---

15. Onuf 1998, 151. The most important documents are General Assembly resolutions 2131 (XX), December 21, 1965; 2625 (XXV), October 24, 1970; and 36/103, December 9, 1981. For other documents, see article E 2 (7) at http://www.un.org/en/sc/repertoire/principles .shtml.
16. Krasner 1999, 20–25.
17. Glanville 2014, 169.
18. This section draws heavily on Thomson 1994.

their borders. States are permitted to use violence—wage war—against one another, but they are now expected to suppress private actors from using their territories to project violence against other private actors and states. In turn, any violence that springs forth from their territory is presumed to be permitted or approved by the state, and thus a possible casus belli. This norm of public responsibility for private violence did not fully emerge until the end of the nineteenth century, and—like the norm of nonintervention—became fairly robust only during the twentieth century.

Prior to the end of the nineteenth century, private purveyors of transnational violence were common. Early modern states, in fact, were heavily reliant on private violence entrepreneurs until they consolidated their own extractive and military abilities. Rather than build their own fleets, states issued letters of marque to privateers, who could then legitimately attack the shipping of enemy states—sharing the "prize" with the sovereign. Without standing armies of trained soldiers, states also turned to mercenaries and, later, mercantile companies that fielded entire armies to supply their fluctuating demands for defense.[19] Prior to the revolution, for instance, about one-third of the French army came from outside France, mostly Swiss regiments and one from Ireland, the original "Wild Geese."[20] Similarly, the overseas trading companies like the Dutch East India Company were licensed to recruit and field their own military forces to protect claims abroad.[21] In the seventeenth and eighteenth centuries, the privatization of violence was a near-universal practice, especially for smaller states and "free cities" that had grown prosperous through international trade but were threatened by larger neighbors. The heads of the mercantile companies became some of the richest men in Europe, in several cases dwarfing the wealth of the monarchs they were hired to protect.

These private violence entrepreneurs, however, posed two central problems to nascent sovereign states. First, given fluctuating demand, "unemployed" purveyors of violence often turned on vulnerable citizens, states themselves, or each other. Privateers became pirates in times of peace, preying on the ships of all flags. Mercenaries became brigands. The mercantile companies formed protection rackets, threatening to use force against states unless they were paid to abstain from further violence. Necessary during war, private violence entrepreneurs became outlaws in peace, threatening social order and the states responsible for that order. Second, seeking employment from the highest bidder, private violence entrepreneurs could act at cross-purposes from their states of origin and muddy the diplomatic waters. States gradually restricted their citizens from becoming mercenaries precisely to avoid aiding their enemies or becoming embroiled in conflicts not of their own making.

19. Avant 2005.
20. McGarry 2013.
21. Phillips and Sharman 2015, chap. 3.

By the end of the nineteenth century, now consolidated states simply stopped using private violence entrepreneurs. With the rise of nationalism and, perhaps more important, national militaries, the market for private violence largely disappeared. Although the timing is complicated, it appears that the norm against private violence entrepreneurs that turned "mercenary" into a term of opprobrium followed rather than preceded the disappearance of the practice. It was only after the Crimean War that nations renounced piracy, in the Paris Declaration of 1856, though some countries continued to issue letters of marque until well into the twentieth century.[22] The status of a mercenary was defined and made subject to criminal law rather than the laws of war only in 1977, in an additional protocol to the Geneva Conventions. The United States de facto outlawed mercenaries only in 1977 as well, when the Fifth Circuit Court interpreted the Anti-Pinkerton Act of 1893 to prohibit such employees—although this was later amended to permit "guard and protective services." By the 1920s, Weber could define the state as holding a *monopoly* of the legitimate use of violence within a territory, a description that might not have made much sense prior to his time.

In turn, violence from any source originating in one country against a second came to be interpreted as intentional and, thus, an act of aggression. While states might deny knowledge of or responsibility for forces operating from within their borders, this was no longer an acceptable excuse. States became responsible, whether they liked it or not, and held each other to account for violence used against each other in all forms. Tellingly, few contested the right of the United States to invade Afghanistan and overthrow the Taliban after the terrorist attacks of 9/11 because it allowed or at least acquiesced in al-Qaeda's use of its territory as a headquarters and for training bases.

This decentralized system of violence control actually worked quite well for a century or more. Never eliminated completely, of course, private violence was sharply reduced. Piracy was understood as a thing of past. Freebooters or "filibusters" lacked secure bases of operation in neighboring countries, raising the costs and difficulties of fomenting rebellions. Mercenarism all but disappeared as a profession, living on only in the French Foreign Legion, which was itself a quasi-state institution.[23] The suppression of private violence, of course, did not preclude states from exercising violence under the "mask" of nominally private actors with whom they maintained plausibly deniable relations, such as U.S. support for the Contras in Nicaragua or Pakistan's support for the Taliban in Afghanistan. That states using private actors were eventually identified and more or less held to account for their support, however,

---

22. The United States issued its last letter of marque in December 1941, to the Goodyear blimp *Resolute* operating out of Moffett Field in California. The navy took over official operation of the blimp, and others, soon thereafter.
23. On the rebirth of private military companies, see Avant 2005.

suggests just how deeply the norm has been accepted. Indeed, the success of this system is most evident today only as it begins to erode in failed states. After Somalia collapsed, for instance, piracy returned as a major problem for shipping in the region, with hundreds of ships attacked since 2005 and over $6 billion of commerce disrupted each year (see chapter 5). As states have weakened in Africa, transnational rebels have flourished, fueling insurgencies and civil wars.[24] Fragile states, most importantly Afghanistan under the Taliban, have been used as safe havens from which to plan and carry out terrorist attacks around the world, including the 9/11 attacks on the United States. Precisely because they permit the return of transnational nonstate violence, failed states have emerged as one of the most important security threats of the twenty-first century.

To date, the primary response to the problem of failed states and ungoverned spaces as havens for producers of private violence has been statebuilding. This is a conservative response, in the more general sense of that word as a commitment to tradition.[25] Statebuilding attempts to bolster states so that they can control what occurs within their borders and, thus, abide by the norm of responsibility for private violence. The goal of the international community, in other words, is to rehabilitate and expand the capacity of states to control their own territories and suppress violent actors who might inhabit otherwise ungoverned spaces. The aim is more state responsibility—more sovereignty. Rather than contemplating alternatives to state sovereignty, perhaps an international force to fight pirates and terrorists, the solution is limited to strengthening governance wherever it is lacking. In this way, statebuilding is a counterinsurgency strategy and defense policy of the highest order.

Sovereign states need sovereign states and, thus, recognize, support, and even promote the principle of sovereignty. Although one might imagine many different ways in which the problem of controlling transnational violence might have been addressed, including reinterpreting sovereignty to allow hot pursuit and other forms of direct intervention, the principle of sovereignty is a useful coordination rule for regulating and managing such violence. By making each state sovereign and the ultimate authority in its realm, it is held responsible for governing all of its territory and regulating any groups that might seek to project violence against others. Interpreting any transnational violence as an act of aggression and therefore subject to legitimate retaliation—an accepted casus belli—states hold each other to account and encourage one another to develop as effective sovereigns who can and do broadcast their legitimate power throughout the entire area they claim. This decentralized system for controlling violence worked remarkably well, such that pirates, freebooters, and mercenaries eventually ceased to exist as viable professions, persisting only in romanticized legends and children's

24. Salehyan 2009.
25. For an extended defense of this response, see Simons, McGraw, and Lauchengco 2011.

stories. Sovereignty was, in this way, a useful fiction that allowed states to agree on effective rules for managing transnational violence. The emergence of failed states in multiple regions of the globe in recent decades, however, challenges this solution.

The Paradox of Sovereignty

The principle of sovereignty, under its nonintervention clause, prohibits external statebuilding. The system of decentralized violence control demands that states take responsibility for violence originating from their territories. Yet when states lack the ability to police their societies and govern all of their territories, the need to control violence requires intervention to promote greater or more effective sovereignty. This is the paradox of sovereignty. To defend the principle of sovereignty and the system of decentralized violence control that follows from it, states must violate that principle.[26]

The practice of sovereignty is very different than the principle, especially the norm of nonintervention. Indeed, the divergence between principle and practice is so great that Krasner has described sovereignty as nothing more than an "organized hypocrisy."[27] Many but not all interventions have occurred under the aegis of statebuilding, including attempts to place sympathetic leaders in power in what we would now call regime change. Indeed, the United States intervened more than twenty times in Central America and the Caribbean between 1898 and 1930 to promote loyal leaders, many of whom later proved to be brutal dictators. Some of these interventions are now classified as statebuilding efforts, though all were at the time and thereafter equally described as instances of informal empire or indirect rule (see table 3.1). The record of intervention into the internal affairs of states, especially fragile states, is extensive and need not be detailed here. What is important is that once states become sufficiently weak that they cannot uphold their responsibilities as sovereign states, other states or the international community more generally has little choice but to intervene to rehabilitate those states.

Failed states have always existed and challenged the norm of nonintervention, though the problem has expanded in recent years as more fragile states created through decolonization have eventually succumbed to their internal divisions.[28] As explained in the previous chapter, authority is always and everywhere negotiated, the product of bargains between rulers and the ruled. Sometimes these bargains prevent states from exercising authority in all of

26. For a discussion of this paradox in the context of U.S. interventions, see Colas 2008.
27. Krasner 1999.
28. Jackson 1990.

their territories. In Pakistan, for instance, by long-standing agreement with the "tribes" that inhabit the area, the central government's sovereignty does not extend fully into the Federally Administered Tribal Areas along the border with Afghanistan.[29] Although this is an unusual case in its formalism, it highlights the fact that governments do not just fail to extend their authority to all corners of their supposed jurisdictions but that such limitations are part of the fundamental bargains over their authority reached with important private authorities. States may sometimes simply lack capacity, through lack of resources, poor training of military and police forces, and so on. But more often, it appears, the lack of capacity is in part an intentional decision by the state to honor the authority of traditional social forces or, at least, not to challenge those authorities. In either case, the state cannot live up to the principle of sovereignty.

This problem has been exacerbated by the shift in the criteria for recognition as a sovereign state that unfolded over the twentieth century. Ironically, at the same time that the decentralized system of violence control was most clearly established, it was being undermined by parallel changes in the notion of sovereignty. Prior to World War I, states recognized polities as sovereign only when they had demonstrated the ability to exercise authority over their territories. This is sometimes called effective sovereignty. Starting with the Paris Peace Conference, which created states in Eastern Europe out of the wreckage of the Austro-Hungarian Empire and recognized those states as sovereign prior to their consolidation, the international community has shifted to a theory of juridical sovereignty, whereby recognition is conferred upon self-declarations of sovereignty by states and their joining some universal international body such as the United Nations.[30] Under this rule, states do not need to demonstrate their ability to regulate their territories before recognition as sovereign equals, but need only claim that status. With the protection that sovereignty provides, fragile states appear to endure longer than was the case in the more brutal and competitive environment that characterized Europe in its formative period.[31] All of this helps set the stage for more frequent state failure, now and in the future.

As a result, the paradox of sovereignty is becoming more salient and self-evident. As fragile states fail, the international community as a whole or states alone must intervene in attempts to rebuild governance in otherwise ungoverned spaces. This presents two perennial problems. First, states intervene to bolster the principle of sovereignty, but must limit the frequency of such interventions and do so on terms that do not fatally undermine that principle. Too-frequent

29. The jurisdiction of the Supreme Court and High Court of Pakistan does not extend to the FATA, according to articles 247 and 248 of the 1973 Constitution of Pakistan. For an overview of the FATA, see Markey 2008.
30. Jackson 1990.
31. Jackson and Rosberg 1982.

interventions threaten to undermine the very system of decentralized violence control that states rely on.

Second, and more important, the international community and states must somehow distinguish between necessary statebuilding interventions and opportunistic ones carried out by self-aggrandizing states that might use such interventions as an excuse for regime change. Although statebuilding in otherwise ungoverned spaces possesses large externalities and might benefit from centralized provision, the international community itself has no mechanism to intervene in failed states. The United Nations or other international organizations may call for action, but any assessments on member states are subject to approval by the permanent members of the Security Council. The system remains dependent on countries willing to step forward and contribute troops to even multilateral operations. In some cases, when the United Nations cannot or chooses not to act, countries choose to engage in statebuilding on their own. In either case, states with strong interests in the failed state are most likely to take on the responsibility of statebuilding. The U.S. intervention in Iraq that caused an otherwise fragile state to fail is one example. Russia's recent intervention in Ukraine, ostensibly to protect Russian-speakers from political instability but ultimately annexing Crimea, is a second. Managing the complex incentives created by sovereignty and self-interest is proving to be a difficult challenge.

Limits on Statebuilding

Current practice attempts to resolve the paradox of sovereignty and reduce opportunistic statebuilding efforts by explicitly limiting the conditions under which states can intervene in each other's affairs, the mandates they carry in their interventions, and the duration of the missions. Practice does this in three ways.

First, external interventions are increasingly expected to be authorized by some international, multilateral body, usually the United Nations, deemed the most important because of its near-universal membership.[32] Some "forum shopping" occurs, as when the United States and Europe, facing certain veto from Russia in the Security Council, turned to NATO to approve the intervention in Kosovo, but this does not challenge the general point. As the case of the Iraq War also makes clear, not all recent interventions have been authorized. States still assert a right to act in self-defense against real or, in the case of Iraq, imagined threats. Still, states increasingly expect that military interventions will be approved by some relevant multilateral body. Indeed, Russia's reliance on the "green men" in the case of Ukraine, apparently

32. On the United Nations as a source of legitimacy, see Hurd 2007 and Thompson 2009.

Russian special forces without official designation, indicates the strength of the emerging norm. President Vladimir Putin had to construct an elaborate ruse under which he could deny any direct intervention or, at least, maintain plausible deniability.

Second, militarized statebuilding efforts are restricted to countries that have clearly "failed." The process is, of course, a continuum, ranging from traditional foreign aid to election monitoring, governance reform, police training, and a host of other activities. The advanced industrialized democracies share their wealth and political practices in ways that certainly constitute statebuilding with a wide range of states. Most of these activities occur at the invitation of the target country—even if the offer is made in such a way that it would be hard to refuse otherwise—and are therefore consistent with the principle of sovereignty. Armed statebuilding, however, is restricted by general agreement to states that have already clearly failed, such as Somalia, Haiti, Liberia, Rwanda, and others.[33] There is no generally recognized right of intervention. Rather, the international community today allows states to act only in the most extreme cases, and then only after the full extent of state disintegration has become manifest.

Third, when authorized, the goals of any intervention are carefully circumscribed by the international community. UN Security Council resolutions authorizing peacekeeping interventions under either chapter 6 or 7 of the UN Charter nearly always affirm that primary responsibility for peace and security remains with the sovereign government of the affected country (or countries, when relevant). Such affirmations make clear that there will be no attempt to usurp permanently or even temporarily the sovereignty of the state. Equally, the responsibilities of the intervening states as defined in the resolution are typically limited. In the case of Somalia in 1991 (see chapter 5), one of the first post–Cold War interventions that set precedents for all others, the initial United Nations mission (UNOSOM I) was restricted to monitoring the cease-fire in Mogadishu, the capital, protecting UN personnel, equipment and supplies, and escorting deliveries of humanitarian supplies in the city and its environs (UNSC Resolution 751), later broadened to the whole country (UNSC Resolution 755). The U.S.-led mission (UNITAF) was limited to establishing only a secure environment for humanitarian relief operations (UNSC Resolution 974). UNOSOM II, begun in March 1993, continued to limit the mission to establishing a secure environment for delivering humanitarian assistance, then specified more clearly exactly what this meant in practice (UNSC Resolution 814). Although UNOSOM II was tasked with rehabilitating Somalia's political institutions, the mandate expanded to include political reconciliation through an agreed cease-fire only in February 1994 (UNSC Resolution 897), after the United States had already decided to withdraw. In Sierra Leone,

---

33. P. Miller 2013, appendix A.

regarded by the United Nations if not others as a more successful case, UN-OMSIL was first authorized to monitor military and security conditions and the compliance of Civil Defense Forces with international humanitarian law. UNAMSIL was established in October 1999 to help implement the peace agreement between the government and rebels with slightly broader but clearly defined and limited responsibilities (UNSC Resolution 1270); it was then marginally expanded again in February 2000 to include providing security at key locations and government buildings (UNSC Resolution 1289). Although in both of these cases there was "mission creep" over time as the complexities of peacekeeping in the midst of civil war became more evident, the responsibilities and permitted actions of the intervening states remained severely restricted.

In addition to limited mandates, authorized interventions are limited in duration, typically requiring reauthorization every six months or less by the UN Security Council, with regular reporting requirements by the secretary-general. It almost goes without comment that statebuilding operations of indefinite duration are prohibited by the international community and the principle of sovereignty. "Imperialism," wherein one country or coalition—however authorized—assumes the sovereignty of the failed state over an undefined period, is ruled out, and "neo-trusteeship" is controversial for the same reason.[34] Rather, all statebuilding attempts must be explicitly temporary, designed to return the failed state to full sovereignty as quickly as possible, and of limited duration. In the case of Somalia, for example, even though the initial UNOSOM I and UNITAF missions were unlimited in duration and did not require any regular reporting, they were nonetheless still intended and expected to be temporary. As the mission became stabilized and expanded under UNOSOM II, reauthorization became mandatory at mostly six-month intervals. In Sierra Leone, UNOMSIL began with renewals every three months, with UNAMSIL expanding with a couple of shorter exceptions to every six months. Few likely expect a peacekeeping mission not to be reauthorized. The UN Security Council typically reviews programs and passes reauthorizing resolutions only days before the current resolution is due to expire, and no mission could be unwound without substantial planning and a phased withdrawal. Nonetheless, at least technically, the missions are kept on a short leash, with all parties—statebuilders and warring factions included—possessing only a limited planning horizon. In no case has authorization been granted explicitly on an indefinite basis. The need for reauthorization, combined with periodic reporting requirements, creates the potential for effective oversight of the mission by the authorizing body.

The "authorized" statebuilding missions contrast with the unauthorized U.S. war against Iraq in 2003, which was, of course, famously not approved by the UN Security Council. As explained in chapter 4, although Saddam Hussein

---

34. On neotrusteeship, see Bain 2003; Parker 2003; Fearon and Laitin 2004; Krasner 2004.

was no doubt a highly repressive autocrat, the Iraqi state had not failed. Indeed, Saddam was understood to be sufficiently powerful to pose a threat to international peace and security. However repressive the regime, and however many norms of international society he violated, the United States could not build a consensus to overthrow Saddam's otherwise stable regime. Equally important in blocking agreement, the United States desired a broad mandate. It did not intend to prosecute Saddam through the International Criminal Court. Nor did it plan to simply deliver humanitarian aid to the regions of the country, particularly the Shite South, that suffered under Saddam's rule and the U.S.-led sanctions regime of the previous decade. Rather, the United States made plain its intent to change the regime of a state that had clearly not failed. In the end, given conditions in Iraq that were not sufficiently extreme and U.S. ambitions that were too expansive, the international community could not support the war, and the U.S. intervention proceeded without explicit authorization. This negative case highlights the conditions necessary for international approval for interventions and makes clear that such interventions will remain rare and quite limited.

Current international statebuilding practice has, thus, reached an uneasy accommodation between the need to protect the principle of sovereignty, along with the decentralized system of violence control that follows, and the need to build states when necessary. Interventions, if they are to be duly authorized by the international community, must be rare, undertaken only in the most dire circumstances, circumscribed, and finite. This is a pragmatic compromise that will, undoubtedly, continue to evolve. Yet this accommodation has important implications for the success of current statebuilding efforts.

Nearly all analysts agree that statebuilding is likely to be most effective when engaged before the state has completely failed.[35] Building from institutions that retain some legitimacy, before groups retreat into their traditional social formations and before violence deepens animosity and fear between groups, is likely to be more effective. It is a widely held belief that an ounce of prevention is better than a pound of cure or, in statebuilding, rehabilitation. Yet under current practice, statebuilding missions are authorized only after the state has clearly spiraled down into large-scale violence and failed. This by itself does not imply that such missions cannot work in postconflict settings, but it does mean that, as explained in the previous chapter, statebuilders begin from extremely disadvantageous positions that make success far less likely.

35. See Jentleson 1998. This conclusion rests mostly on common sense, not empirically verified patterns. As statebuilding efforts before failure are typically "lighter" and nonmilitarized, we do not observe the same types of interventions before and after failure and, thus, cannot assess their respective efficacy.

As discussed in chapter 1, the promise of statebuilding is the ability of a powerful external state or coalition to credibly install a new regime that will "stick," and thereby encourage the vesting of social interests in a particular social order produced by the new state. By limiting the mandate and the duration of missions, however, the international community makes it more difficult for statebuilders to credibly commit to guarantee any social order they might seek to construct. Limited to providing humanitarian aid or monitoring cease-fires, the statebuilder cannot defend a social order in general. Even with more expansive mandates, expectations of only a short-term role and a nearly constant need for reauthorization prevent statebuilders from committing credibly to the defense of social orders into the indefinite future. If social actors cannot expect the social order to endure, and must at least consider the possibility that the country will once again fall into renewed violence, they will not invest in ways that are specific to any social order. Without credible guarantees, instability becomes a self-fulfilling prophecy.

Even though the international community may believe it has reached a pragmatic accommodation between the conflicting principle of sovereignty and practice of statebuilding, the accommodation itself undermines international statebuilding. Effective statebuilding requires broad mandates to guarantee social order and missions of indefinite duration through which external powers can commit to playing a constructive role in the process over the long term. Paradoxically, the more credible the commitment to guarantee a social order, the less power the statebuilder will actually have to exercise and the shorter will be its mission. The more effective the statebuilder is in creating expectations of stability and the conditions necessary for successful vesting of social groups in the new state, the quicker social forces will be to develop indigenous interests in their own state. With limited mandates and time, statebuilders lack credibility, undermining the catalytic role they might otherwise play.

Sovereignty and the Statebuilder's Dilemma

The statebuilder's dilemma, explored at greater length in the remainder of this book, is itself rooted in the principle of sovereignty and, by implication, the absence of an authoritative governance structure at the global level. As a result, statebuilders must volunteer for the responsibility. As statebuilding is a costly undertaking—sometimes very costly, as in Iraq—only states with some significant interest in the failed state are likely to take up the necessary effort. But it is precisely those interests that cause statebuilders to favor loyal leaders and undermine the legitimacy of the states they seek to build.

Effective states police their territories. Although nearly every country has some areas of weak governance, such as Brazil's favelas, where police presence is very weak and rare, in principle consolidated states can tax citizens and mobilize coercive force to impose control on those regions. Those that cannot do so are considered to be more or less fragile states. In most, though, it is the ability to mobilize the resources of citizens authoritatively that allows states to broadcast power to all corners of their territories.

The international community as a whole, however, lacks any similar authority to police its ungoverned spaces. There is no supranational authority able to command contributions or demand forces to be used to broadcast power to all corners of the globe. Policing ungoverned spaces would provide positive externalities for all countries now plagued by existential threats of transnational terrorism. Historically, the most effective solution to the free rider problem has been the creation of a centralized authority with the power to tax members and act on their behalf. Yet statebuilding remains a voluntary undertaking. States engage when and where they desire and, as with the United States in Somalia in 1993, withdraw their forces when they choose.

Thus, the statebuilder's dilemma is necessarily a product of the principle of sovereignty. Until such time as the international community has independent authority to govern when and where states fail, statebuilding will remain a voluntary practice, and states with interests in the failed state will step forward to take the lead role. When doing so, they will seek to place a leader more or less sympathetic to their interests in power. Present limitations by multilateral organizations do not resolve this dilemma, though they do in fact limit the practice of statebuilding in ways that may render it even more ineffective.

The statebuilder's dilemma is a real one in the sense that it defies solution. It can be managed but not escaped. The paradox of sovereignty arises as an unintentional consequence of choices made over time for other reasons. Different choices could be made, although not without cost and, potentially, other unforeseen consequences. The principle of sovereignty is not fixed or exogenous, but a dynamic, negotiated, and ultimately endogenous package of ideas. The norm of nonintervention did not develop until the eighteenth century or gain widespread recognition until the mid-twentieth; the restrictions on private violence did not arise until the late nineteenth or early twentieth century and were codified only in the 1970s; and the idea of juridical sovereignty did not fully blossom until the founding of the United Nations and the later movement toward decolonization. The practice of sovereignty, which has always differed from the principle, is even more open and fluid. One could imagine bringing the principle of sovereignty into greater alignment with practice. The current accommodation for statebuilding already moves in that direction, as does the emerging norm of "responsibility to protect," sharing a similar intent but more focused on human rights practices of states. The international community could return to a conception of effective sovereignty and assert the authority to identify fragile states at risk of failure, impose structural reforms on existing governance structures as appropriate, and intervene militarily early on an indefinite basis when necessary. Though such changes would likely be resisted by national leaders jealously guarding their autonomy in order to exploit their populations for their own ends, the point is that reforms are possible, at least in theory. As long as a system of sovereign states continues to dominate the imagination of states, however, the state-builder's dilemma will remain a fundamental impediment to the success of current and future statebuilding efforts.

3

Legitimacy and Loyalty

The promise of statebuilding is that an external power—a state or coalition of states—can create and guarantee a social order with a particular set of rules and institutions and, by doing so, catalyze a process of vesting social groups into a state that can eventually become self-sustaining. Yet this promise is undermined by the statebuilder's dilemma, explored in this chapter. Any statebuilder has, at a minimum, two goals. First, it wants to build a state that will be legitimate in the eyes of those over whom it will rule. Although the weight attached to building legitimacy for the target state has varied over time and across cases, such legitimacy is necessary for the state to govern effectively and endure over the long term. Second, the statebuilder wants a leader and state that will share or protect its interests in that country. Any state willing to bear the costs of building a new state in some foreign territory will have interests of its own in that state and over the policies it is likely to adopt. Though the statebuilder may want to create a state that is legitimate, its interests in that country's policies also create an incentive to install a loyal leader who is sympathetic to those interests and will protect them. Although the trade-off between legitimacy and loyalty will vary between different statebuilders and target countries, that there is a trade-off is inevitable and unavoidable. The deeper the interests of the statebuilder in the failed state and the greater the distance between the policy preferences of the statebuilder and those of the citizens of that state, the more intense the statebuilder's dilemma will be and the less likely statebuilding is to result in a legitimate state.

This chapter examines the core trade-off between legitimacy and loyalty and explores the factors that render the dilemma more or less acute. I then discuss three contemporary and still influential theories of legitimation. None succeeds in overcoming the dilemma.

The Statebuilder's Dilemma

All statebuilders want regimes and, in turn, leaders who will be able to govern their territories effectively, exerting control over otherwise ungoverned spaces that threaten international peace and stability. To govern effectively, leaders need some measure of political legitimacy. Although political repression can keep an authoritarian leader in power for some time, as explained in chapter 1, coercion is not only costly but ultimately ineffective in maintaining political order over the long run. Indeed, even in an authoritarian state, the ability to coerce citizens requires support from at least some significant fraction of the political community that is willing to pay taxes, serve in the coercive apparatus, work in the propaganda office, and fulfill other essential roles. Hardly a democrat, Thomas Hobbes recognized that "the power of the mighty (the Leviathan) has no foundation but in the opinion and belief of the people."[1] Although a regime need not be legitimate in the eyes of all its people to sustain a state, it must be legitimate for at least some key social groups. Attaining some minimal level of legitimacy is the sine qua non of statebuilding. Without legitimacy, the state will likely fail again in the future.

Yet the statebuilder also wants leaders who will serve its own interests in the country, whatever they may be. The goal of effective governance is an existential concern to all states in the international system and, as such, is prone to free riding. Statebuilders willing to bear high costs in creating and maintaining a new state in some foreign land, however, will always have some more specific or immediate concerns in that country as well. Interests may include strategic objectives, such as securing neighboring sea lanes or forward military bases; economic ambitions, such as protecting foreign investments or access to vital raw materials; or ethnopolitical ties, such as defending co-ethnics at risk in the fragile state. Statebuilders may also have the more aggressive goals of acquiring additional territory and encouraging secession to weaken rivals, or more defensive intentions, such as removing an aggressive leader and regime from power and preventing the acquisition of weapons of mass destruction. The goals of statebuilders will be many and varied. They may arise from "national" interests of the statebuilder in strategic locales or from the narrow interests of particularistic or special interests within its own society. There may also be debate within the statebuilder's society over the appropriate goals to be pursued. The Iraq case, examined in the next chapter, illustrates all of these different levels of interests, as well as vigorous debate over their pursuit. In this book, I do not inquire deeply into the sources of these interests or their content. Rather, I posit only that states with some specific interests in the target state will be more likely to undertake a statebuilding mission than others. When statebuilders have interests in the failed state, it is not enough to have just any leader in power, no matter how effectively

---

1. Quoted in Williams 2006, 265. See also Flathman 1980, 29, quoted in the introduction.

that leader may govern. Rather, statebuilders want a leader who will advance their interests. In short, statebuilders desire a *loyal* leader willing to do their bidding.

The statebuilder's dilemma is that the goals of legitimacy and loyalty are always in conflict with one another, at least at the margin. As discussed in the next section, the intensity of the conflict will vary—especially depending on the distance between the policy preferences of the statebuilder and those of the citizens of the target state—but the dilemma is always present to some degree. To illustrate this point, figures 3.1a and 3.1b depict a single dimension of policy along which the statebuilder and the target population disagree (the difference between figures 3.1a and 3.1b is explained below). Assuming that there are perhaps many issues of domestic politics about which the statebuilder is indifferent, the dimension here is equivalent to issue 1 (the horizontal dimension) in figure 1.2. This might be a specific issue, such as basing rights, or an ideological dimension, perhaps reflecting differing conceptions of the roles of the market or religion in public life (equivalent to the left-right dimension often posited in U.S. politics). Conceptually, it does not much matter how or why the statebuilder and the target population disagree, only that they differ in some degree. In the case of the United States in Iraq, discussed in chapter 4, Washington likely desired to integrate the country into the Pax Americana as an exemplary democratic and Muslim country, to use its territory as a forward operating base in the region, and to recruit it as an ally in the global war on terror—all goals that were opposed by the average Iraqi. In Somalia, Ethiopia was adamantly opposed to the popular irredentist program adopted by the Union of Islamic Courts, which seized power in Mogadishu in early 2006.

Whatever the issue in dispute, in turn, the statebuilder has some preference or an "ideal point" over the policy adopted by the target state, fixed for analytic purposes at the left end of the continuum. The statebuilder's ideal point, once again, could simply reflect the interests of the leader of that country, a majority of its citizens, or a national consensus.[2] The target population, in turn, has policy preferences that vary around some ideal point representing,

2. One of the many simplifications in this heuristic is the assumption of a single ideal point for the statebuilder. In reality, there will be a distribution of preferences in the statebuilder, potentially subject to cycling as well, but normally assumed to aggregate through some institutional mechanism into a preferred policy. In any multidimensional policy space, it is possible that the ideal point of an elected leader may not be identical to that of the median voter. In the case of Iraq, discussed in the next chapter, for instance, it appears that the preferred policy of the Bush administration was more aggressive and inclined toward preventive war than that preferred by the median voter in the United States. Unpacking the domestic politics of the statebuilder would enrich any explanation of a case. However, doing so would not alter the basic point here that the further apart the ideal point of the statebuilder and the target state, the more acute the statebuilder's dilemma will be and the more the statebuilder will favor loyalty.

a.

Range from which the statebuilder
selects a leader

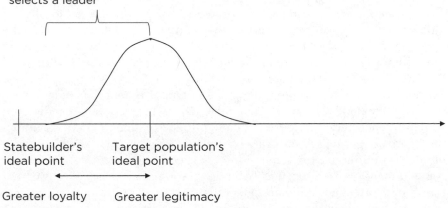

Statebuilder's   Target population's
ideal point   ideal point

Greater loyalty   Greater legitimacy

b.

Range from which the statebuilder
selects a leader

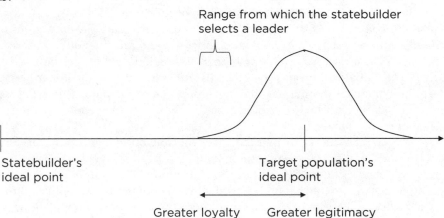

Statebuilder's   Target population's
ideal point   ideal point

Greater loyalty   Greater legitimacy

Figures 3.1a and 3.1b. The statebuilder's dilemma.
(a) Similar policy preferences between the statebuilder and the target state population. (b)
Distant policy preferences between the statebuilder and the target state population. The area
under each curve represents a possible distribution of policy preferences in the target population. The statebuilder will always select a leader from the population to the left of the target
population's ideal point. The closer to the target state's ideal point the leader's own political
preferences are, the more legitimate the leader will be. Likewise, the closer to the statebuilder's ideal point the leader is, the more loyal to the statebuilder the leader will be. At an extreme, the statebuilder will choose a leader whose preferences are at the far left of each distribution. Holding the statebuilder's valuation of legitimacy versus loyalty constant, more-distant
policy preferences shrink the range of the population from which the statebuilder will select
a leader and from which the leader's support coalition will be drawn.

in this case, the preference of the median member of that society.[3] Several key points follow from this simple heuristic.

The statebuilder will always select a leader—or back a regime likely to select a leader—with policy preferences between its ideal point and the ideal point of the target population. Under no circumstance does the statebuilder have an incentive to select a leader that it knows to be to the right of the target society's ideal point. As in principal-agent models, the statebuilder will attempt to "screen" possible leaders ex ante on the basis of their own policy preferences, selecting a leader whose preferences are sincerely held and close to its own. By selecting a leader who prefers the same policy, the monitoring and enforcement costs to the statebuilder are minimized.[4]

Statebuilders who emphasize legitimacy over loyalty will select leaders with policy preferences closer to (but still to the left of) the ideal point of the target population. Such leaders will share the interests of more of their citizens and, as discussed in chapter 1, find it easier and less costly to build a larger coalition of supporters who will legitimate their rule. It follows that when legitimacy is emphasized over loyalty in leaders, statebuilding is compatible with democracy or, at least, some broad-based form of political participation. A legitimate leader may or may not choose to govern democratically; this depends on the cultural traditions of the society, the degree of popular support, and many other local factors. But importantly, when statebuilders emphasize the legitimacy of leaders over their loyalty, statebuilding is not—in principle—incompatible with democracy.

Statebuilders who emphasize loyalty over legitimacy will select leaders whose policy preferences are closer to their own. At an extreme, statebuilders who weigh loyalty above all else will choose leaders from the left tail of the distribution of policy preferences. In this case, the leader will prefer and, to the extent possible, pursue policies very similar to those the statebuilder itself would under direct rule, suggesting that under this circumstance statebuilding is similar to other forms of informal imperialism or indirect control.[5] Five further implications follow from an emphasis on loyalty.

---

3. In this illustration, policy preferences in the target state are assumed to be single-peaked or normally distributed. In more complicated distributions of policy preferences, such as a bimodal distribution, policy in the target state might not converge to the position of the median voter. The median voter theorem begins with Black 1948 and Downs 1957. For one of many possible reviews, see Holcombe 1989. In a multidimensional policy space, the ideal point is the intersection of the medians or a range of points within the Pareto set (see figure 1.2 and surrounding discussion). Whether preferences are distributed in more complex ways or multidimensional, the central argument here on the distance between the policy preferred by the statebuilder and the target state will still hold.
4. For a review of principal-agent models, see Hawkins et al. 2006. In cases where screening fails, of course, the statebuilder can also attempt to control the actions of the leader through ex post punishments.
5. Doyle 1986. For a more general typology of international hierarchies, see Lake 2009.

First, leaders selected for their loyalty to the statebuilder will be less likely to govern democratically. The further leaders are from the ideal point of the target population, the more difficulty they will have in assembling broad-based coalitions that will support them over other possible contenders. When their own policy preferences are far from those desired by their own populations, leaders cannot rely on popular support, whether at the voting booth or in public. The most loyal leaders—those far to the left of the target state distribution in figures 3.1a and b—can remain in power only through some autocratic structure that insulates them from popular opinion and sanctions. Loyal leaders will also engage in greater political repression than their more legitimate counterparts. This syndrome of authoritarian and repressive rule long characterized "client" regimes supported by the United States in Central America in the early twentieth century and by the Soviet Union in Eastern Europe during the Cold War. As President Franklin Delano Roosevelt quipped about General Rafael Leonidas Trujillo y Molina of the Dominican Republic, one of the more repressive and odious dictators supported by the United States, he may be an S.O.B., but "at least he's our S.O.B."[6] The statebuilder can, of course, always "buy" more public support for a loyal leader by providing more aid to that leader to distribute; this may allow the leader to rule more democratically as long as the flow of benefits continues. But buying more public support raises the costs of statebuilding and leads to the next implication.

Second, the more loyal are leaders and the smaller their political base within their populations, the more likely they are to direct foreign assistance to their core supporters than to broader publics. This is similar to the central proposition of selectorate theory, which posits that rulers with small minimum winning coalitions will provide private goods limited to their supporters at the expense of public goods that benefit society at large.[7] This smaller group of supporters is also likely to be located in the left tail of the distribution along with the leader (as drawn in figures 3.1a and b). In the case of statebuilding, aid routed to the failed state intended to strengthen governance will be confronted with the same calculus.[8] Unable to count on domestic support for policies they and their statebuilders prefer, loyal leaders will channel resources not to broader publics—which are unlikely to support them anyway, or which will support them only with substantially greater per capita transfers—but to their smaller support coalitions, who are themselves more favorable to the policies preferred by the statebuilders, typically the economic elites, who are tied to international markets, and the military, who

---

6. Lowenthal 1995, 24. This quip is often described as having been directed by FDR toward other leaders in the region. That the observation appears to apply broadly merely signifies the similarity in relationships constructed by the United States during this period.
7. On selectorate theory, see chapter 1 and Bueno de Mesquita et al. 2003; Bueno de Mesquita and Smith 2011.
8. Girod 2015.

are dependent on infusions of foreign weapons and training. Where legitimate governments might distribute aid broadly to society to build even deeper public support, loyal leaders will concentrate aid from the statebuilder among their smaller groups of supporters. To outsiders, this will appear to be "crony capitalism," appeasing the military, or simple corruption—a complaint widely voiced about U.S. aid to Hamid Karzai in Afghanistan during his presidency.[9] Nonetheless, this "diversion" of resources is integral to the political survival of leaders who support the statebuilder's preferred policies rather than the desires of their own populations.

Third, the greater the emphasis placed on loyalty by the statebuilder, the smaller the pool of candidates from which the statebuilder can select leaders. Whatever the distribution of policy preferences within the target society, the greater the desire of the statebuilder to select a leader who shares its preferences, the thinner is the tail from which it can choose.[10] Assuming that the policy preferences of those with the political will and capability to be leaders are similar to those of the population as a whole, the more emphasis is placed on loyalty, the fewer possible leaders there will be, perhaps leaving the statebuilder with only a handful of viable candidates from which to select, or, at an extreme, a single viable alternative. Despite the considerable frustration of President George W. Bush with his hand-selected Prime Minister Nouri al-Maliki of Iraq, discussed in more detail in chapter 4, the administration was consistently thwarted by the absence of a "plan B" or an alternative leader to support.

The smaller the pool of political leaders, in turn, the harder it is for the statebuilder to control the individual selected.[11] Knowing that statebuilders have no choice but to support them, leaders can then shirk by deviating from the preferences of their statebuilding patrons. This is why screening leaders for similar policy preferences is so important; but screening is also imperfect. Again, knowing there are few viable alternatives, leader can extort even greater resources from statebuilders and direct this aid to their own political or even personal financial ends. Electoral fraud, corruption, and other forms of malfeasance will be rampant. And having solidified their support coalitions, leaders will become increasingly willing over time to defy or extort greater resources from the statebuilders.

Fourth, given the small pool of possible replacements, any of whom would likely face the same incentives as the anointed leader, statebuilders will be forced to acquiesce in undemocratic rule and the diversion of aid to leaders and their supporters. Though it may complain loudly, there is little any statebuilder

---

9. The litany of complaints is documented in any of the *Quarterly Reports* of the Special Inspector General for Afghanistan Reconstruction (SIGAR), https://www.sigar.mil/quarterlyreports/index.aspx?SSR=6.
10. The only exception is when the statebuilder and the target society's policy preferences overlap.
11. Chiozza 2013.

can do in this situation. Indeed, to the extent that statebuilders emphasize loyalty over legitimacy, political repression of the broad public and the diversion of aid by the leader to build a small support coalition are entirely predictable and a natural consequence of the statebuilder's own desire to see its preferred policies followed in the new state. Thus, regardless of their desires, the more statebuilders emphasize loyalty, the more likely they are to support or be forced to acquiesce in undemocratic regimes with high levels of political and economic corruption that manage to stay in power only through electoral fraud and repression and by extorting ever greater quantities of aid from their patrons. This is precisely the syndrome that emerged in both Iraq and Afghanistan after the U.S. invasions. Maliki and Karzai are not anomalies who somehow escaped U.S. control. Rather, the inability to control the corruption, fraud, and domestic partisanship of these leaders, although they were loyal on key dimensions of foreign policy, was integrally related to their selection for loyalty.

All of these problems are exacerbated the shorter the time horizon of the statebuilder (discussed in chapter 2) either because of limits imposed by a multilateral authorizer of the intervention or because it wants to withdraw as quickly as possible for its own reasons. Perhaps given enough time, the statebuilder might be able to guarantee policies that bolster its supporters within the country such that they can become a permanent winning coalition, itself sufficiently vested in the new regime that it becomes self-sustaining. As discussed below, this took many decades in the case of U.S.–Central American relations. But with short time horizons, statebuilders are limited to supporting loyal leaders who, they hope, share their aspirations and can quickly solidify coalitions able to sustain them in power. Statebuilders will, therefore, increase the resource flow and accept the diversion of aid from the general public to the leader's supporters.

Finally, for all of the above reasons, political opponents of the loyal leader will also be opposed to better relations with the statebuilder. Because the leader did not follow policies preferred by the public, funneled resources to a narrow support coalition rather than to the public broadly, and engaged in corrupt, repressive practices, opposition to the loyal leader will inevitably arise, even when repressed for long periods. Given its support for the loyal leader, the opposition—once organized—will undoubtedly charge the statebuilder with complicity in the leader's autocratic and corrupt practices and, perhaps, crimes. By backing the loyal leader, the statebuilder taints relations with any future opposition, creating an incentive for the statebuilder to double down in the short run and making the problems even harder to solve. The long-term reaction to the U.S. role in Central America, for instance, was widespread anti-Americanism that it has taken a generation to overcome even after President Jimmy Carter reversed course. U.S. support for loyal leaders in the Middle East today, in part, led al-Qaeda to divert its initial focus from the near enemy, the Saudi regime, to the far enemy on 9/11.[12] We saw similar trends in the opposition to Maliki in Iraq, most prominently in the violent opposition of ISIS. Statebuilders reap what they sow.

If statebuilding is likely to fail, why do states continue to engage in this effort? Knowing that the leader will likely rule repressively and corruptly, rely on a small group of supporters, and fail to earn legitimacy from the broader population, why do statebuilders nonetheless seek to build new states with loyal leaders? The answer is deceptively simple. They do so, in part, because some state, however illegitimate and fragile, is likely better than no state, and, more important, because they ensure that the new state adopts policies they prefer. Statebuilders decide that continued fragility is of less importance than having leaders who will protect their interests. In this way, statebuilding is typically not about legitimacy for the long term, though that remains part of the calculus, but really about promoting leaders who share or will follow the policy preferences of the statebuilder.

Variation in the Intensity of the Dilemma

The trade-off between legitimacy and loyalty always exists, though it can vary in intensity. The intensity of the statebuilder's dilemma is a function of at least three factors: how the statebuilder weighs legitimacy versus loyalty at any given time or in any particular case; the strength of the statebuilder's interests in the failed state; and the distance between the policy preferences of the statebuilder and those of the target population. Variations in the intensity of the dilemma are illustrated in the cases of Central America, on the one hand, and West Germany and Japan, on the other.

Balance between Legitimacy and Loyalty

As implied above, different states will weigh legitimacy and loyalty differently. In Central America in the early twentieth century, discussed below, the United States focused almost exclusively on loyalty. Since the end of the Cold War, it appears that the United States has placed greater emphasis on legitimacy. We do not, unfortunately, have good theories of how states evaluate the trade-off in different ways at different times. The weight attached to each goal is an empirical question—albeit one that is difficult to answer definitively—that is addressed in the cases that follow.

Legitimacy may be, of course, a value in itself, for both the statebuilder and the new state. Under any circumstances, legitimacy makes it easier and less costly to govern society, and likely more effective. The main benefit, however,

---

12. Gerges 2009. On variations in anti-Americanism in the Middle East, see Jamal 2012.

is that it provides stability over the long run, transforming the failed state into a potentially consolidated state better able to deter challengers to its rule and to govern its territory. If successful in creating legitimacy for the new state, the statebuilder will be less likely to have to intervene again in the future. An emphasis on loyalty, on the other hand, is more likely to ensure that a pliable leader rules the country and produces policies consistent with the statebuilder's interests—at least in the short run. Depending on the other variables discussed in this section, however, the more loyal are the leaders, the less support they will receive at home, the more precarious their political positions will be, and the more often they will be challenged by domestic opponents. By emphasizing loyalty, the statebuilder increases the likelihood of getting favorable policies, but this comes at the cost of greater political instability and the risk that it will have to intervene again in the future.

The effect of a statebuilder's time horizon or discount rate would appear to affect this trade-off, but it does so in complicated ways.[13] On the one hand, the longer the statebuilder's time horizon (the lower its discount rate), the more it might be expected to emphasize legitimacy and the ability of the state to survive over the long run. On the other hand, the longer the statebuilder's time horizon, the more it will care about the specific policies adopted by the leader—presuming he can hang onto office—as more favorable policies will also redound to its advantage for a longer period. Thus, the shadow of the future extends both ways, with indeterminate effects on the statebuilder's dilemma. On balance, a longer time horizon likely favors legitimacy except when the costs of intervention are likely to be low in the future.

The international environment might also matter, much as it did in prompting imperialist strategies in the nineteenth century.[14] Less competitive or threatening political environments may induce statebuilders to invest more in legitimacy, whereas more competitive environments will likely increase the need for loyalty to more securely lock countries into their respective spheres. Without competition from another superpower, for instance, the United States today appears less concerned about the loyalty of leaders and more willing to invest in legitimacy for the longer term than during the Cold War era. This is, however, only one factor that likely affects how states weigh the trade-off between legitimacy and loyalty. In Central America, with virtually no regional competitors by the period between the world wars, the United States still leaned toward loyal leaders. And after the Cold War, in the most favorable environment for legitimacy in decades, the United States clearly preferred a loyal leader in Iraq.

Whatever the specific balance, even statebuilders that weigh legitimacy more heavily than others will be willing to take on the responsibilities of re-

13. This is analogous to the bargaining and enforcement problem more generally. See Fearon 1998.
14. See the discussion of systemic pressures in Doyle 1986.

building a foreign state only when they have at least some specific interests in the future policies of that state and will, thus, attach some importance to the leader they help put in power. Only when a statebuilder values legitimacy or loyalty exclusively is the dilemma moot.

Strength of Interests

The greater the interests of the statebuilder in the failed state, the greater emphasis it will place on installing and maintaining a loyal leader in power. Statebuilding can be an enormously costly undertaking. Only states with strong preferences about the policies followed by the failed state are likely to incur this expense willingly. When specific interests in the target state are lacking, statebuilders will not volunteer or, if they do, will withdraw at the first sign of significant costs, much as the United States did in Somalia in 1993. Only states with strong interests in the failed state are likely to step forward as volunteer statebuilders. The more intense these interests, however, the more the statebuilder will emphasize loyalty over legitimacy in the choice of leader.

The greater the interests of the statebuilder, in turn, the higher the costs it is willing to bear and the more resources it will provide to the failed state in order to support a more loyal leader. This might appear to promise greater odds of success on its own. Yet in the hands of a loyal leader, the net effect may be the opposite. Knowing that the statebuilder has deep pockets, loyal leaders have less incentive to cultivate broad-based legitimacy. They can make larger demands on the statebuilder and concentrate the resulting resources more narrowly on their support coalition. Ironically, the greater the interests of statebuilders in the target country, the less likely statebuilding will result in regimes that are regarded as broadly legitimate by the populations over which they rule. Instead, the more intense the interests of the statebuilder are, the narrower the leader's base of support will be, the more corrupt the government will be, and the less stable the regime will be. In short, the greater the interests of the statebuilder, the more likely statebuilding will fail to build a legitimate state.

Distance in Policy Preferences

Most important, the policy preferences of the statebuilder and the failed state can differ by degree. Although policy preferences are never likely to overlap completely, they are likely to vary more or less, depending on the statebuilder and target populations. The closer the ideal points of the statebuilder and target population, the less acute the trade-off between loyalty and legitimacy. If both states prefer pretty much the same policies, as in figure 3.1a, leaders selected by the statebuilder will also be regarded as legitimate by their citizens. With some quantity of aid from the statebuilder, even a relatively "extreme" leader within the population of the failed state—one in the left "tail" of the distribution with personal policy preferences close to the statebuilder's—might be able to build a broad-based coalition of sympathetic supporters. This is, in part, the story of West Germany and Japan after 1945, which received massive aid during their respective occupations and are often regarded as two of only a handful of successful statebuilding attempts (see below).

The greater the distance between the ideal points of the statebuilder and the target population, all else being constant, the more acute the trade-off between legitimacy and loyalty. If the distance is too great, of course, the statebuilder may choose not to become involved: no leader in the target state may be available to safeguard its interests, and thus the statebuilder either stays home or—as was more common in the nineteenth century—assumes direct control in some form of imperialism. Up to the point where the statebuilder fails to enter or withdraws, however, it will select a leader closer to its ideal point, as in figure 3.1b. This is true even for statebuilders that emphasize legitimacy. As long as the statebuilder has any preference over the policies of the target state, the more distant the failed state's ideal point is, the more likely the statebuilder will be to choose a leader with relatively more extreme preferences and, thus, a smaller and smaller support coalition. In essence, as policy preferences become further apart, it is as if the statebuilder places increasing weight on loyalty over legitimacy—increasing the intensity of the statebuilder's dilemma. The effect is greater the stronger the interests of the statebuilder in the target state. Iraq and Afghanistan are examples where distant policy preferences—along with intense interests in the countries—led to deep concerns with the loyalty of newly installed national leaders, who then used their nearly unique positions within their societies to exploit the United States even while failing to use the resources provided by Washington to build stronger states. The more distant the policy preferences of the two countries, the less likely statebuilding is to fail to produce legitimate states.

The great irony of statebuilding, in turn, is that the more distant the policy preferences of the statebuilder and target state are, and the more emphasis is placed on the loyalty of the leader, the more displeased the statebuilder will be with the outcome. Even if statebuilders appoint leaders with the most extreme preferences from within their society—on the left of the distribution of preferences in figure 3.1b—the policies enacted by those leaders will still be far from what they desire. This explains the paradox that, although statebuilders may be quite unhappy with the leader's actions, it sticks with them despite the corruption at home and the less-than-desired policies abroad. Given the gap in policy preferences, this is the best outcome the statebuilder can achieve, but it is still not what it would want in some ideal world. In the end, the more distant the policy preferences, the more emphasis the statebuilder places on loyalty, the more corrupt and repressive the leader will be, the more statebuilding is likely to fail, and the unhappier the statebuilder will be with the policies pursued! But even here, the statebuilder still undertakes the effort because the policies adopted are better than what a more legitimate target state would do left to its own desires.

Illustrations from History: Central America, West Germany, and Japan

In addition to the case studies of Somalia and Iraq in the following chapters, we can also see variations in the statebuilder's dilemma at work in the examples of Central America in the early twentieth century and in West Germany and Japan after 1945, often touted as the two statebuilding successes of the postwar era. In Central America, moderate differences in policy preferences led to an emphasis on loyal leaders, who then governed through highly repressive dictatorships. These cases also show, however, how vesting over time can change the interests of target state populations. In West Germany and Japan, intense interests and smaller policy differences allowed loyal leaders to govern legitimately.

The United States had long claimed an area of exclusive control in Latin America under the Monroe Doctrine, proclaimed in 1823, but lacked the ability to enforce it, relying instead on British dominance in the region to police the other European powers. Likewise, the United States had lusted after a trans-isthmian canal. Only as the Panama Canal moved toward reality, however, did the United States begin to worry about the fragile states on the Caribbean littoral that, unable to protect property claims or repay their debts to European bankers, might become objects of renewed imperial interest. As U.S. concern with the region expanded, it developed new interests in the stability of its southern neighbors, leading to the Roosevelt Corollary to the Monroe Doctrine, which asserted a right of intervention in the event of what we would now call state failure, setting off a series of statebuilding interventions (see table 3.1).[15]

The policy preferences of the United States and those of the median citizens of various states in Central America were also likely quite different. Though policy preferences are hard to know in the absence of public opinion polls or other instruments unavailable from this period, and the articulated views available in the secondary literature are largely from the educated elite, it does not seem unreasonable to assume that policy differences between the United States and the various populations resembled those illustrated in figure 3.1b. In Central America, the United States inherited, so to speak, states with highly unequal societies already dominated by landowning, agro-exporting elites put in place under prior Spanish rule and integrated into the international economy under British hegemony.[16] Rather than side with the broad populations of these countries in favor of land redistribution and other forms of populism, which might have threatened U.S. investments in the

15. On the Roosevelt Corollary, see LaFeber 1994, 247–248; Smith 1996, 57.
16. Sokoloff and Engerman 2000.

Table 3.1 U.S. statebuilding efforts in Central
America, 1898–1933

Country	Years
Cuba	1898–1902
Panama[a]	1903–1936
Cuba	1906–1909
Nicaragua[a]	1909–1933
Haiti	1915–1934
Cuba[a]	1917–1922
Dominican Republic	1916–1924
Nicaragua[b]	1927–1933

Sources: Pei, Amin, and Garz 2006; P. Miller 2013.
[a] Pei, Amin, and Garz 2006 only.
[b] P. Miller 2013 only.

region, the United States allied itself with the existing elites, who were highly
vested in their autocratic regimes and the U.S. market. In doing so, it reinforced
the highly unequal and unstable political orders within these societies,
which benefited the elites and shut off possibilities of political and economic
reform that might have improved the welfare of the broader populations.[17]

Throughout this era, the United States appears to have cared little about
the legitimacy of the governments it supported. Although opposed to renewed
European colonialism, by the interwar period this was likely not a major source
of concern. Without major regional competitors, the United States might
have been expected to take a long view of its role in the region and seek legitimate states able to stand on their own over time. In weighing legitimacy and
loyalty, however, the United States clung to a doctrine of social Darwinism,
reinforced by deep racism, that denied that the "colored" majorities of these
countries were capable of effective self-governance.[18] Supporting the more
"Europeanized" elites, the United States ignored pleas for independent, democratic rule and more than acquiesced in—indeed favored—authoritarian governments led by members of the elite or military officers allied with the elite
who were loyal to their northern patron.[19] In these cases, the statebuilder's
dilemma was acute because of the policy differences, leading to a strong emphasis on loyalty. The United States simply chose to ignore one-half of the
trade-off and was willing, if not eager, to support repressive regimes as long as
they supported U.S. policy in the region.

17. LaFeber 1983.
18. Loveman 2010.
19. See Kinzer 2006.

Although the Good Neighbor policy of President Franklin Delano Roosevelt is often seen as a decisive change in attitude toward Latin America, it is better understood, in my view, as the culmination of U.S. efforts to stabilize pro-American regimes in the region.[20] Having installed loyal leaders in power, the United States could now step back and enjoy the fruits of its labors. Although the statebuilding efforts of this period are often judged to be failures or, at best, mixed successes, this is because they are assessed largely for their democratic qualities.[21] For the United States, what mattered more was the stability of rule under pro-American leaders. Even after the advent of the Good Neighbor policy, whenever opposition to the U.S.-supported regimes became manifest, the United States was still willing to intervene, as it did through direct intervention in the Dominican Republic in 1965, indirect intervention in Nicaragua via the Contras in the 1980s, and failed invasions (Bay of Pigs), failed assassination attempts, and perennial sanctions against Cuba from the revolution onward.

More recently, U.S.–Central American relations have been reset on a new track that permits greater democracy in the region. Under the press of globalization, itself the result of integration into the Pax Americana, many states on the Caribbean littoral have gradually reoriented themselves as labor-intensive export platforms, shifting the median voter away from opposition to the traditional agro-exporting elite to broader support for policies of greater economic integration favored by the United States. As the old vested interests in raw materials and primary products have depreciated over time, and new vested interests in labor-intensive manufacturing have expanded, the circumstantial interests of states and especially of the average citizen in the region have shifted dramatically. The Dominican Republic is, perhaps, the exemplar of this trend.

As the interests of states in the region have converged, the trade-off between legitimacy and loyalty has slowly diminished. As interests moved from something like figure 3.1b to figure 3.1a, the United States could support loyal leaders who were also more legitimate in the eyes of their own people. In the wake of the Vietnam War and the anti-Americanism this conflict brought to a head, President Jimmy Carter sought to reorient the U.S. relationship with Central America. He withdrew U.S. support for the most oppressive dictators in the region and returned the canal to Panama as a signal of his commitment to this new course. This strategy was, in part, reversed by President Ronald Reagan, especially in his support for the Nicaraguan Contras. Nonetheless, as the policy preferences of the United States and populations in the region have narrowed around the so-called Washington Consensus on neoliberal economic policies—with the notable exceptions of Cuba, Venezuela, and

20. On the Good Neighbor policy, see LaFeber 1994, 375–379; Smith 1996, chap. 3.
21. P. Miller 2013; Pei, Amin, and Garz 2006.

Bolivia—Carter's approach has generally prevailed, and U.S. support for democracy has steadily expanded, attenuating the statebuilder's dilemma and, by implication, the need to back less legitimate leaders.

This attenuation has been made possible by the increasingly similar interests, at least at the margin, of the United States and the broader populations of the Central American states. Statebuilding and the vesting of interests in a new policy regime can, over time, work a fundamental transformation of state interests. With broad movement toward neoliberalism at home and abroad, great democracy is now more consistent with the loyalty of leaders to Washington. Yet this has been a century-long process. It is not clear today that statebuilders have sufficient patience or will be allowed by the international community to enforce specific policy regimes over such extended periods of time.

The outcomes in West Germany and Japan after 1945 were dramatically different. The United States also possessed new interests in the two defeated powers, likely even more intense than those in Central America around the turn of the past century. Having fought two world wars in Europe and a devastating war in the Pacific, all blamed on the autocratic regimes in Germany and Japan, the United States vowed to resolve the problem once and for all through statebuilding on a massive scale. With the emergence of the Cold War beginning in 1947, the United States also sought to rehabilitate the defeated powers as stable allies against the Soviet Union and to integrate them into its forward-based defense strategy. In West Germany, the United States originally planned an occupation force of 404,500 troops, reduced due to budgetary pressures to 200,000 by the end of 1946.[22] In Japan, the initial occupation force included 354,675 U.S. soldiers.[23] In both, the occupations were expected to last up to four decades and represented substantial commitments of time, effort, and resources.[24] From the point of view of Germans and Japanese after the war, this must have seemed like an occupation of indefinite—indeed, permanent—duration. This helped convince citizens in both West Germany and Japan of the credibility of the U.S. role and the new regimes it installed.

After the war, at least, the policy preferences of the United States and the average citizen in West Germany and Japan were also relatively similar or, perhaps more accurately, were made to be similar. The United States clearly desired to integrate both states into the emerging Pax Americana, open their economies to trade and investment, recruit them as active allies in the struggle with the Soviet Union, and ensure that their foreign policies did not at the very least contradict its own. It is more difficult, of course, to discern the pol-

22. Dobbins, McGinn, et al. 2003, 9–10.
23. Ibid., 34. On statebuilding under the occupation in Japan more generally, see Dower 1999. On Japan in comparative perspective, see Dower 2003 and Monten 2014.
24. Lake 1999, 176–182.

icy preferences of the average German or Japanese during the early postwar period in the absence of hard evidence through public opinion surveys or other instruments. Nonetheless, it appears clear that, at a minimum, the interests of Germans and Japanese were in flux. Nazism and militarism had been thoroughly defeated and delegitimated. The interests vested in the old order were either destroyed in the war or greatly depreciated. The previously autocratic state had few defenders left in either country. Without clear moorings, under U.S. occupation and with the promise of integration into the Pax Americana dangling before them, pro-American moderates centered on Christian Democrats under Konrad Adenauer in West Germany and Liberal Democrats under Shigeru Yoshida in Japan rapidly emerged and consolidated their coalitions with considerable assistance from the United States in the form of Marshall Plan aid and other programs. Despite significant socialist and communist oppositions in Europe and Japan, once the Cold War got under way average citizens in West Germany and Japan likely feared the Soviet Union, although not to the same degree as their U.S. counterparts. And despite some dissent on the Left, nearly all supported the international political order favored by the United States, with its reliance on embedded liberalism and its permissive attitude toward export-led growth.[25] By the late 1940s, it seems reasonable to assume, the policy preferences of the defeated states had substantially converged with those of the United States. These cases approximate the distribution of preferences illustrated in figure 3.1a, with the median citizen now quite close to the United States. As a result of the convergence in policy preferences, the statebuilder's dilemma essentially evaporated. Democracy was not only possible in West Germany and Japan but preferred, as was a return to sovereignty far quicker than originally anticipated.

The degree of West Germany's and Japan's transformation over time cannot be overstated. These were previously fascist and militarist regimes that fought total wars against their neighbors and the United States. After its victory, rather than allow policy differences to become reified, the United States supported Christian Democrats and Liberal Democrats in both states who were willing to cast their lot with Washington. Once West Germany and Japan were induced into this order, their domestic political economies quickly coalesced around a strategy of export-led growth and became vested in the Pax Americana and support for the United States. The success of statebuilding in West Germany and Japan after World War II, often a source of mystery to contemporary analysts, had less to do with the particular strategies or institutions employed by the United States and much more to do with the propitious circumstances created by the openness of policy preferences in the two defeated states and the convergence around policies desired by Washington. As we shall see in chapter 4, this happy outcome contrasts sharply with the case of Iraq.

25. Ikenberry 2001, 2011.

Theories and Practices of Legitimation

Statebuilders employ different theories of how and when states become legitimate to motivate and structure their interventions. Not all statebuilding efforts, of course, emphasize legitimacy. Some, as we have just seen in the case of the United States in Central America, have focused almost exclusively on the loyalty of the leader. In other cases, though, the statebuilder has had more mixed motives, or the dilemma was sufficiently real that explicit consideration needed to be given to how to build a legitimate state. In these instances, three theories of legitimation have predominated over the past half century, especially in the United States. These theories understand the trade-off between legitimacy and loyalty differently, but all either seek to dismiss the statebuilder's dilemma by positing an underlying if not yet realized harmony of interests or propose a flawed strategy for overcoming it. In this section, I summarize briefly each of the theories and major criticisms that have grown up around them, and then demonstrate that none of them successfully reconciles the statebuilder's dilemma.

Modernization Theory

Modernization theory aims to describe and explain the processes and path of transformation from traditional or underdeveloped societies to liberal, democratic states characteristic of "advanced" industrialized societies.[26] As summarized by Stuart Eisenstadt, a prominent proponent: "Historically, modernization is the process of change towards those types of social, economic, and political systems that have developed in Western Europe and North America from the seventeenth century to the nineteenth and have then spread to other European countries and in the nineteenth and twentieth centuries to the South American, Asian, and African continents."[27] As a shorthand, development or modernization is synonymous with "Westernization."

The theory posits that countries develop through evolutionary stages. Walter Rostow, one of the most influential advocates, described five progressive steps as traditional, precondition for takeoff, takeoff, drive for maturity, and mass consumption society.[28] Development is understood, in turn, as a process of increasing social complexity. Early stages are propelled forward by increased specialization and differentiation, which then encourage further specialization and differentiation, leading to the discovery and adoption of certain universal social structures, notably markets, money, bureaucracy, and industry. Through this process, societies become more urbanized and secular, with

---

26. Key works on modernization theory, from which this synthesis is drawn, include Smelser 1966; Binder 1971; Almond, Flanagan, and Mundt 1973.
27. Eisenstadt 1966, 265.
28. Rostow 1960.

weaker kinship ties and smaller nuclear families. Along with these social trends come increased demands for democracy, respect for human rights—especially civil and political rights—and political accountability. Critically for purposes of statebuilding, modernization theory assumes that development entails a shift from extended family, tribe, clan, and other private authorities that compete with the state to a single national identity with authority consolidated in a single apex or sovereign. With this shift, politics becomes increasingly open, liberal, and democratic.

The causes of underdevelopment, in turn, are understood to lie in traditional social structures that inhibit change and lack opportunities for productive investment. Although the problem of underdevelopment is seen as largely internal in origin, statebuilders, in today's parlance, can jump-start the process of modernization through the provision of foreign aid and technical assistance. This view of statebuilding underlay the Alliance for Progress and the Peace Corps, both adopted under President John F. Kennedy during the heyday of modernization theory. Focused largely on Latin America, and spurred by the recent Cuban Revolution, the Alliance for Progress nearly tripled U.S. aid to the southern continent in 1961, reaching $1.4 billion per year through 1967 ($3.3 billion if private investments and other international sources are included).[29] The Peace Corps also grew rapidly, with the first members being sent overseas in August 1961 and growing to 15,000 volunteers serving in over forty-four countries by 1966.[30] Later, emphasis changed to creating the political and economic institutions necessary to encourage domestic investment and the proper use of foreign aid.[31] Nonetheless, the consequences of institutional reform were still expected to be a natural process of development through which currently underdeveloped states would become more modern and similar to their already "developed" counterparts.

As a theory of statebuilding, modernization theory did not see any substantial conflict between the legitimacy of states and the loyalty of leaders. Indeed, state legitimacy was expected to follow naturally—perhaps inevitably—from modernization itself. As traditional social formations gave way and authority was consolidated in the state, modernizing societies would come to resemble developed states in which public authority trumps private authorities. As they developed, all societies would also become more similar in social structure and, implicitly, in their policy preferences. Even if societies were now far apart in their desired social orders, as in figure 3.1b, they would grow together over time in a natural convergence. The main aim of statebuilding, then, was to ignite the "takeoff" to self-sustaining economic growth that would, at some future date, reduce the tension between states that are legitimate to

29. Smith 1996, 151.
30. Peace Corps n.d.
31. Discussed in the introduction as the still dominant institutionalist approach to statebuilding.

their own societies and leaders beholden to and sympathetic to the interests of external statebuilders. Although there might be some incompatibility between Western-supported leaders and their more traditional societies prior to the takeoff, these differences would erode as the target societies modernized. The statebuilder's dilemma, in short, was a temporary phenomenon that modernizing states would eventually outgrow. Indeed, given the constraints of traditional societal structures on development, the statebuilder might even have an obligation to support an authoritarian but modernizing leader who could act outside the constraints of democratic institutions to propel the country to an early takeoff or sustain it through rocky starts.[32] In this case, there might be no trade-off at all, despite the paternalism implied by modernization's advocates.

Modernization theory reigned supreme in the academy in the 1950s and early 1960s. Since then, it has been variously and appropriately criticized for its teleology, unidirectional theory of change, and ethnocentrism.[33] The idea that all developing states are hidebound traditionalists and that there is but a single path to higher per capita national income—and that it was blazed by the Europeans—was thoroughly debunked by the rise of the newly industrialized countries of East Asian.[34] Now largely dismissed by scholars, modernization theory continues to hold considerable sway in policy circles and the public imagination at least in the United States. The emphasis in development policy—the term itself is indicative of the hegemony of modernization theory—on raising per capita incomes and building state capacity further suggests the tenacity of its ideas. Blended with liberalism, modernization theory still informs much of the current thinking about statebuilding.

Liberal Statebuilding

At the end of the Cold War, statebuilders found themselves freed from the shackles of ideological competition. Rather than single-mindedly supporting leaders loyal to their side in an ideological struggle, the default strategy under superpower competition, statebuilders could now give greater emphasis to building legitimate states. As we shall see in the case studies of Iraq and Somalia, the end of the Cold War created a political opening for statebuilders to accord legitimacy a higher priority than before. In the euphoria of the end of the Cold War—indeed, the end of history—the international community reached to political and economic liberalism to guide its statebuilding efforts.

Four tenets of liberalism are important and fit together into an integrated strategy for building legitimate states. First, democracy legitimates states by

---

32. Huntington 1968.
33. Among other critiques, see So 1990; Billet 1993; Inglehart 1997; Roberts and Hite 1999.
34. Haggard 1990.

promoting deliberation by citizens in a public sphere.[35] Although the conditions for ideal deliberation remain contested and are rarely approximated in the real world, liberals nonetheless posit that democracy comes closest of all known political systems to meeting these conditions. By encouraging the exchange of ideas and information among individuals, competition between parties for votes, and a free press to stimulate debate and verify information, democracy allows the will of the people to be determined more accurately than would be otherwise possible. Second, democracy legitimates states by ensuring government responsiveness to citizen demands and desires. Here, again, democracy is imperfect. Politicians may write the rules of political competition to insulate themselves from the will of the people. Special interests may pull policy away from the median voter. But compared to the alternatives, liberals believe democracy does respond to the demands of average citizens and provides public goods more effectively than the alternatives.[36] Third, democracy legitimates states because it is procedurally fair.[37] Under democracy, the rules of politics are established and more or less clear, permitting smooth successions of power from one set of elected officials to another. In addition, democracy equalizes more or less the voices of citizens in the political process. Special interests, of course, play a major role even in consolidated democracies, enjoying access to politicians that average citizens do not—as their name implies. But through the rule of "one person, one vote," democracy is relatively fair—or at least more fair, again, than the alternatives. For all three reasons, participating in the political process, especially for citizens previously repressed by the state, can often have a powerful legitimating effect. Iraqis proudly showed off their purple fingers after their first elections in 2005, dyed to inhibit election fraud but quickly reinterpreted as a symbol of their new ability to vote for their leaders. Such moments visually and emotionally attest to the legitimating power of democracy.

Finally, liberal economic policies of competitive markets, limited regulation, and openness to trade are understood both to maximize social welfare, and thereby legitimate the state, and constrain the state in ways that help preserve democracy over the long term. By minimizing the scope of the state and maximizing the sphere of private property and private rights, economic liberalism creates social forces with vested interests in protecting those rights against state encroachment. By keeping resources out of the hands of the state, economic liberalism reduces the benefits of holding political office and, therefore, incentives for individual leaders to appropriate political power for themselves. In short, economic liberalism, good on its own terms, also reinforces and preserves democracy.

35. Cohen 1989; Dryzek 2001.
36. On public goods provision by democracies, see Lake and Baum 2001; Levi, Sacks, and Tyler 2009.
37. Tyler 1990.

These pillars of liberalism—democracy and free markets—fit together into a persuasive whole that promises to legitimate otherwise failed states, just as they legitimate the state in advanced industrial democracies. Drawing on well-established liberal theory and their own subjective historical experiences, the victors of the Cold War in North America and Europe deeply embraced this new mode of statebuilding in the decades following the collapse of communism.

As implemented in the now "standard" model, liberalism focuses on rebuilding the political institutions of failed states on inclusive, democratic principles.[38] As soon as practicable after the end of hostilities, the principal parties are brought together in a constitutional convention composed of all stakeholders within the country, usually excluding only those responsible for widespread atrocities or who represent an overthrown faction (for example, the Taliban in Afghanistan). This convention is charged with writing inclusive rules of political participation and creating a new structure of democratic politics tailored to the unique experience of the country. As part of this process, an interim government is often created. Once the constitution is ratified, internationally monitored elections are quickly held. Participatory institutions are clearly seen as a priority and perhaps even a panacea. In addition to reconstructing the political institutions of the state, liberals also advocate for economic reform. Along with political liberalization, liberal statebuilders in the 1990s sought to implement the Washington Consensus on economic policy, including reducing barriers to international trade and investment and stimulating the growth of private enterprise.[39] Pushed by international financial institutions and others during this period, the Washington Consensus was part of the "good governance" movement that was applied far beyond failed states.

Problems in the liberal theory of legitimation were manifested as early as the humanitarian intervention in Somalia; they reached a nadir in postwar Iraq. First, although proponents believe it can be broadly applied, liberalism is not a universally shared philosophy. Where it is accepted as a broad ideological interest, it appears to have played a positive role in legitimating the state, as in Bosnia. But in many regions of the world where it is not generally accepted, it does not automatically have this effect. In Islamic countries, for instance, God's law as embodied in the Koran is understood as superior to human law. For religious Muslims, man-made law, no matter how participatory the political process through which that law was made, can never trump Sharia or the teachings of religious scholars.[40] In less religious societies that nonetheless lack experience with democratic institutions, liberalism may clash with local practices and political thought, and will also fail to confer le-

38. Paris 2004.
39. Ibid., 19; Barbara 2008.
40. Sisk 1992.

gitimacy on states. Notions of "fairness" differ dramatically across cultures,[41] as do notions of individualism central to liberalism versus clan or collective identities.[42] It was a supreme act of Western hubris to expect liberalism (the "freedom agenda") to apply equally to all societies and political cultures around the globe.

Second, democracy necessarily alters the balance of political power between social groups and challenges interests vested in the ancien régime. All political institutions privilege some social interests over others. In autocratic regimes, the military, individuals with personal ties to the leadership, or industries that share their economic rents with leaders tend to dominate the political system. Democracy shifts political power from these interests toward the majority of citizens. For its proponents, this is one of democracy's key benefits. Yet, by disrupting the political equipoise, democracy can be extremely destabilizing.[43] In Somalia, as explained in more detail in chapter 5, the United Nations initially negotiated with the principal warlords, who enjoyed political power roughly proportional to the size of their militias. By spring 1993, however, it began a process of democratization by building elected district-level councils with the ultimate goal of creating a new countrywide representative body. This enraged the warlords, who correctly saw it as a deliberate attempt to sideline them and empower others in society. The strongest warlord, General Mohamed Farrah Aidid, quickly broke with the United Nations process. The United Nations subsequently convinced the United States that Aidid was an obstructionist, and an intense conflict broke out between the peacekeepers and his militia, ultimately resulting in the failed attack on his headquarters in Mogadishu in October 1993, the deaths of eighteen U.S. servicemen, and the pullout of U.S. forces from Somalia. Similarly, attempts to build democracy in Iraq, which would empower the majority Shiites, fed the insurgency among the Sunnis, the religious minority that was previously privileged under the Ba'athist regime.

Democracy will never appear legitimate to former power holders who lose influence within the new, democratically constructed state. But any rules that preserve the power of formerly privileged groups will, by definition, not be democratic. The evidence to date, as Roland Paris ably shows, is that democratization has, at best, no effect on building effective states and may even have a detrimental effect by reifying divisions and distrust.[44] Although it is an unquestioned article of faith in developed counties that democracy is a "good thing" and desirable for all—and I will admit to sharing this faith—there is little evidence that democracy per se can legitimate governments in weak states.

41. Henrich et al. 2004.
42. Weiner 2013.
43. Mansfield and Snyder 2007.
44. Paris 2004.

Third, economic reform has an effect similar to democratization on economic interests in a country. Economic reform necessarily strips away economic protections, reduces the rents of those individuals and industries that had prospered through their connections to the old regime, and shifts returns toward industries and entrepreneurs who can compete effectively in domestic and international markets. Again, liberals see this process of economic and political change as one of the benefits of market reform. Yet these economic disruptions also undermine state legitimacy. The economic losers will seek to block reforms, and if they fail will likely judge the state that caused their new "plight" as illegitimate. Pointing to Iraq again, the minority Sunnis, with no oil resources in their region of the country, were nonetheless economically privileged and the wealthiest group in the country before the war. The economic reforms championed by the Coalition Provisional Authority, regarded by Ambassador Paul Bremer as his greatest accomplishment, created a "fearsome" backlash from the former economic elite and drove them into the insurgency.[45] Even more so in Somalia, the breakdown of normal economic intercourse during the humanitarian crisis allowed the warlords to profit from control over external aid and, indeed, from criminal behavior, including now piracy. Any return of the rule of law would necessarily diminish their activities. As now perhaps the only prosperous groups in Somalia, the warlords, smugglers, and pirates use their illicit returns to build public support and through continued violence undercut prospects for the return of political stability.[46]

In short, despite the tenets of liberal theory, on no dimension does liberalism in practice automatically legitimate a state.[47] Political and economic reforms disrupt the ancient regime and weaken interests vested in the old order, and these interests are likely to oppose any state founded on different principles. Neoconservatives have sometimes averred that it is a form of racism to imply that developing peoples are not yet ready for democracy and freedom, but it is equally an act of Western intellectual arrogance to assume that democracy alone is sufficient to legitimate new state institutions, especially in countries without a tradition of democratic rule.[48]

Perhaps most critically, liberalism assumes that, once empowered through democratic institutions, societies will have similar or at least compatible interests. In this way, liberalism is the successor to modernization theory—or, more accurately, modernization theory shares fundamentally liberal intellectual roots. In liberal statebuilding theory and practice, however, democratic institutions and market reforms are believed to be appropriate regardless of the level of economic development of the society and to produce an align-

---

45. Chandrasekaran 2006, 70, 134, 328; Allawi 2007, 198.
46. Bradbury 2003, 20–21; Menkhaus 2003, 417.
47. Beate 2007.
48. Fukuyama 2006a, chap. 5.

ment of interests across all societies. This assumption has been particularly strong in the United States, especially in the administration of President George W. Bush. Implicitly, Americans have assumed that democratically elected leaders would support the United States and its interests around the globe. This rests on the notions that "small d" democrats are inherently alike and that democracies favor the status quo and are, therefore, innately peaceful—all of which largely complements the position of the United States in the world today. This belief may also rest on the lessons learned from the successful statebuilding efforts in West Germany and Japan after World War II, although, as noted above, both cases were more complicated than any simple notion of democratization can explain. Thus, like modernization theory, the liberal theory of legitimation assumes away the trade-off between legitimacy and loyalty that lies at the core of the statebuilder's dilemma. Yet the dilemma remains whether policymakers want to acknowledge it or not. Indeed, in most cases since 1990, the United States has claimed to be following the liberal model even while it hand-picked leaders with whom it shared similar interests and then sought to sustain those leaders in power. Although the end of the Cold War allowed a greater emphasis on legitimacy in statebuilding, statebuilders themselves did not yield entirely in their demands for loyal leaders.

Winning Hearts and Minds

Counterinsurgency (COIN) warfare as a statebuilding theory arose from the wreck of liberal statebuilding in the deserts of Iraq. Yet even as Iraq imploded in sectarian violence, deviations from the liberal model led to apparent success in some parts of Iraq, especially the area around Mosul occupied until February 2004 by the U.S. Army's 101st Airborne Division under the command of General David Petraeus. The U.S. military quickly recognized these pockets of relative success and generalized the practice into a new doctrine, embodied in the *U.S. Army/Marine Corps Counterinsurgency Field Manual* (*CFM*), released in December 2006.[49] It might seem odd to treat COIN as statebuilding, but according to the *CFM* counterinsurgency *is* statebuilding, a battle to win the "hearts and minds" of the local population for the nascent state and thereby undercut support for the rebels.

The COIN model grew out of a long history of guerrilla warfare and analysis, but was "field-tested" by the United States through President Bush's surge in Iraq, a policy shift much broader than simply increasing the number of troops on a temporary basis, and through President Barack Obama's expanded efforts

49. United States, Department of the Army 2007 (hereafter *CFM* 2007). The *CFM* overlaps with and appears informed by substantial case studies and lessons learned compiled by the RAND Corporation and echoes other recent manifestos. See Dobbins, Jones, et al. 2007 and Ghani and Lockhart 2008.

in Afghanistan. Like liberal statebuilding, COIN aspires to create legitimate states. Unlike its predecessor, however, COIN eschews democracy and free markets in favor of providing security and essential public services to the population. If the mantra of liberal statebuilding was "democracy first," COIN clearly places public security first, with democracy relegated to a distant priority. The theory of legitimation embodied in COIN rests on a social contract view of the state and its core tenet that legitimacy follows from providing effectively for the basic needs of the people.[50] In this approach, authority derives from a mutually beneficial exchange in which the state provides a social order of benefit to its citizens, and those citizens in turn comply with the extractions (for example, taxes) and constraints on their behavior (for example, law) that are necessary to the production of that order. As Hobbes reasoned in *Leviathan*, individuals will voluntarily subordinate themselves to a ruler only in return for protection, and in doing so they escape a condition of anarchy and enter a civil society.[51] In this way, "outcome" legitimacy arises from results, especially an improved standard of living, rather than from political participation or ideology.

COIN begins with a core insight that the struggle between insurgents and counterinsurgents is over political power, a battle in which "each side aims to get the people to accept its governance or authority as legitimate."[52] Essential here is the competition for the "uncommitted middle," which lies between "an active minority supporting the government and an equally small militant faction opposing it."[53] Legitimacy, in turn, is expected to follow from the ability of an actor—be it the insurgents or the state—to provide essential public services, especially security. As the *CFM* states: "A government that cannot protect its people forfeits the right to rule. Legitimacy is accorded to the element that can provide security, as citizens seek to ally with groups that can guarantee their safety."[54] Explicitly recognizing that legitimacy can follow from many sources, including tradition and religion, the field manual nonetheless leaves no doubt that "the ability of a state to provide security—albeit without freedoms associated with Western democracies—can give it enough legitimacy to govern in the people's eyes, particularly if they have experienced a serious breakdown of order."[55] Clearly downgrading democracy as a basis for legitimacy, the *CFM* asserts that security is a necessary and possibly sufficient condition for legitimacy.

To win hearts and minds, according to an overlapping RAND study, statebuilders should prioritize goals and activities in the following order:

50. North 1981; Olson 2000; Barzel 2002.
51. Hobbes 1651/1962.
52. *CFM* 2007, 2; see also 3, 15.
53. Ibid., 35.
54. Ibid., 16.
55. Ibid., 37.

Security: peacekeeping, law enforcement, rule of law, and security sector reform;

Humanitarian relief: return of refugees and response to potential epidemics, hunger, and lack of shelter;

Governance: resuming public services and restoring public administration;

Economic stabilization: establishing a stable currency and providing a legal and regulatory framework in which local and international commerce can resume;

Democratization: building political parties, free press, civil society, and a legal and constitutional framework for elections;

Development: fostering economic growth, poverty reduction, and infrastructure improvements.[56]

Operationally, the *CFM* makes clear that security, whether provided by U.S. forces or host nation forces, is the highest priority, even though this means that at the tactical level troops will be placed at greater risk by protecting the people rather than themselves, being visible and present in the streets, and living among the population rather than in secure bases. Conversely, democracy and economic development, central to liberal statebuilding and modernization theory, are demoted to lower priorities overall, and, strikingly, elections and support for a free market are the last, not the first, steps in statebuilding practice.[57] Although the goal remains building legitimate states, the field manual completely flips the theory of legitimation on its head. While in liberalism states that are legitimated by democratic processes are then expected to provide services demanded by citizens, COIN aims to provide those services first in order to legitimate the state, with democracy and economic reform following only once stability has been achieved.

By January 2007, President Bush was forced to acknowledge that the model of liberal statebuilding initially followed by his administration had failed in Iraq. He altered course in the surge, expanding the number of troops deployed by some twenty thousand and replacing General George Casey with Petraeus. Focusing on providing basic security and essential public services to Iraqis, the new statebuilding strategy dispersed the newly enlarged U.S. forces more widely, adopted population-centric protection measures, engaged in outreach to the armed antagonists, and developed new, more precise counterinsurgency tactics made possible by better intelligence provided by Iraqi civilians. Using an "oil spot" strategy, the military established control over an area through a large initial deployment, provided services and especially the security desired by the population, elicited information from the population about local insurgents, and then used that information to target insurgents

56. Dobbins, Jones, et al. 2007, xxiii.
57. *CFM* 2007, 156.

and expand its area of control. By progressively repeating these steps, the military was able to tamp down the violence in Baghdad. Critically, before and in the new breathing space opened by the surge, the largely Sunni insurgents organized into new Awakening Councils also simply decided to stop fighting.[58] The new statebuilding strategy dramatically reduced U.S. military and Iraqi civilian casualties. By December 2008, the overall level of violence in Iraq had dropped by 80 percent from its peak (see chapter 4).[59] In this new environment, the United States negotiated a Status of Forces Agreement with the Iraqi government that set a timeline for the withdrawal of all U.S. combat forces from the country by December 31, 2011, ending the direct U.S. role in statebuilding in Iraq.

Despite its success in creating the conditions for the withdrawal of U.S. forces, COIN experienced significant failures as a means of legitimating states.[60] First, although small-project aid under COIN appears to have increased support at the local level for the government, there is no evidence that this strategy "scales up" to the national level, especially after the stabilizing hand of external patrons is removed.[61] Services provided by the state or an external statebuilder—as in Iraq and Afghanistan, where COIN has been most fully implemented by the military and studied by scholars—may well influence hearts and minds in any particular village, but the legitimacy earned at this level may not necessarily extend to the central government. Each village may gladly accept a new well, but when the question shifts to how to allocate always scarce resources across the country and between previously warring groups, traditional authorities are likely to mobilize their supporters to demand greater shares and thereby reignite competition between factions.

Second, even if providing essential public services is necessary for legitimacy, it may not be sufficient. A central problem with all states, as recognized by James Madison, is that any government effective enough to enforce the rule of law is also strong enough to abuse its power, at least in the short run. Granting coercive power to a ruler to create and enforce a social order necessarily gives that ruler the ability to use coercion in her own self-interest as well. This is often not a pressing issue in fragile states, where the problem is typically a lack of authority, but it is a key impediment to rebuilding strong states: the fear of future exploitation prevents groups from subordinating themselves to a new central authority, and thus they block the state from gaining significant legitimacy by denying it their support or actively fighting against

58. Robinson 2008, 324–325.
59. Kruzel 2009.
60. Biddle, Friedman, and Shapiro 2012 claim that the success of the surge and COIN was dependent on the "turn" of the Sunni tribes in the Anbar Awakening. See chapter 5. Porch (2013) argues that COIN shatters society and makes it more difficult to build consolidated states. On the complex relationship between service provision and legitimacy, see McLoughlin 2015.
61. Berman, Shapiro, and Felter 2011. Discussed in more detail in chapter 4.

it. Such fears of abusive central authority, for instance, are critical to the problems of statebuilding in Somalia today.[62] The favoritism and corruption of the Karzai regime in Afghanistan also eroded popular support for the central government. To grant legitimacy to a state, citizens must be relatively confident that the authority so given will be used for the intended purpose of fulfilling the social contact. To receive this grant, therefore, the state must credibly commit not to abuse the authority it acquires.

Democracy has, historically, been one of the most effective ways of controlling state power. By diffusing authority and ensuring that popular preferences are represented in the policy process, democracy ties the sovereign's hands, in Douglass North and Barry Weingast's classic rendition of this problem.[63] Democracy is not, however, the only means of constraining a state. Limited government existed before democracy and has existed without democracy. Indeed, if a single majority exists within a society, democracy may even lead to the abuse of vulnerable minorities, and less participatory and more consociational forms of government may be preferred.[64] Federalism and other divided forms of government can also limit state power, as can freer markets and private property rights.[65] No single institutional solution is likely to be universally appropriate. Although providing essential public services is important, limiting potential abuses by the ruler may also be a necessary and prior step in any statebuilding effort, even under COIN. In this way, COIN errs by downgrading the importance of democracy and economic reform not because they are themselves legitimating institutions, as in liberalism, but because they help constrain the authority of overly strong states.

Finally, and most important, COIN does not resolve the statebuilder's dilemma. The theory assumes that by pumping resources into the failed state, the statebuilder can provide enough security and other public goods to win—or, more accurately, buy—the hearts and minds of the people. Unlike modernization theory and liberalism, which assume that all people will eventually agree on the broad contours of policy and come to share similar preferences, COIN does not presume a harmony of interests now or in the future but does assume that people can be brought to support the regime with sufficient effort and resources. This might be true in principle, if resources are unlimited and flow indefinitely, but it raises the costs of statebuilding significantly, and especially so as the policy preferences of the statebuilder and population in the failed state increasingly diverge. In this context, it is worth noting that the vast majority of the costs of the Iraq War were incurred after the end of formal combat operations and during the statebuilding phase. Paradoxically, the high price of COIN limits statebuilding to those instances where

62. Bradbury 2003, 15, 21; Menkhaus 2003, 408.
63. North and Weingast 1989.
64. Lijphart 1968.
65. Weingast 1995; Lake and Rothchild 2005; Myerson 2006.

the statebuilder has significant interests in the failed state. These are, as noted above, precisely the circumstances under which the statebuilder will emphasize installing a loyal leader rather than a legitimate state. Indeed, given the opportunity costs of resources and time, all statebuilders will, at the margin, substitute a more loyal leader for additional effort in COIN. In those cases where policy preferences are distant and, therefore, the price of winning or buying hearts and minds is highest, statebuilders will be tempted to back a loyal leader—along with all the implications of that choice, including, most importantly, the diverting of resources from providing public goods to building the leader's private support coalition. Even though COIN is designed to win hearts and minds for the new state, it is most likely to be employed by statebuilders in exactly those countries where they have the strongest interests and, thus, will be most likely to back a loyal leader. Though COIN may promise to overcome the statebuilder's dilemma, when the stakes are high enough statebuilders will still favor loyalty over legitimacy.

When and Why Statebuilding Succeeds and Fails

All states require legitimacy to be successful over the long run. To govern effectively, some significant fraction of the individuals within a society must recognize state authority as rightful, obligatory, and something with which they should comply. When the state is perceived as legitimate or expected to be legitimate—often the same thing—social interests vest themselves in the state, becoming a further force for stability in the face of uncertainty. As suggested by the persistence of authoritarian regimes, political repression can substitute for legitimacy, but not forever. The more citizens regard the state as legitimate, the more enduring, resilient, and capable it will be.

As explained in chapter 2, states want other states to be capable of policing their territories effectively. Statebuilders can catalyze expectations of stability in failed states—and thus, the vesting of social interests—but this requires a credible commitment by the external power to the new social order and its protection. This is the great promise of statebuilding. Yet the system of Westphalian sovereignty that requires strong states also limits what statebuilders can do. Direct external control is prohibited. Statebuilders must work indirectly through proxies to achieve their aims, whatever they may be. And to limit self-interested interventions, the international community imposes limited and temporary mandates on statebuilders, undermining the credibility of their commitments. Statebuilding is an enormously fraught undertaking. It is both essential to the maintenance of the Westphalian system and a threat to it.

This is the environment in which contemporary statebuilders must operate. Statebuilding remains poorly understood and even harder to implement effectively. It is also an enormously costly task. The greater the interests of states in target states, the more likely they will be to step forward and take on this responsibility voluntarily. It is precisely because statebuilders are likely to be self-interested that the international community imposes limited and temporary mandates on them. But these interests nonetheless create a fundamental and inescapable dilemma between enhancing the legitimacy of the state and securing the interests of the statebuilder. Though they have varied in popularity over time in the academy and among policymakers, none of the theories of legitimation just described obviates this central dilemma. Modernity, even if easily imposed, does not necessarily produce harmonious interests, nor do democracy and free markets. Winning or buying hearts and minds increases the costs of statebuilding, only making it more likely that those states willing to accept the challenge will have intense interests in the future policies of the target state. The statebuilder's dilemma may be more or less acute, but it is inescapable.

The dilemma is least intense when statebuilders emphasize only one goal—legitimacy or loyalty—at the expense of the other. A realpolitik view of statebuilding privileges the interests of the statebuilder and, in turn, the loyalty of the leader. This was largely the strategy pursued by the United States in Central America in the opening decades of the twentieth century. Fearing that popular opinion would challenge its political and economic interests in the region, the United States sided with the landed elites and supported several of the more odious dictators in modern history. Although legitimacy was understood to be desirable—all else considered—it was clearly and consistently subordinated to loyalty. The dilemma became apparent only when opposition movements arose and turned stridently anti-American.

What might be called "enlightened" statebuilding, never realized in practice, emphasizes legitimacy for its own sake. This is the ideal behind the statebuilding efforts of several European states and NGOs today, who provide assistance for security sector reform (SSR); disarmament, demobilization, and reintegration (DDR); and other strategies for strengthening civil society in the aftermath of widespread political violence. These efforts are fundamentally altruistic and commendable, and may be effective at the margin, but they are typically limited in scale and scope precisely by their altruism. Truly neutral statebuilders willing to devote substantial resources to the task are rare. Efforts to date, moreover, typically operate under the shadow of a more self-interested statebuilder willing to use military force to end the violence and guarantee a settlement, so it is difficult to assess the independent effects of SSR and DDR programs in and of themselves. Non-self-interested statebuilders cannot be ruled out, but this is a weak reed on which to rely. Overall, the greater the interests of the statebuilder in the target state, the greater the emphasis it will put on loyalty.

The most propitious circumstance for statebuilding is when the policy preferences of the statebuilder and the target society are not too distant from one another. When the statebuilder and the people of the failed state want essentially the same policies, any leader appointed by the statebuilder will act in ways that are supported and seen as legitimate by the population. This was the favorable condition found in West Germany and Japan after 1945. Conversely, the least favorable circumstance is when policy preferences in the two societies are quite distant from one another. In these cases, leaders preferred by the statebuilder will be opposed by the people, and vice versa. The greater the distance in policy preferences, the more acute the trade-off between legitimacy and loyalty, the more statebuilders favor loyal leaders, and the less likely statebuilding is to succeed in creating legitimate states able to govern themselves effectively over the long run.

Today, unfortunately, the dilemma is most intense where statebuilding is most necessary. The states most likely to fail are either in Africa or the Middle East. Of the twenty-five states at greatest risk of failing according to *Foreign Policy* magazine in 2015, eighteen are in Africa, four are in the Middle East, and only three are elsewhere.[66] At the same time, only the United States has the capacity to lead militarized statebuilding efforts or cajole others into contributing on a substantial scale. Even in the case of Ethiopia's intervention in Somalia, described in chapter 5, the United States heavily subsidized the military effort. For the foreseeable future, the United States will continue to be the world's primary (but not exclusive) statebuilder.

In Africa, U.S. interests are not sufficiently deep, and Washington is unlikely to undertake large-scale, militarized statebuilding efforts. Here, fragile states will fail and remain that way or be captured by neighboring states with their own statebuilder's dilemmas, as in Somalia. In the Middle East, as in the case of Iraq, U.S. interests are greater and policy preferences are far from those of the average citizen in those societies (discussed in chapter 4). Easy cases where the interests of the United States and the preferences of the target society coincide are not likely to arise in the years ahead. Rather, it is precisely in those states where the policy preferences of the United States and the target populations are furthest apart that Washington will be called on to rebuild failed states. The statebuilder's dilemma has always been with us. In the foreseeable future, and in those countries where the United States is most likely to intervene, the dilemma will be more intense than ever.

66. *Foreign Policy* magazine, Fragile States Index 2015, http://foreignpolicy.com/2015/06/17/fragile-states-2015-islamic-state-ebola-ukraine-russia-ferguson.

4

Statebuilding in Iraq

Iraq is the crucible in which post–Cold War theories of statebuilding were tested, found wanting, and then, in the heat of battle, forged anew. As described in chapter 3, liberal statebuilding emphasizes democracy and free markets as the primary means toward legitimating state authority. This model was implemented in Iraq between 2003 and 2006 by the administration of President George W. Bush in extreme form, almost in caricature. The insurgency that followed the initially successful military invasion laid bare the inadequacy of liberal statebuilding. Small islands of apparent success in Iraq, in turn, directly informed a new model of the process which, as a form of counterinsurgency (COIN) warfare, emphasizes winning the hearts and minds of the local population. This new model eventually became the centerpiece of U.S. statebuilding efforts from the announcement of the Bush "surge" in January 2007 to the withdrawal of U.S. forces from Iraq in December 2011.

Yet despite its efforts and trillions of dollars, the U.S. strategy in Iraq failed, most visibly in 2014 when the government in Baghdad lost control of more than one-third of its territory to insurgents from the Islamic State of Iraq and Syria (ISIS). Regardless of the problems inherent in both the liberal and COIN models of statebuilding, and inadequate planning and botched implementation, detailed below, the failure of the Iraqi state followed directly from the statebuilder's dilemma.

Prior to 2003, Iraq was not plagued by ungoverned spaces that might be exploited by global insurgents, but the United States was concerned about a regime that might actively support terrorists. After toppling Saddam Hussein, the United States found itself responsible for a truly failed state plagued by sectarian rivalries long suppressed under authoritarian rule. The country quickly split along religious and ethnic lines, and large areas of territory fell out of the control of the central government. Foreign fighters poured into the Sunni areas of the country, especially Anbar Province, both to defend their now beleaguered coreligionists and to fight the Americans. Shiites turned to support from neighboring Iran. Although the collapse was precipitated by the U.S. invasion, Iraq soon became a classic failed state with large ungoverned spaces. As intragroup violence and fear spiraled out of control, the United States had little choice but to engage in a major statebuilding effort.

Throughout the U.S. experience in Iraq, the statebuilder's dilemma was acute. In pursuit of its freedom agenda, the Bush administration certainly aspired to create a new regime that would, through democracy and free markets, win the legitimacy of its people. At the same time, however, the United States had intense interests in Iraq, given its status as a major supplier of oil, its strategic position within the Persian Gulf and the Middle East more generally, and its demonstrated potential for regional disruption. As the United States attempted to extend its influence in the Persian Gulf after the end of the Cold War, Iraq was a critical piece of the puzzle that had to be brought under the indirect rule of the United States. These deep interests in the country required that any leader placed in power by the United States would have to be pro-Western, supportive of the regional status quo, willing to host American bases and follow the U.S. lead in foreign policy, and—perhaps most important—willing to serve as an ally in the global war on terror. The divergent interests of Iraqis and the United States rendered the statebuilder's dilemma acute and limited the pool of leaders from whom Washington might select. Once it became clear that the exiles hand-selected by the Pentagon before the war were unacceptable to Iraqis, the United States had to choose from a small set of Iraqi leaders willing to work with it. This limited choice allowed the eventual leader, Nouri al-Maliki, to turn the tables on the United States, construct a mostly Shiite coalition rather than the broader power-sharing regime desired by Washington, divert aid to his political purposes, and eventually force the United States out so that he could pursue his own designs more freely. In this case, the failure of statebuilding was not one of design or implementation but inherent in the statebuilder's dilemma.

In contrast to U.S. strategy in Central America in the early twentieth century, Iraq is not a case where the United States focused exclusively on loyalty. Rather, in the absence of competition from other major powers in the region, and looking toward the future, the Bush administration sought to balance its desire for legitimacy to stabilize Iraq over the long term against the need for a leader who would at least be sympathetic to U.S. policy goals. Indeed, by the end, the United States might have placed greater weight on legitimacy than did Maliki, the leader it chose to govern in its place. Nonetheless, the case of Iraq shows clearly that when the interests of the statebuilder are perceived to be important and the policy preferences of the target state and the statebuilder are far apart, the statebuilder's dilemma is acute, and even a limited emphasis on loyalty can fatally undermine the statebuilding project.

This chapter does not address the causes of the war. Rather, my focus is on the lessons for statebuilding that we can draw from this case. The chapter proceeds in seven steps. The first section briefly surveys the state of the state in Iraq on the eve of war. The second section examines the Iraq War and its aftermath, with a focus on the theory and practice of statebuilding between 2003 and 2006. The third section outlines the surge and the change in doctrine and practice that began in early 2007. Although drawn from secondary sources, these sections provide one of the first comprehensive evaluations of statebuilding in Iraq and, thus, are somewhat more detailed than a focus on the statebuilder's dilemma alone might otherwise require. With the theory and practice of statebuilding in Iraq as background, the fourth section concentrates on this dilemma, especially the selection of Maliki as prime minister and the consequences of this choice for statebuilding in Iraq. The fifth section compares Iraq as a whole to the Kurdish region, which was insulated from much of the statebuilding activity during this period and did not suffer from an acute form of the statebuilder's dilemma. The sixth section briefly describes the failure of the new Iraqi state in 2014. The seventh and concluding section draws lessons from the Iraq experience for statebuilding more generally.

The Iraqi State on the Eve of War

The United States went to war with Iraq in 2003 for many reasons, including Iraq's threats to U.S. allies in the region; its long history of human rights abuses; the fear that it had weapons of mass destruction (WMD) and the possibility—however vague—that it might share these weapons with terrorists; and its potential to disrupt international oil markets. At least some Americans, especially the neoconservatives clustered around the Bush administration, also desired to set an example of successful democratization in the Middle East and possibly settle old scores from the 1991 Persian Gulf War. At the largest scale was a desire pursued continually from at least the administration of George H. W. Bush to extend the Pax Americana into the Middle East, and especially the Persian Gulf. In return for stabilizing the region politically and militarily, every president since the end of the Cold War has hoped to expand trade and investment in this otherwise volatile region. No one reason was decisive, but for the Bush administration and many Americans, including substantial majorities in Congress, together they justified the invasion. Central to all of these motivations, however, was the goal of "regime change" and the removal of Saddam Hussein and his Ba'athist supporters from political power.[1]

1. Why the United States undertook a war to overthrow the regime of Saddam Hussein in Iraq remains a matter of dispute. This is, in part, due to the shifting rationales offered by the Bush administration in both the run-up to the war and especially after the promised

Iraq was a predatory but far from failed state in 2003. It suffered from long-standing social cleavages, especially between Sunnis, who occupied a privileged position within the society and regime; Kurds, who had carved out a somewhat autonomous region in the North after the Persian Gulf War (roughly 17 percent of Iraq's population); and the majority Shia (65 percent of the population), increasingly repressed following their ill-fated rebellion in the weeks after the U.S. victory in 1991.[2] Yet prewar Iraq enjoyed a measure of cosmopolitanism. Other forms of self-identification by clan, city, or class were sometimes as strong if not stronger than religion. Intermarriage across the Sunni-Shia religious divide was not uncommon.[3] Nonetheless, sectarian cleavages were rubbed raw after 1991 and eventually became bleeding sores. Playing on fears of sectarian violence were he to fall—fears that turned out to be realized—Saddam likely increased his support from the Sunni minority that had prospered under his rule and served as his primary support coalition.

Despite this underlying and growing sectarianism, however, the regime was relatively stable and would likely have endured were it not for the U.S. invasion.[4] Although he had significant support among his Sunni backers, Saddam led, no doubt, an authoritarian, highly repressive government that was regarded as illegitimate at least in the eyes of the Shiite and Kurdish communities.[5] At least one analyst called it a "fierce" state rather than a failed one.[6] Similar to Siad Barre in Somalia, as described in chapter 5, Saddam was a dictator who built a robust and long-lived regime through a combination of repression toward out-groups and favored access for in-groups, all the while deepening the cleavages that would likely emerge if he were deposed.[7] Moreover, repression worked. Brutally crushing the Shiite rebellion in the South that broke out immediately after the Persian Gulf War successfully

---

WMD were not found. It is also likely that any major event like the Iraq War has multiple causes, each of which might have individually led to conflict but together overdetermine the outcome. Isolating any one factor, one decision, or one personality that "caused" a singular event of such magnitude is a fool's errand but will continue to give analysts much to write about in the decades ahead. Much of the increasingly voluminous literature on the war—used in this chapter and cited extensively below—is largely descriptive and written by journalists who observed the conflict closely and interviewed key decision makers at length. For analytic treatments of the cause of the Iraq War, see Lake 2010–2011; Harvey 2012; Debs and Monteiro 2014.

2. On the deep-seated cleavages, linked back to British colonialism, see Dodge 2003.
3. Herring and Rangwala 2006, 148.
4. On the long-term fragility of the state, see Bouillon 2012. For more pessimistic views, see Cockburn 2007, 15; Pedersen 2007. What was not obvious to outsiders was just how badly the economic infrastructure had decayed during the 1990s, suggesting that the state was more fragile than many realized. See below.
5. Herring and Rangwala 2006, 51. Note that although most Kurds are Sunni Muslim, some segments in the East and South of the country are Shiite. Gordon and Trainor 2012, 23.
6. Rowswell, Bouillon, and Malone 2007, 9.
7. On the pervasive crony capitalism of Saddam's regime, centered on the Sunni community, see Bremer 2006, 64–65.

deterred further challenges to Saddam's rule. Both predictions of internal dissent and rebellion and promises of popular aid should the United States invade, offered by the exile community in the years before the 2003 war, proved to be unrealistic. Even as it became clear over the course of 2002 that the Bush administration was committed to removing Saddam from power, no indigenous opposition arose to challenge the regime or liberate the country.[8] The majority of Shiites were politically cowed by the regime, and there was no clear expectation that this would change in the foreseeable future.

Militarily, the regime may have been increasingly fragile, but it remained quite formidable.[9] As was often repeated to bolster support in the United States for the Persian Gulf War, Iraq reportedly had the world's sixth largest military and, more important, was a significant threat to its neighbors— including Saudi Arabia, one of the richest countries in the region, which had used its oil wealth to purchase a world-class military from the United States. Although its defeat in one hundred hours in 1993 spoiled this reputation, Iraq remained a military power with, it was feared, an extensive WMD program, the output of which it might use itself or give to terrorists who might use it against the United States and its allies. Despite punishing economic sanctions that disproportionately affected the poorest segments of society, any state capable of posing such a threat not only to its neighbors but to U.S. interests in this important region of the world was hardly lacking in capacity. Indeed, if it had been, even the Bush administration might have waited for the regime to fall on its own.

Iraq was fragile but not failing precisely because it retained some legitimacy, at least from Sunnis, effectively repressed its opponents, and was still strong enough to control all of its territory and threaten its neighbors. If the regime were to be changed, it had to be pushed—hard—off an otherwise stable ledge. Iraq did not fail because of "natural" causes or internal breakdown, but because the United States and its coalition intervened militarily to change the regime. As it was forced to "fail," Iraq is a slightly unusual case compared to other statebuilding episodes in the past two decades. Nonetheless, once the state was destroyed it faced the same problems as other failed states: sectarian conflict broke out immediately, and the statebuilder's dilemma quickly became evident.

8. This was true even after the passage of the Iraq Liberation Act in 1998, which stated: "It should be the policy of the United States to support efforts to remove the regime headed by Saddam Hussein from power in Iraq and to promote the emergence of a democratic government to replace that regime." Quoted in Bolger 2014, 113–114.
9. On "stacking" the military and increased fighting potential, see McMahon and Slantchev 2015.

Statebuilding in Iraq, 2003–2006

As is now well known, the United States invaded Iraq on March 19, 2003, and won a rapid and decisive victory. On May 1, President Bush, in his famous "Mission Accomplished" celebration onboard the USS *Abraham Lincoln*, declared an end to major combat operations. Having deposed Saddam, however, the United States confronted the need—somewhat unexpectedly for leading administration officials—to build a new state that could govern effectively and legitimately. Statebuilding in Iraq is almost entirely a story of U.S. policy and practice. The new Iraqi state was quite literally "made in the USA." In the war and its aftermath, the United States operated largely outside the United Nations and its imprimatur, drawing in the international organization only for assistance with elections and the political transition.[10] The United States also thoroughly dominated the ad hoc coalition that fought the war, and responsibility for postwar statebuilding passed entirely to Washington. President Bush, for instance, appointed Ambassador L. Paul Bremer as head of the Coalition Provisional Authority (CPA) without consultation with his coalition partners. In turn, the failure or success of the effort rests almost entirely on the United States.

Initial statebuilding efforts in Iraq proved highly problematic for three unrelated reasons that nonetheless combined in a devastating failure of vision and policy. First, the United States was intentionally unprepared for statebuilding in postwar Iraq, leaving it intellectually and materially ill equipped for challenges it should have anticipated. Second, when finally forced to accept responsibility for statebuilding, the United States simply implemented the liberal model without significant attention to the circumstances of postinvasion Iraq. All of the structural problems with this model, already made clear in earlier statebuilding attempts in the 1990s, were immediately apparent, ultimately leading to the new COIN strategy in 2007. Third, as discussed in more detail below, although attentive to the need for legitimacy for the new state, the United States also sought to control and manipulate the democratic process it put in place to ensure that leaders loyal to its interests rose to power. Predictably, its handpicked prime minister, Maliki, then built a political coalition composed almost entirely of Shiites previously excluded under the previous regime. The remainder of this section focuses on the first two

10. Although I do not detail the United Nations' involvement here given its minor role, the status of coalition forces in Iraq was affirmed and reaffirmed in a series of United Nations Security Council (UNSC) resolutions. UNSC Resolution 1511 recognized the CPA in October 2003 and authorized the multinational force to "take all necessary measures to contribute to the maintenance of security and stability in Iraq"; it also extended this authorization after the return of Iraqi sovereignty in June 2004 through UNSC Resolution 1546. This mandate was subsequently renewed in UNSC Resolution 1637 in 2005, UNSC Resolution 1723 in 2006, and UNSC Resolution 1790 in 2007. Note the limited duration of each of these resolutions. The United States, on behalf of the coalition, was requested to report to the UNSC every six months.

errors as context for the larger problem embodied in the statebuilder's dilemma.

Winning Blind

There is considerable debate over whether there was adequate planning within the Bush administration for postwar Iraq. Opinions about the administration's planning vary from the charitable conclusion that it was "not well thought out" to the more critical assessment that it was "mired in ineptitude, poor organization and indifference."[11] The debate is hard to resolve, as all of the major players within the administration have attempted to fix the blame for the postwar fiasco on each other.[12] It now appears that there was a significant planning effort before the war, led by the State Department, that was subsequently ignored by the civilian and military leadership, who regarded it as inadequate. David Kay, a CIA weapons inspector on the initial team of the Office for Reconstruction and Humanitarian Affairs (ORHA; see below), described the State Department's "Future of Iraq Study" as "unimplementable," more "a series of essays to describe what the future could be" rather than a plan that would have made a difference.[13] Meanwhile, having wrested control of reconstruction from other agencies, the Pentagon carried out a parallel planning effort under the supervision of Secretary of Defense Donald Rumsfeld and Undersecretary of Defense for Policy Douglas Feith. This plan was also not well developed and rested on a series of erroneous assumptions.

The lack of an adequate plan was not an accident. As summarized by the journalist George Packer, "if there was never a coherent postwar plan, it was because the people in Washington who mattered never intended to stay in Iraq," at least as a nation-building force.[14] The Bush administration entered office hostile to the notion of statebuilding. During the campaign, candidate Bush bluntly declared, "I don't think our troops ought to be used for what's called nation-building."[15] In this spirit, Rumsfeld insisted on taking the lead on Iraq policy but did not want to get bogged down in stabilizing the country after the fall of the regime. As Fred Kaplan writes, Rumsfeld (and in turn the Pentagon) "didn't plan for the postwar because he didn't want a postwar. It wasn't an oversight; it was deliberate."[16]

---

11. Ricks 2006, 179, quoting an anonymous general involved in postwar planning at the Pentagon. See also Diamond 2005, chap. 2; Packer 2005, 114, 116–117; Chandrasekaran 2006, 35, 59; Allawi 2007, 83.
12. For retrospective defenses of the planning efforts, see Feith 2008, 274–298; Bush 2010, 248–250; and Rice 2011, 188–195. Although defiant to the end on the justification of the war, Vice President Dick Cheney (2011, 433) simply acknowledges that the administration underestimated the difficulties of rebuilding a "traumatized and shattered society."
13. Gordon and Trainor 2006, 159; see also Isikoff and Corn 2007, 191–200.
14. Packer 2005, 147; see also Robinson 2008, 20.
15. Washington 2004.
16. F. Kaplan 2013, 59.

Consistent with this limited ambition, the administration set itself the goal of liberating Iraqis to rebuild their own country, not occupying them. By April 15, two weeks before the Mission Accomplished celebration, Bush was already meeting with his top aides to plan the withdrawal of U.S. forces from Iraq, a task expected to begin within sixty days and result in as few as thirty thousand troops in Iraq by September.[17] From the first outbreaks of civil violence until the surge began in 2007, the sole U.S. military strategy was to tamp down the insurgency sufficiently that responsibility could be transferred to the Iraqis themselves and U.S. forces withdrawn as soon as possible. In this sense, "victory" over the insurgents was never a military or political goal of the administration.[18] Rather, it desired above all a quick handoff of responsibility to the Iraqis—whether or not they were actually prepared to accept it. Embodying this view of the United States as a liberating but not occupying force, former UN ambassador John Bolton subsequently said that the administration's only mistake in the war was not turning the country over to the Iraqis sooner, giving them "a copy of the *Federalist Papers*," and saying "good luck."[19]

The planning effort, such as it was, rested on five ultimately naïve and incorrect assumptions. Buying fully into the liberal orthodoxy that would inform their eventual statebuilding efforts, administration officials assumed that inside the heart of every Iraqi was a "small d" democrat yearning to be free.[20] As Vice President Richard Cheney stated, "I really do believe that we will be greeted as liberators."[21] In explaining why few occupation troops would be needed, Chair of the Defense Advisory Board Richard Perle similarly observed that there would be "no one fighting for Saddam Hussein once he is gone."[22] As described by Major General Carl Strock, the dramatic ouster of Saddam was expected to create a "*Wizard of Oz* moment" in which "after the wicked dictator was deposed, throngs of cheering Iraqis would hail their liberators and go back to work."[23]

With Rumsfeld envisioning elections within months, the administration simply assumed that Iraqis would intuitively understand and immediately adopt democratic institutions.[24] Within months of the invasion, for instance, the United States called on Iraqis to hold caucuses to select representatives for new provincial councils, much like the Iowa caucuses back home. Even though the councils would have neither power nor money, this was understood to be an important initiative and the first step toward democracy. But

17. Gordon and Trainor 2006, 457–460; Herring and Rangwala 2006, 13.
18. Gordon and Trainor 2012, 212.
19. Interview with Jeremy Paxman on the BBC show *Newsnight*, "Iraq 4 Years On," March 21, 2007. For a transcript of the interview and link to the televised interview, see Fertik 2007.
20. Daalder and Lindsay 2003, 125; Herring and Rangwala 2006, 10.
21. Packer 2005, 97.
22. Ricks 2006, 65; see also Feith 2008, 415.
23. Gordon and Trainor 2006, 463.
24. Herring and Rangwala 2006, 12.

as one Iraqi told Dexter Filkins, a reporter for the *New York Times*, "the word for 'caucus' does not exist in Arabic," and the participants in this process had no idea how to proceed.[25]

Reflecting the desire for loyal leaders, both the State Department and Pentagon plans also relied heavily on expatriate Iraqis, some of whom had spent most of their lives and careers in the West, and assumed that these pro-American leaders would be immediately welcomed into the new democratic regime. The Pentagon's ties to Ahmed Chalabi are, of course, well known. A darling of the neoconservatives even while they were out of office during the Clinton years, Chalabi was director of the Iraqi National Congress (INC), an umbrella group of anti-Saddam exiles. Distrusted by the CIA, the State Department, and many uniformed military, Chalabi nonetheless had broad support within the civilian leadership of the Pentagon and was expected to head a new Iraqi government after Saddam's fall.[26] Indeed, belying his serious intent, Feith once joked with Lieutenant General Jay Garner (retired), head of ORHA and the first American "in charge" of Iraq, that when he got to Iraq "we could just make Chalabi president."[27] INC fighters were even flown into southern Iraq on U.S. military planes to assist in fighting Saddam's fedayeen, a move widely interpreted as aimed to give Chalabi a leg up on both internal and external rivals for the presidency. Even the State Department relied heavily on expatriates in the Future of Iraq study group that produced its massive if inadequate report.[28] Given relations between the United States and Iraq under Saddam, and the authoritarian nature of the Iraqi government, there were few lines of communication between U.S. officials and potential indigenous Iraqi leaders.[29] Nonetheless, the Bush administration assumed that its interlocutors could figuratively parachute into Iraq and gain popular support. Perceptively summing up the problem, one senior coalition official quipped that the U.S. political strategy in Iraq "relied on two things: exiles and optimism."[30] As one prominent Iraqi politician later assessed the exiles and, indirectly, the U.S. government: "The exiles—they made a big mistake, thinking that because they have the Americans on their side, they . . . can ride an American tank into Baghdad, they can gain legitimacy. It just doesn't work that way."[31]

In addition, the plan for the postwar period failed to anticipate the decrepit state of Iraq's infrastructure. According to Ali Allawi, Iraq's first postwar minister of defense and minister of finance, the country "was in an advanced

25. Filkins 2008, 83.
26. On early CIA interactions with Chalabi, see ibid., 262–263.
27. Ricks 2006, 104.
28. Packer 2005, 124–125. Cheney (2011, 387) blames the State Department for excluding so-called externals (exiles) from the planning process.
29. On networks between the United States and Iraq, see MacDonald 2014, chap. 6.
30. Quoted in Herring and Rangwala 2006, 12.
31. Allawi 2007, 140.

state of decay." Under international sanctions and threatened by domestic unrest throughout the 1990s, Saddam had withdrawn from detailed management of the economy, focusing on his immediate survival. Large areas of southern Iraq and Kurdistan were deliberately starved of basic services, with Sunni areas north of Baghdad faring only marginally better. Overall, "the standard of living had precipitously crashed" after the Persian Gulf War.[32] Much of the country's economic infrastructure, including its oil pipelines, was allowed to deteriorate radically. Yet officials in Washington declared repeatedly that Iraq could easily pay for its own reconstruction.

The plan also did not anticipate the tensions that would be released between religious groups once the Sunni-dominated government was defeated. In a joint news conference with British prime minister Tony Blair before the war, President Bush remarked that it was "unlikely there would be internecine warfare between the different religious and ethnic groups" in Iraq, and Blair agreed.[33] Likewise, Paul Wolfowitz testified before Congress that postwar force requirements might be low because "there's been none of the record in Iraq of ethnic militias fighting one another."[34] Nonetheless, other observers foresaw severe problems. As early as 1999, Central Command (CENTCOM) chief General Anthony Zinni, expecting the government and the military to "fall apart like a cheap suit" after Saddam's fall, conducted a classified war game that "brought out all the problems that have surfaced" after the invasion.[35] Although "it shocked the hell" out of him, he was unable to interest other parts of the government in preparatory work.[36] As Allawi concludes, "none of this should have come as a surprise."[37]

Finally, the plan was premised on the expectation that the Iraqi military and police forces would remain intact to provide political stability after the war. Encouraged by the mass desertions during Desert Storm in 1991, the CIA predicted that Iraqi forces would simply switch sides en masse with their equipment. The plan was that these army units would then control the country's borders and take on other tasks that overstretched U.S. troops could not. Instead, as U.S. forces moved closer to Baghdad, the Iraqi military dissolved before their eyes. As the journalist Michael Gordon and Lieutenant General Bernard E. Trainor observe, "rarely has a military plan depended on such a bold assumption."[38]

These flawed assumptions, together with the quick military victory, led the Bush administration to "grievously misunderstand" the nature of the conflict

---

32. Ibid., 114; see also Pedersen 2007.
33. Isikoff and Corn 2007, 180.
34. Ibid., 194.
35. Gordon and Trainor 2012, 6.
36. Ricks 2006, 20.
37. Allawi 2007, 12. The lack of knowledge about Iraq before and during the war is a central theme of Filkins (2008), who argues that the Bush administration and the military, especially early on, made no serious attempt to understand the country.
38. Gordon and Trainor 2006, 89.

that began in Iraq after the fall of the regime.[39] The United States chose to interpret the violence as resistance to the shift in political and economic power that would follow spontaneous democratization and economic reform. In this view, not unreasonable at the time, the insurgency was composed of former regime supporters who feared losing political power and their privileged position in the economy and society. Any moves toward democratization, redefining the basis of political power through votes, and greater reliance on market mechanisms, especially the breaking up of the state-owned enterprises from which many in the elite benefited, would necessarily reduce the political position of Sunnis and benefit the Shia and Kurds. Whether or not the insurgency was planned before the invasion took place remains a topic of debate.[40] After 1993 Saddam had created the fedayeen, a dispersed militia that was designed to suppress revolts by Shiites in the South and slow the U.S. advance toward Baghdad if war came, and weapons caches were hidden around the country, suggesting a measure of foresight. On the other hand, the insurgency lacked a centralized leadership, which would have followed from an intentionally designed force, and no evidence has emerged that Saddam expected to lead an insurgency if his military forces were defeated. Nonetheless, whether planned or not, elements of the former regime were well placed and well equipped to fight U.S. forces once the regime fell. This understanding of the conflict led naturally to the U.S. military strategy in Iraq—or perhaps the military's favored strategy reinforced this understanding of the conflict. If the primary opposition was from elements of the former regime, U.S. forces needed only to isolate and destroy the likely small number of insurgents. Once the "dead-enders" were defeated, to use Rumsfeld's frequent description, the new regime could be quickly consolidated.

Yet this understanding was either incorrect from the start or soon became obsolete. Iraq unraveled quickly, combining the paths to failure blazed by other predatory and factionalized states identified in chapter 1. Once the regime was toppled, U.S. forces proved insufficient to protect the population against generalized violence, as demonstrated in the rioting and looting that occurred immediately after Saddam's flight from Baghdad, or against violence from the insurgents, which grew over the next few months. Each communal group then pulled inward and began to arm to defend itself against violence from the others. Very quickly, cosmopolitanism disintegrated and society realigned itself almost entirely on ethnic (Kurds) or religious (Sunni versus Shiite) lines.[41] Iraq, in essence, spiraled down into a classic security

39. Gordon and Trainor 2012, 356, summarizing the JSAT review, initiated by Petraeus as he assumed command of U.S. forces in Iraq.
40. See Herring and Rangwala 2006, 167–168.
41. Ibid., 155–157; Dodge 2007b. Cheney (2011, 434) claims that the Shia resisted being dragged into the sectarian violence until after the al-Askariya Mosque attack in February 2006, but the Mahdi Army was already in place in 2003 and a source of concern to other U.S. officials. See Bremer 2006.

dilemma in which the absence of centralized authority able to protect groups from one another, communal fears stimulated by past abuse, and threats of violence interact to force groups to turn to self-help for their own safety. Each group's arming inevitably threatened other groups, bringing about the very insecurity and violence each dreaded.[42] In such situations, self-identification matters less than prevailing socially constructed identities; one became a Shiite or Sunni regardless of one's own identity as others identified and treated strangers and even friends as members of the feared and possibly opposed group. Questions about which side started the violence then become almost irrelevant. Groups may even anticipate violence from others and act preventatively to protect their interests, which then sparks the vicious cycle regardless of actual behavior.

This essential security dilemma was propelled by extremists on all sides who then engaged in outbidding within their communities in the struggle for intracommunal leadership.[43] For the Sunnis, this entailed an alliance with indigenous and foreign fighters affiliated with al-Qaeda and other extremist organizations that promised to defend their interests against the Shia, at least until 2006, when the Awakening movement began to take hold (see below). For Shia, many flocked to Muqtada al-Sadr and his Mahdi Army, who in April 2003 took over a large area of eastern Baghdad known as Saddam City and renamed it Sadr City, and the Badr Brigades, associated with the Supreme Council for the Islamic Revolution in Iraq (SCIRI), one of the major political parties. Both of these militias were funded and supported by Iran.[44]

The security dilemma became particularly intense after Shiites took over the Interior Ministry, which controlled the National Police Force. This was a natural result of relying on loyal Shiite allies, as explained below, but important nonetheless in expanding the violence. This force, virtually "indistinguishable from a Shiite militia," soon began carrying out attacks on Sunnis under official cover and often in uniform.[45] Unable to trust the police, Sunnis were driven further into self-help, relying exclusively on their own militias for support. The more the police preyed on the Sunnis, the more the Sunni militias retaliated with bombings and attacks.[46] This had the bizarre follow-on effect of bringing in U.S. troops to punish the Sunnis for fights actually provoked by the Shia-dominated police.[47] By 2005 the security forces that might have mitigated the security dilemma if they played an even-handed and neutral role in Iraq had become clearly partisan and a major driver of the vicious cycle of fear, self-help, and violence. The National Police were not protectors of public order; rather, they were uniformed death squads murdering and kid-

42. See Posen 1993; Lake and Rothchild 1996.
43. On outbidding, see Lake and Rothchild 1996, 54.
44. See Cole 2007.
45. Ricks 2009, 177.
46. Herring and Rangwala 2006, 158.
47. Gordon and Trainor 2012, 223, 227.

napping Sunnis in broad daylight without fear of official sanction.[48] In November of that year, 80 percent of Shiites responding to a national poll reported that they felt safe in their neighborhoods, but only 11 percent of Sunnis felt the same.[49] By 2006 intercommunal violence was escalating rapidly, manifested most dramatically in the February bombing of the al-Askari Mosque, one of the holiest Shia religious sites. This was the moment when initial U.S. statebuilding efforts can be pinpointed as having failed.[50] There was not a single insurgency but multiple insurgencies, united only by a common desire to see the United States withdraw from Iraq so that each could pursue its own ends.[51]

A side effect of the security dilemma was an increase in the power and influence of traditional tribal or clan authorities in Iraq, which, though organized along sectarian lines, dominated in specific localities. Because Iraq was a secular state dominated from the center and, indeed, by a single leader, traditional authorities had waned under three decades of authoritarian rule under Saddam. With the outbreak of violence after 2003, and the turn to self-help, local leaders reestablished their centrality and, in fact, moved to invigorate localized forms of rule that coordinated poorly if at all with the central government and the CPA.[52] Some of these local authorities were recognized and incorporated into the new state, with the Kurdish Regional Government (KRG) being the largest and most important (see below). Some cities gained new autonomy under traditional leaders, such as Falluja under Sheikh Abdullah al-Janabi, but took up arms against outsiders, including the Americans.[53] Still other groups evolved into freestanding militias, most of whom fought against the United States until late 2006 (when the Anbar Awakening began) and their sectarian rivals. As the old regime disappeared, Iraqi society fractured along multiple lines, and political power was decentralized across myriad groups. Local leaders took on renewed responsibility for tribal justice and became the primary intermediaries with U.S. forces, both distributing resources on behalf of the coalition and negotiating with the Americans for their constituents. Their critical role as intermediaries, which arose spontaneously in early 2003, was later reinforced as official U.S. policy.[54]

Having allowed the security dilemma to take hold and create a multisided civil war, however, the United States was ill equipped to respond. More troops would have been required to provide the security necessary to prevent the

48. F. Kaplan 2013, 180.
49. Herring and Rangwala 2006, 152.
50. Bolger 2014, 214.
51. Herring and Rangwala 2006, 162.
52. Local leaders were distinct from the political parties that formed largely at the center. This center-periphery cleavage was yet another dividing line in postwar Iraqi politics that deepened as the local leaders sought to establish political support independent of the national political parties. Ibid., 105–127.
53. Ibid., 52–53.
54. Ibid., chap. 2 and 86–88, 124, 136–137.

turn to self-help strategies, and even more were eventually needed to tamp down the violence after it escalated. Encouraged by the handpicked moderates from the Shiite community whom it placed in positions of power (see below), the United States also began targeting not just Sunni insurgents but also Sadr and his Mahdi Army, who competed with the moderates for support within the community.[55] In challenging the Shia extremists, the United States managed to alienate all sides, provoking attacks against itself from both communities even while violence between the militias exploded. The failure was not just a problem of too few troops, as critics of Rumsfeld often aver, but stemmed from a complete misreading of the situation in Iraq after the fall of Saddam.

The United States may have even contributed to the violence itself, not only through the inadequate number of troops it committed but also because of its military doctrine, which continued to rely on the use of massive and overwhelming firepower against the various enemy groups. The collateral damage created by this strategy served to alienate all groups in Iraq. In the battles for Falluja (2004), for instance, U.S. forces destroyed the city to save it. In one firefight, described by Filkins, who was embedded with the unit, twenty soldiers facing a single sniper used thousands of rounds of ammunition, called in airstrikes to deliver both two-thousand- and five-hundred-pound bombs, and eventually deployed two M-1 tanks; the building in which the sniper was hiding was destroyed, yet he eventually escaped by the back alley.[56] This unrestrained use of firepower was not atypical. Untrained in counterinsurgency warfare and understandably seeking to protect the lives of soldiers, the U.S. military tolerated enormous collateral damage, affecting Sunnis and Shia alike. Any male within a combat area was automatically treated as an insurgent, and deaths of women and children were tolerated as a necessary cost of battle. This strategy of war fighting, in turn, alienated the Iraqi population and was a major reason that all segments of society, regardless of whether they supported the overthrow of Saddam, wanted the Americans to leave as soon as possible.[57]

Understanding the insurgency as a continuation of the war, but now fought against pro-Saddam Sunni irregulars, the Bush administration and military leaders logically concluded that the very presence of the United States in Iraq was a leading cause of the insurgency. The reasonable strategy, it followed, was to build up Iraqi forces, turn the fight over to them, and withdraw as quickly as possible. This remained U.S. military doctrine until the surge in 2007. However, the Joint Strategic Assessment Team (JSAT), commissioned by General David Petraeus as he assumed command over U.S. forces in Iraq, correctly diagnosed the real problem.[58] The heart of the insurgency, in their

55. Ibid., 28.
56. Filkins 2008, 200–203.
57. On the implications of collateral damage, see Crawford 2013.
58. F. Kaplan 2013, 260.

view, was, first, the collapse of the Iraqi state, which set off a communal power struggle that, second, allowed the Shiites to successfully co-opt the new Iraqi state and turn it into a sectarian force.[59] The insurgency was not a product of the victory and continued presence of the United States in Iraq but arose from the failure of statebuilding after the so-called end of combat operations. As Eric Herring and Glen Rangwala concluded in 2006, before a COIN strategy was even envisioned by the Bush administration, the United States had broken "every rule in the counter-insurgency book if the aim [was] to build a state which has vigorous popular support."[60]

Altogether, the violence, personal and economic insecurity, and instability served mostly to reinforce sectarian cleavages. As Colonel Derek Harvey, an intelligence officer deployed at the military's headquarters in Iraq and charged with deciphering the enemy threat, later told an army historian, "The normalcy of life has been ripped asunder, the people are falling back on two things: the mosque and their family, which was the clan, the tribe."[61] Throughout this period, however, the military strategy remained one of Iraqi self-help. General George W. Casey, the U.S. military commander in Iraq from June 2004 to February 2007, and Rumsfeld shared a strong view that the more the United States did, the less the Iraqis would do for themselves. The goal was to pull back U.S. troops and involvement, have the Iraqi troops participate in all aspects of all military operations, and withdraw U.S. troops as soon as possible.[62] This strategy was consistently combined with devastating optimism; Casey's 2005 "transition for self-reliance" strategy assumed in the face of countervailing evidence and common sense that the insurgency would stay at similar levels in Sunni areas but weaken in the rest of Iraq—a prediction proved horribly wrong by subsequent events.[63] Yet, as Gordon and Trainor write, "behind closed doors, defeating the insurgency was not the goal. Rather, the goal was to whittle it down to manageable proportions so that the Iraqi forces could handle the fight for a protracted period."[64] The United States had a plan for bringing its troops home as soon as possible, but not one for building a new, stable, and democratic state. Indeed, the "Red Team" report, a joint civilian-military review initiated by Zalmay Khalilzad soon after he arrived in Baghdad as the new U.S. ambassador in July 2005, suggested that this strategy might well be counterproductive. "Fears of abandonment," the report noted, might lead Iraqis to rely instead on Iran and to be more reluctant to cut the political deals necessary for a stable government.[65] As explained in chapter 1, the lack of a credible commitment by the United States

59. Gordon and Trainor 2012, 356.
60. Herring and Rangwala 2006, 174.
61. Quoted in Gordon and Trainor 2012, 38.
62. Ibid., 90.
63. Ibid., 137.
64. Ibid., 159, 212.
65. Ibid., 161.

to establish a rule of law in Iraq provided no incentive for any Iraqi faction to become vested in the new order. Continuing instability and violence were the natural results.

Whether the sectarian violence could have been prevented through better planning and more U.S. troops will remain a counterfactual without possible answer. Had an adequate plan been in place with sufficient troops to provide security for all groups in Iraq, the violence would have been lessened and, perhaps, the security dilemma might not have taken hold. Yet, with any likely plan, the United States would still have adopted a liberal model of statebuilding and sought to elevate leaders loyal to its interests, actions with their own problems that would have likely led to internal violence in the failed state that it had created. Separating out the lack of planning from other possible causes of violence remains difficult. Nonetheless, the inadequate plan for postinvasion Iraq was clearly a factor contributing to the failure of the eventual statebuilding effort.[66] One can rarely do well what one has not anticipated.

Liberal Statebuilding

In the 1990s, the United States fully embraced the theory and practice of liberal statebuilding. In all such efforts, the United States promoted rapid movements to new, more democratic constitutions with broad-based elections and pressed for market-oriented economic reforms. Even before Iraq, of course, problems with this liberal approach to statebuilding were evident. Democracy and free markets were not necessarily embraced by all societies, especially those with no history of liberalism. Social groups empowered and advantaged under the old regime resisted broadening political participation and freeing commerce. Nonetheless, liberal statebuilding was the prevailing orthodoxy, which the Bush administration inherited. President Bush thoroughly embraced the tenets of democracy promotion and market liberalization as core principles of his "freedom agenda." Indeed, the president's minimal requirements for any new government in Iraq were that it be democratic and an ally in the war on terror.[67] Forced by the anarchy in Iraq to rebuild the state it had destroyed, the administration then implemented an extreme version of liberal statebuilding, ultimately undermining the orthodoxy on which it was built.[68] Ironically, as we shall see in the section on the statebuilder's dilemma in Iraq below, the statebuilding failure came not from too much democracy but from promoting a leader expected to be loyal to the United States. Indeed, had the Bush administration pushed harder for a truly legitimate and more democratic regime, the statebuilding strategy might have had greater prospects for success.

66. Dodge 2005, 2007a.
67. Gordon and Trainor 2012, 178.
68. Dodge 2013a.

The postwar statebuilding effort, limited though it was, was originally em-bodied in the minimalist but appropriately named ORHA, headed by Gen-eral Garner, who had led the relief effort in northern Iraq in 1991. The ORHA team arrived in Baghdad on April 21, 2003—three weeks late, small and poorly staffed, and grossly underfunded. As but one example, Garner had a budget of just $25,000 to resurrect the devastated Iraqi government.[69] In keeping with his limited mandate, Garner planned to administer the country through government ministries, which he assumed were intact, remove only senior Ba'ath Party members, and recall the Iraqi Army to rebuild infrastruc-ture and secure the population and borders.[70] General Tommy Franks, the CENTCOM commander, told subordinates that the Iraqi government would be functioning in thirty to sixty days.[71] Designed largely as a humanitarian effort, ORHA was immediately overwhelmed by the outbreak of violence in Baghdad.[72] At a first meeting with locals in Baghdad on April 28, which fo-cused on the need for a liberal constitution to protect individual rights, a tribal sheikh complained, "I have no running water, no electricity, no security—and you are talking about a constitution?" Another demanded, "Who's in charge of our politics?" To which Garner tellingly replied, "You're in charge."[73]

As violence swept through Iraq, Garner was informed three days after his ar-rival that he and ORHA would be replaced by Bremer and the new CPA, an announcement that was made public on May 6. Bremer immediately took the occupation in a completely new direction. Whether directed to do so by the Bush administration or not, Bremer switched the mission from a humanitarian operation to full-on statebuilding. In Bremer's own vision, he was the head of an occupation authority, albeit one charged with nurturing a Western-style democracy. As he informed the Iraqi Governing Council (IGC) in his first meeting with the group, he came with the full support of the United Nations Security Council, although on what basis he made this claim is unclear, and "was the legitimate authority in Iraq in the eyes of the international commu-nity under the law of occupation."[74] On May 12, four days after his arrival, Bremer declared the CPA to be the supreme authority in Iraq and assumed sovereignty over its people and territory, overturned plans for the creation of a provisional Iraqi government, disbanded the Iraqi Army, began a purge of Ba'ath Party officials, and in general took up the previously denigrated task of statebuilding. Following the liberal blueprint for such missions, Bremer then outlined a seven-step, 540-day strategy for drafting a new constitution, passing an election law, and holding national, regional, and local elections

69. Packer 2005, 143.
70. Gordon and Trainor 2012, 11.
71. Ibid., 12.
72. Herring and Rangwala 2006, 12.
73. Packer 2005, 144.
74. Gordon and Trainor 2012, 13, 16.

for a new government, and announced plans to reform the economy.[75] Like ORHA, the CPA was inadequate to the task, though this time neither under-staffed nor underfunded.[76] Rather, the mistakes now were ones of policy rather than resources.[77]

Why Bremer changed what was called the "inside-out" approach antici-pated in the skeletal plan for postwar Iraq to an "outside-in" approach to statebuilding remains controversial.[78] In doing so, he abandoned the model of indirect rule embedded in the ORHA for direct governance, perhaps because the widespread violence required a firm hand or, more likely, because continued opposition from other U.S. agencies and Iraqis themselves pre-cluded putting the Department of Defense's handpicked leader, Chalabi, in power, and there was as yet no clear successor. Some administration officials claim that this change was a surprise and was not vetted in high-level policy committees.[79] Nonetheless, when criticism of his initial moves immediately exploded, Bush told Bremer that he "had his back," indicating the president's approval of the change in direction.[80]

Bremer's disbanding of the army and his policy on de-Ba'athification were the most controversial of these new directions. The de-Ba'athification policy originated with Rumsfeld and Feith, and was planned even before Bremer left Washington for Baghdad. On the other hand, the decision to formally disband the army appears to have begun with Bremer himself but was also cleared at the highest levels. Both decisions were justified under the perceived need to demonstrate credibly to Iraqis that Saddam's instruments of repres-sion could not be reconstituted.[81] Although most Iraqi troops had simply melted away during the war, formally dissolving the army ended any linger-ing hopes that the Iraqi military would take responsibility for defense in the near future. Yet the Bush administration still proceeded with planning to reduce the American "footprint" in Iraq over the summer. Disbanding the army and expelling high-ranking officials also ended any hopes by Iraqi sol-diers and those with close ties to Saddam that they might have a place and a job in the future Iraq, driving at least some of these individuals and their

75. Ibid., 14–15.
76. Although policy was centralized in the CPA, the U.S. military remained autonomous and, through sheer numbers and dollars, far superior to the U.S. civilians supposedly leading in Iraq. At its height, the ratio of CPA to military personnel was 1:250. Herring and Rang-wala 2006, 97–105.
77. For Bremer's reflections on these mistakes, see Bush (2010, 259–260) and Rice (2011, 238). An underreported problem was the incompetence of many CPA officials, at least some of whom were picked for their party credentials and past work on Bush's election campaign. See Chandrasekaran 2006, 103–104.
78. The terms are from Gordon and Trainor 2012. For a critique of the "top-down" approach pursued by the Bush administration between 2003 and 2005, see Papagianni 2007.
79. F. Kaplan 2013, 196.
80. Gordon and Trainor 2012, 32.
81. Bremer 2006, 39, 54–36, 224.

weapons into the growing insurgency.[82] Although less controversial at the time, the decision to abandon the promised provisional government had a larger long-run effect by undercutting indigenous forces supporting democratization.[83] This also undermined the credibility and hopes of those Iraqi elites with whom "the USA had been engaged, with varying degrees of enthusiasm, for the better part of a decade."[84]

Despite the new centralization of authority within the CPA, Bremer and his team followed the liberal statebuilding script closely and focused on moving rapidly toward a new constitution and democratic elections as well as economic reform. An interim government was formed, and the CPA was officially disbanded in June 2004, returning nominal sovereignty to Iraq. It was hoped that, with these moves, the spreading violence would abate, as Iraqis would formally be in charge of their own affairs, and the anti-Americanism of the rebels might dissolve. But "why," asked Wayne White, the State Department's Iraq expert, should "the Sunnis welcome the hastening of a government dominated by Shiite exiles?"[85] When the violence continued to escalate, the United States then pinned its hopes on elections and the creation of a more democratic government.

Following the creation of the interim government, elections for a National Assembly to write a new national constitution were then scheduled for January 2005, a mere six months later. This near-impossible condition was demanded by Grand Ayatollah Ali al-Husseini al-Sistani, the preeminent Shiite cleric in Iraq, in exchange for his cooperation with the occupation and the rebuilding of the political process. With all hopes then focused on these elections, time was short. Unable to conduct a census and allocate seats in parliament by province or other units, all of Iraq was treated as a single electoral district with party lists. As was entirely predictable, this gave well-funded religious parties a major advantage, increased the power of party leaders who controlled the positions of candidates on the lists, and magnified the consequences of any election boycott. The last factor was, perhaps, the most devastating in the long run, and was anticipated by U.S. analysts even prior to elections.[86] Many Sunnis did eventually boycott the election or, equivalently, stayed away from the polls out of fear. Despite the images of Iraqis waving their purple fingers that were widely replayed on Western televisions and in newspapers— the sign that they had exercised their newly found right to vote—only 2 percent of Sunnis in Anbar Province, home to the insurgency, actually participated in the election.[87] Only a handful of seats went to the various Sunni political parties. By contrast, the major Shiite parties coordinated on a single list—the

82. Robinson 2008, 3.
83. Galbraith 2006, 118–124; Isikoff and Corn 2007, 225.
84. Allawi 2007, 110.
85. Gordon and Trainor 2012, 66, quote on 82.
86. Ibid., 81, 84, 143.
87. Ibid., 135.

United Iraqi Alliance—and increased their weight in the electoral scale.[88] Nonetheless, the January elections became an immovable marker of progress for the Bush administration and could not be delayed for any reason.[89] The result was that the drafting of the constitution proceeded without substantial Sunni representation, and no Sunni politician endorsed the text.[90]

A National Assembly took office in April 2005, electing Ibrahim al-Jaafari prime minister. Jaafari defeated Ayad Allawi, who, even with American support, had garnered only 14 percent of the vote in the January elections. Jaafari was a compromise candidate, in part, because he was a weak "placeholder" leader.[91] He proved as inept and weak as many feared.[92] The new constitution was approved in a national referendum in October 2005. Elections for a new legislature, the Council of Representatives, were held in December 2005, a second major marker of progress for the United States. Having been shut out of government by the earlier boycott, vigorously encouraged to participate by the United States, and fearful that any Shiite-dominated regime would lean increasingly toward Iran, the Sunnis participated in this election in greater numbers and won eighty-seven seats in parliament. With considerable wrangling among competing leaders, however, it took until the following May to form a government. With the Americans determined to block a full term for Jaafari, a coalition was finally formed with his deputy, Nouri al-Maliki, as prime minister (see below).[93] Written to guard against the rise of another dictator like Saddam, the new constitution required a supermajority to elect a new prime minister. With multiple parties, factions, and sectarian cleavages, it produced predictable gridlock.[94] With the new government finally taking power in May 2006, the transition to democracy—at least on paper—appeared complete. As Major General David Fastabend reflected, "we needed elections in the worst kind of way in 2005—and we got them."[95] Just like the return of sovereignty, the elections did little to stem the violence. As many feared, the process of elections over the course of 2005 hardened rather than softened the sectarian divide.[96]

Along with democratization, the CPA also began a massive liberalization of the previously state-owned socialist economy, dramatically opening Iraq to foreign investment and trade.[97] Bremer writes that the goal was to get Iraq's oil production to prewar levels by October 1, 2003, issue a new currency to

88. Herring and Rangwala 2006, 36.
89. Gordon and Trainor 2012, 128.
90. Herring and Rangwala 2006, 39.
91. Gordon and Trainor 2012, 142, 144.
92. Bolger (2014, 193) describes Jaafari as "openly beholden" to al-Sadr and "much tougher to influence" than Allawi.
93. Gordon and Trainor 2012, 197.
94. Ibid., 135.
95. Ricks 2009, 31.
96. Gordon and Trainor 2012, 135.
97. Foote et al. 2004.

replace the devalued Saddam dinar, create the country's first-ever indepen-dent central bank, and "liberalize Iraq's commercial and investment laws."[98] Thomas Foley, director of private sector development for the CPA, under-stood his goal as the transformation of Iraq's state-led economy into a "fully thriving capitalist economy" with low taxes and tariffs that was simultaneously open to foreign investment. CPA Order 37, issued in September 2003, just months after the invasion, instituted a flat tax of 15 percent on all individuals and corporations; CPA Order 39 permitted 100 percent foreign ownership of all businesses in Iraq, except those in resource extraction and banking and insurance, and complete repatriation of all profits; and CPA Order 54 liberal-ized trade by removing all tariffs, duties, import taxes, and surcharges. The CPA also endorsed a 1987 Ba'athist law that banned all labor unions from public enterprises.[99] Thus, Iraq was subject by decree to many of the same policies that the Bush administration had wanted but been unable to achieve at home.

Liberalization was extremely destabilizing, both economically and politi-cally. The minority Sunnis, with no oil resources in their region of the coun-try, were nonetheless economically privileged and the wealthiest group in prewar Iraq. The economic reforms championed by the CPA stripped the Sun-nis of their base of power and prosperity and redirected it to the Shiites in the South and the Kurds in the North. It should not have been a surprise that the new politically and economically empowered Shiite majority would attempt to consolidate its power or that the politically and economically weakened Sunni minority would have a very different vision of Iraq's future. Yet, even though it was soundly rejected by average Iraqis, with only 5 percent of re-spondents in a 2004 poll preferring a smaller role for the state in the econ-omy, Bremer regarded economic reform as his greatest accomplishment in Iraq.[100]

The CPA began a number of massive infrastructure projects, but these gen-erated few opportunities for budding entrepreneurs in Iraq or jobs for work-ers. Despite billions spent on reconstruction, most of the projects went to large foreign and mostly U.S. corporations. Of the fifty-nine prime contracts awarded by the United States in 2004, forty-eight went to U.S. companies.[101] Some of these contracts could have gone to Iraqi firms. The General Com-pany for Water Projects, an Iraqi firm that had built most of the existing in-frastructure, was prohibited from bidding on new contracts under rules barring previously state-owned firms, with most of the water construction bids then going to Bechtel, a major U.S. construction firm, which lacked experience

98. Bremer 2006, 116.
99. Herring and Rangwala 2006, 226–228.
100. Chandrasekaran 2006, 70, 134, 328; Allawi 2007, 198. On the opinion data, see Herring and Rangwala 2006, 233.
101. Herring and Rangwala 2006, 237–238. The NGO Iraq Revenue Watch reported that 74 percent of the value of such contracts was awarded to U.S. firms.

working in the country.[102] Many projects, in turn, were delayed because of continuing security concerns.[103] Nearly all projects suffered from a combination of corruption and shoddy work. Bechtel was constructing or refurbishing large power and sewage treatment plants but neglecting to string electrical wires or lay the pipes to bring the electricity and clean water to the neighborhoods.[104] By June 2005, of the $200 million of U.S. funds spent on water and sanitation projects in Iraq, approximately $52 million had been spent on projects that were either not operating or operating below capacity.[105] In short, the economy was deeply disrupted by the war and then liberalization, even while the United States failed to stimulate Iraqi businesses, build a safety net for Iraqis, or provide the public goods they needed. In February 2005, returning from a fact-finding trip for the new secretary of state, Condoleezza Rice, Philip Zelikow wrote that despite billions of dollars of aid, Iraq "remains a failed state shadowed by constant violence."[106] In this environment of instability and fear, few Iraqis invested their own resources or became vested in the new system.

Fiasco

Despite apparently meeting various institutional benchmarks defined by the Bush administration, neither military success, political stability, nor legitimacy followed as hoped. As is clear in figures 4.1a and 4.1b, military and civilian casualties climbed steadily over the first four years of the war. Rather than reducing violence, the statebuilding mission was floundering. Support among Iraqis for the United States declined accordingly. According to Lieutenant General Thomas Metz, Casey's corps commander who oversaw day-to-day operations of the military: "At best, we have only the most grudging support of the Iraqi people, who are waiting to see if we can bring them security and some measure of economic development. Beyond that, most of them want us to leave as soon as possible."[107] In October 2004, over 70 percent of respondents in the geographic center of Iraq near Baghdad and 95 percent in the largely Shiite South opposed the presence of coalition forces. In January 2006, 88 percent of Sunnis, 41 percent of Shia, and even 16 percent of Kurds in Iraq supported attacks on U.S. forces.[108] As predicted, the Sunni opposi-

102. Ibid., 67.
103. Gordon and Trainor 2012, 26, 130, 171, 238. By 2006, of the $200 million in reconstruction projects promised to Anbar, none had been started. At the same time, many payments to Iraqi subcontractors ended up in the hands of the insurgents. Ironically, some projects aimed to earn the good will of Iraqis had to be unveiled in secret for fear of attack. Filkins 2008, 175.
104. F. Kaplan 2013, 185.
105. Herring and Rangwala 2006, 68.
106. F. Kaplan 2013, 193.
107. Gordon and Trainor 2012, 98.
108. Herring and Rangwala 2006, 201, 205.

a.

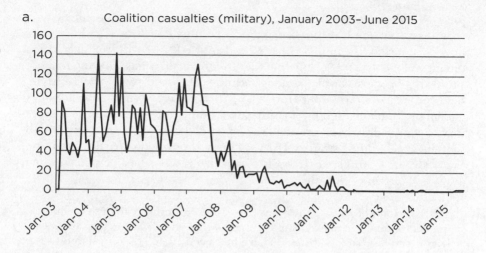

Coalition casualties (military), January 2003–June 2015

b.

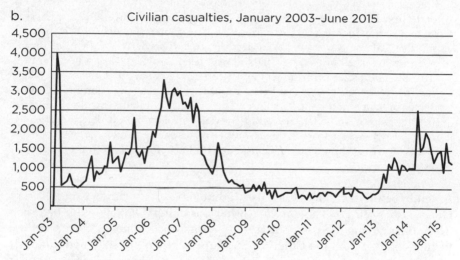

Civilian casualties, January 2003–June 2015

Figures 4.1a and 4.1b. Iraq War casualties by month.
Coalition casualties come from iCasualties, http://icasualties.org/Iraq/index.aspx. Civilian casualties are from Iraq Body Count, http://www.iraqbodycount.org/.

tion to the U.S.-created state was becoming increasingly and violently anti-American.[109]

Although the Bush administration tried to ban the word "insurgency," it was eventually clear that Iraq had fallen into civil war, with the United States as a major cause and player.[110] By March 2005, Bob Earle, assistant to Ambassador

109. Arango and Schmitt 2014.
110. On the sensitivity of the word "insurgency," see F. Kaplan 2013, 229. Although the political scientist James Fearon was certainly not the first to declare that Iraq was facing a civil

John Negroponte, concluded in a memo to the president that "democracy remains possible in Iraq, but Iraq is a post-conflict failed state."[111] In an intelligence report for the military in late 2006 entitled "The Perfect Storm," Lieutenant Colonel Nycki Brooks wrote that the insurgency was "shifting to a self-sustaining armed conflict among ethno-sectarian groups."[112] Testifying before the Iraq Study Group, formed in 2006 to review the war and suggest alternatives, and chaired by Howard Baker and Lee Hamilton, former secretary of state Colin Powell presented an extended critique of the war and subsequent statebuilding strategy. Drawing on notes from one participant in the Study Group, Gordon and Trainor summarize Powell's bleak remarks, which are worth quoting at length.

> There had not been enough troops from the beginning. The Bush team did not understand the demands of the occupation and had somehow assumed Iraq would just "snap together." There had been complete confusion on the American side. Jay Garner's background as a former Army air defense officer made him ill-equipped for the job of dealing with post-invasion Iraq. Jerry Bremer had made his own job harder. . . . The decision to disband the army was a mistake and was not properly discussed. The de-Ba'athification program was hijacked by Ahmed Chalabi, who used it to purge a vast number of officials. There had been "no common superior" in Baghdad, meaning that the lines of authority between Bremer and Rick Sanchez [a major general, in charge of Combined Joint Task Force 7, the largest combat operations center in Iraq] were never clear. Sectarianism was a greater threat there than the insurgency, and American forces had little capacity to stop it or control events. The goal should not be democracy . . . but reform of the Iraqi political system.

Asked by future secretary of defense and member of the Study Group Robert Gates, "Does our government know what it is doing?" Powell—who had seen everything during the past four years—pointedly responded, "No."[113] As the former chair of the Joint Chiefs of Staff and secretary of state had famously warned in his "Pottery Barn rule," the United States had broken Iraq, and it now owned it—only, despite the prescient warning, it did not know what to do with the pieces. The violence and lack of legitimacy meant that the country was mired in deep political turmoil. The overall effort, such as it was, and the liberal paradigm of statebuilding had failed miserably, much to the consternation of its proponents in the Bush administration and, more important, to the Iraqis who were its victims.

---

war, his testimony before Congress, subsequently published in revised form in *Foreign Affairs*, legitimated the description. See Fearon 2007.

111. Gordon and Trainor 2012, 131.
112. Ibid., 239
113. Ibid., 271.

COIN as Statebuilding, 2007–2011

The "surge" announced by President Bush on January 4, 2007, is often portrayed as simply an increase in the number of troops deployed in Iraq, a move aimed primarily at reversing the underdeployment that had plagued U.S. efforts since 2003. It is also frequently depicted as a singular event and, in retrospect, a turning point in the war. In actuality, it was a series of three interconnected changes in U.S. statebuilding strategy that played out in late 2006 and early 2007, of which the deployment of twenty thousand additional troops was perhaps the least important.[114]

Central to the greater success of U.S. efforts in Iraq starting in 2007 were the Anbar Awakening, the shift to the new COIN strategy by the U.S. military, and political reconciliation. These three developments together embodied a new theory and practice of statebuilding that departed radically from the liberal model. Unlike its predecessor, the new approach eschewed democracy and free markets and emphasized, instead, the provision of essential goods and services to the population, especially security (see chapter 3).

The Anbar Awakening began slowly in mid-2006, months before the surge was announced.[115] Anbar is one of the few almost entirely Sunni provinces in Iraq and was the cradle of the insurgency and a haven for al-Qaeda in Iraq. The province was split between Iraqi nationalist groups like the Islamic Army, which sought to drive the Americans out of Iraq, and the radical Islamists of al-Qaeda and Ansar al-Sunnah, who fought in Iraq as part of a larger war against the West.[116] Encouraged by their U.S. military liaisons, the moderate Sunni sheikhs in Anbar decided to throw their future in with the Americans for two primary reasons.[117] First, Sunnis began to realize they were losing the civil war and had little choice but to turn to the United States. With at least a modicum of concern for the legitimacy of the new state, Washington would likely insist on a more inclusive Iraq than would the Shiites alone if the latter won a decisive victory.[118] Although the Sunni sheikhs continued to oppose the U.S. presence in the country, at this stage of the conflict the friend of their enemy was their friend. Decisive here in solidifying their support was a subsequent decision of Petraeus to go on the offensive against the Shiite militias in a serious way and thereby put pressure on Maliki. With evidence that a police brigade in southern Baghdad was murdering Sunnis, Petraeus withdrew

114. Ricks 2009, 165. The number of additional troops deployed varies depending on whether the units already in Iraq whose terms were extended are included or not. On the relative importance of the components of the surge, see Biddle, Friedman, and Shapiro 2012.
115. Ricks 2009, 59–72. There were several earlier aborted attempts to reach out to the tribes in Anbar. See Gordon and Trainor (2012, 170) for one particularly notable instance. On the chicken-and-egg debate about which came first, the Anbar Awakening or the surge, see ibid., 691.
116. Filkins 2008, 273.
117. Robinson 2008, 252.
118. F. Kaplan 2013, 268.

all support for the brigade, depriving it of fuel, money, and equipment, and prohibited its members from entering U.S.-controlled areas. When Maliki complained vigorously, he received no sympathy.[119] Second, the sheikhs were increasingly put off by the agenda of the foreign jihadists who flooded Anbar after the fall of Saddam.[120] The sheikhs slowly recognized that the foreign fighters who dominated the insurgency in Anbar were not fighting for Iraq but were playing a larger international game that did not always coincide with their interests. With the new U.S. support and commitment, the sheikhs reasoned that if they joined the political process and helped create stability in Iraq, the United States would likely go home more quickly.[121] As a result, the sheikhs turned their own militias against the foreign insurgents. The United States reinforced this turn by redeploying more troops to Anbar to assist the Awakening groups and to secure the gains they were achieving, lending some credibility to U.S. promises of support.[122] The Awakening thus became the foundation of the surge even before the surge had begun.[123] This same strategy, along with often substantial cash payments or other targeted benefits, was later extended to "turn" much of the Sunni-based insurgency.[124]

The second step was the introduction of the new COIN strategy. COIN was a long time coming.[125] Following Vietnam, the U.S. Army intentionally forgot nearly everything it had learned about counterinsurgency warfare.[126] The Persian Gulf War of 1991, in turn, reinforced the military's desire to fight large-scale conventional armies rather than lightly armed insurgents in urban settings.[127] Yet several commanders in Iraq did try innovative counterinsurgency strategies, especially the 101st Airborne Division, deployed in Mosul until February 2004 and led by then major general David Petraeus. As Fred Kaplan describes it, Petraeus even then propounded the idea, consistent with the theory of statebuilding outlined in chapter 1, that the object "was not to get the people of . . . Iraq to love America; rather, it was to get a critical mass of these people to develop a *vested interest*—to feel a stake of ownership—in the new Iraq, because unless that happened, the country would spin out of control."[128] The general was subsequently brought home from Iraq in September 2005 to rewrite the *U.S. Army/Marine Counterinsurgency Field Manual*, discussed in chapter 3.[129] Armed with his new field manual, General Petraeus

119. Ibid., 262–264.
120. Ibid., 247.
121. Ricks 2009, 66.
122. F. Kaplan 2013, 246.
123. Rice 2011, 590; Robinson 2008, 324.
124. Ricks 2009, 202.
125. On the efforts to promote COIN within the U.S. military, see F. Kaplan 2013.
126. Packer 2005, 201; Ricks 2006, 226, 267.
127. Ricks 2006, 132.
128. F. Kaplan 2013, 74, italics added.
129. *CFM* 2007; Robinson 2008, 76.

then returned to Iraq to lead the surge and moved quickly to impose the new COIN doctrine on the military even as additional troops were pouring into the country.[130] It is unlikely that the increased troops by themselves would have changed the dynamics on the ground. Central to the success of the surge was the way both old and new forces were used.

As explained in chapter 3, the *CFM* outlines a very different approach to warfare and, in turn, to statebuilding. Recognizing that you "can't kill your way out of an insurgency," COIN aims to win the hearts and minds of the local population. By providing security and other basic public goods such as potable water, sanitation, and health services, COIN seeks to gain the loyalty of locals, who, in turn, are more likely to provide the intelligence necessary to identify and defeat the insurgents. It does not attempt to defeat the enemy directly by breaking its ability and will to fight, but rather to win over the local population and thereby deny insurgents the safe havens they require to operate. It is, in part, a confidence game. By providing locals with essential public services that make them better off, especially security against retaliation, and by convincing them that victory is likely, COIN aims to draw citizens into the new regime and turn them against the insurgents—similar to what had happened somewhat more spontaneously in Anbar Province. Using an "oil spot" strategy of pacifying one area and then proceeding to its neighbor, COIN progressively chokes off the ability of the insurgents to hide within sympathetic populations. Given the multisided nature of the Iraq conflict, COIN also implied in this case that the U.S. military shift from a defense of the government, as is normal in counterinsurgency operations, to "balanced operations" that targeted groups on both sides of the sectarian divide. Along with the surge, the U.S. military attempted to recast itself as an arbiter between groups.[131]

Interestingly, COIN explicitly reverses the priorities of the liberal orthodoxy that dominated the first phase of statebuilding in Iraq. That model presumes that democratization and economic reform will lead to a consolidated state that will then step up and take control of the war and defeat any remaining insurgents. COIN focuses on the provision of goods and services to earn the loyalty of the public and demotes democracy and freer markets to the lowest priority and last steps in statebuilding.[132] On this point, the political strategy out of Washington and the military strategy developed in Iraq diverged. The Bush administration remained adamant that whatever government they left in place in Iraq must be democratic. For the president, at least, this was a necessary

---

130. Success has many fathers. Robinson (2008) largely credits the surge and COIN to Petraeus, while Ricks (2009, esp. 107) highlights the roles of General Jack Keane (retired) and Lieutenant General Raymond Odierno.
131. Ricks 2009, 156.
132. *CFM* 2007, 156, esp. figure 155–152; Dobbins et al. 2007, xxiii.

condition for success and, eventually, the withdrawal of U.S. forces.[133] In this sense, the administration did not fully embrace the new priorities of the counterinsurgency strategy.

Unsurprisingly, given its provenance, Petraeus implemented COIN "by the book." Combined with the additional troops from the surge, the strategy worked, at least at the local level. After an initial increase in U.S. and Iraqi casualties, fully anticipated as troops moved out of fortified bases and into the neighborhoods they were protecting, the change in strategy dramatically reduced the violence previously spiraling out of control. As Figures 4.1a and 4.1b indicate, casualties spiked in the first half of 2007 and then began to fall as the full complement of troops was deployed and the new strategy was fully rolled out.

Providing basic public services at the local level also began to win the hearts and minds of Iraqis.[134] As Petraeus learned from his time in Mosul and repeated frequently thereafter, "money is ammunition" and "the best weapons for COIN don't fire bullets," ideas that were incorporated into the *CFM*.[135] As Petraeus repeatedly claimed, counterinsurgency is 20 percent military and 80 percent political, and its effectiveness must be evaluated on that score as well.[136] Altogether, the United States spent approximately $25.3 billion on reconstruction projects in Iraq through 2008, with nearly 88 percent going to "large projects" and the remainder to local public goods projects under a variety of programs but grouped under the Commander's Emergency Response Program (CERP).[137] As discussed above, many of the large projects were designed by the CPA or later by the U.S. embassy, contracted with U.S. firms, canceled or substantially delayed by security concerns, and carried out without sufficient oversight, resulting in high levels of corruption and shoddy work. These big projects, in turn, had no effect on levels of violence in Iraq, measured by the number of military engagements between U.S. forces and insurgent groups (tracked as "significant activities" or SIGACTs). Large projects by district between March 2003 and December 2008, including the first two years of the surge, had no or perhaps even a weakly positive effect on the number of SIGACTs. CERP funding, however, had very different effects. CERP funds, totaling approximately $3 billion over the same time period and at least some of which came from hoards of cash found in Saddam's palaces, were administered quite differently from large-project aid. As the name implies, CERP funds were explicitly designed to provide military commanders with resources to engage in small-scale projects (under $100,000) to meet the

---

133. Gordon and Trainor 2012.
134. The results here are from Berman, Shapiro, and Felter 2011and Berman, Felter, et al. 2013.
135. F. Kaplan 2013, 142, 151.
136. Ibid., 164.
137. See Berman, Shapiro, and Felter 2011, 791.

needs of the local communities in which they were deployed.[138] Since they were small-scale and local, CERP projects more likely reflected the public goods desired by communities, though the funds were also used to bribe local officials and pay compensation to people whose houses were destroyed or whose family members were killed.[139] Key is that, unlike the large projects, the small amounts were paid directly to Iraqis. Prior to the surge, controlling for previous levels of violence and preexisting trends, CERP funding did not significantly reduce violence against U.S. troops. From 2007 to 2008, however, the correlation between CERP spending and the number of military engagements is strongly negative, with each dollar of per capita CERP funding producing 1.59 fewer violent engagements with U.S. forces per 100,000 residents over a six-month period (the mean number of incidents was 58.6 each period). Though this number may seem small, it implies that an increase in CERP spending of $37 per Iraqi (all else constant) would have driven the level of violence to zero.[140] CERP spending in Iraq was also most effective in reducing violence when projects were small, development expertise was available, and troop strength was high—indicating that aid and military deployments are complementary.[141] COIN had a real effect in winning hearts and minds not only by providing security but by providing public goods desired by the population.

COIN succeeded sufficiently to permit the withdrawal of U.S. troops in December 2011. By 2009, as indicated in figures 4.1a and 4.1b, casualties of all sorts had declined dramatically from their 2004–2007 heights. Withdrawing U.S. forces had been, of course, the goal all along, to "step up" the Iraqi military so that the Americans could go home. Some military leaders never gave up the idea that they were as much a cause of as the solution to the insurgency. Everyone envisioned the surge as temporary. In this limited sense, however, COIN was a success.

Hoping to establish a permanent basis for the U.S. role in Iraq beyond his administration, President Bush opened negotiations with Iraq for a Status of Forces Agreement (SOFA) in late 2007. Going into negotiations, the Iraqis had four main aspirations: (1) a commitment from the United States to defend Iraq against external attack, (2) a promise from the United States to defend the regime against a potential coup, (3) an assurance that the United States would work to dismiss Iraq's debts from the Saddam era, and (4) the lifting of Saddam-era sanctions.[142] The United States had three essential goals: any SOFA had to have the support of the government of Iraq—ideally through the ratification of the agreement by parliament, authority for continued military operations

---

138. Herring and Rangwala 2006, 78.
139. F. Kaplan 2013, 75.
140. Berman, Shapiro, and Felter 2011.
141. Berman, Felter, et al. 2013.
142. Gordon and Trainor 2012, 525.

by U.S. forces, and legal protections for U.S. troops in Iraq.[143] Using the Americans' desire for parliamentary ratification as leverage, Maliki negotiated hard for fixed dates of withdrawal, with Bush eventually compromising on mid-2009 to remove U.S. forces from the cities—giving Maliki a freer hand in the use of force for his own ends—and the end of 2011 to remove all forces from the country. These dates were, however, never taken seriously by the Americans, especially the military. Anticipating that Iraq's armed forces would remain weak and inept, the expectation all along was that Maliki would have no choice but to invite U.S. troops to remain, perhaps under an extended UN mandate.[144] Despite the deadlines, the military planned on keeping up to fifty thousand troops in Iraq for the foreseeable future. Once President Barack Obama was elected, however, these numbers were scaled back to under ten thousand and then to thirty-five hundred, both to fulfill the newly elected leader's campaign promises and to make the permanent force more palatable to the Iraqis. This may have been a misreading of Iraqi priorities, which focused much more on issues of sovereignty than on the absolute number of U.S. troops.[145] With the Obama administration insisting that Maliki once again get parliamentary approval for the new troops and the revised SOFA, the issue of immunities for U.S. troops became a roadblock. The president declared negotiations over in a video conference on October 21, 2011, and the final troops withdrew in December. Critics charged that had Obama really wanted the accord and to keep troops in Iraq, a bargain would have been possible—and perhaps this is true, though the counterfactual is unknowable.[146] The final withdrawal reflected the exhaustion of the United States with the war, the "good enough" status of Iraq, and the need to forge a new relationship with the sovereign government of the country. For the second time, the United States declared victory in Iraq, but this time it really did go home—thus ending the U.S. experiment in statebuilding in Iraq.

The Statebuilder's Dilemma in Iraq

Mistakes were certainly made in failing to plan for statebuilding in Iraq and, once recognized as a necessity, in following the liberal blueprint. Although COIN eventually created the conditions for withdrawal and hope for a minimalist state that might be able to govern on its own, it did not produce a consolidated state with broad-based legitimacy. Although one might argue that these mistakes alone were enough to doom the U.S. effort in Iraq, the failure of statebuilding in this case, as in others, was ultimately rooted not in strategy

143. Ibid., 528.
144. Ibid., 548.
145. Ibid., 667.
146. Ibid., 674.

but in the statebuilder's dilemma. Throughout its intervention, the United States sought to balance the twin objectives of legitimacy and loyalty. The United States did not seek loyalty over any other goal, as in Central America in the early twentieth century. Legitimacy via democracy and then service provision always remained an important ambition.[147] Nonetheless, even while trying to create a legitimate Iraqi state, the Bush administration simultaneously intervened in the political process to ensure that a leader at least sympathetic to U.S. interests came to power. This narrowed the pool of potential leaders quite dramatically, as we shall see, to a Shiite who was willing to work with the United States. With few alternatives, Maliki was anointed and consistently supported by the Bush administration as prime minister.

Once in power, in a surprise to the administration but perfectly predictable in terms of the theory described in chapter 3, Maliki ruled as a Shiite partisan. Instead of building a broad coalition, he sought to consolidate his base of support within his core constituency.[148] With no Plan B, as it was called by the Bush administration, the United States acquiesced in Maliki's domestic political strategy, even after recognizing that his partisanship was driving the insurgency and preventing the United States from being able to withdraw as quickly as had been hoped.[149] Ironically, having consolidated his base of support, Maliki was then able to ignore U.S. wishes and refused to countenance a long-term presence for U.S. forces, who would otherwise have continued to constrain him from governing as narrowly as he wished. In the end, the United States placed greater emphasis on legitimacy than did its handpicked leader.

No tweaking of strategy at the margin would have vitiated the dilemma. Indeed, even had adequate troops been sent and COIN implemented from the outset, the statebuilder's dilemma would have undermined the effort. In this case, the trade-off between legitimacy and loyalty was acute. Any degree of emphasis on loyalty was likely to result in a leader who would govern in a narrow, partisan, antidemocratic fashion and exploit the position of the United States to divert resources to his preferred ends and constituency. The tragic consequences of this dilemma, however, accentuated the violence, undermined the capacity of the new state, and finally led to the second failure of the Iraqi state in the summer of 2014.

Policy Preferences

The gap in policy preferences between Americans and Iraqis is hard to ascertain but nonetheless appears to be fairly large. It is this difference in policy

147. For a critique that the United States did not emphasize legitimacy enough, see Roy 2004.
148. Robinson 2008, 123; F. Kaplan 2013, 207–208.
149. Some U.S. officials, notably Lieutenant General Pete Chiarelli, the number two commander at CENTCOM, began to doubt whether turning responsibility for governance over to this partisan government was a viable solution to the insurgency. F. Kaplan 2013, 207.

preferences that makes the statebuilder's dilemma particularly intense in this case. Any leader acceptable to the United States would likely favor policies far from those of the median citizen in Iraq, creating a conflict between legitimating the state and appointing a leader on whom the United States could rely.

There is, of course, continuing debate about U.S. motivations in Iraq and the war. Given that the Bush administration floated many possible arguments in favor of intervention and focused on those that appeared to resonate with the American public, it is hard to separate the marketing of the war from the "true" motives of the administration and the country more generally.[150] Despite the slogans in 2002 and 2003 protesting "No blood for oil," there does not appear to be any evidence that the Bush administration was narrowly focused on the issue of Iraq's oil resources. Although the administration was concerned about Iraq's ability to destabilize international oil markets if allowed to export freely, this appears to have been at most an existential worry rather than a compelling motivation. More generally, the United States seems to have desired to integrate Iraq into the Pax Americana, much as its former enemies Germany and Japan had been after World War II, in which its new partner would (1) give up some control over its own foreign policy in return for U.S. security guarantees, (2) provide forward operating bases in the region as necessary, and (3) open its economy to international trade and investment. The security and basing relationship was key after U.S. troops withdrew from Saudi Arabia in early 2003. Above all, at least according to the president's public statements, the United States wanted to recruit Iraq as an ally in the war on terror and, for the neoconservatives in his inner circle, serve as an exemplar of a new, liberal, and democratic Muslim state in the Middle East.[151]

As hard as it is to identify the goals of the United States in Iraq, it is even harder to discern the policy preferences of average Iraqis before and immediately after the invasion. There are few public opinion polls prior to 2003, and the polls since then are, unfortunately, largely focused on changes in well-being and attitudes since the war began and often tainted for my purposes by actions undertaken by the United States during the fighting. Few polls attempt to tap into underlying attitudes toward different policy dimensions in ways that are comparable between the United States and Iraq. Nonetheless, some broad and tentative conclusions about varying policy preferences can be drawn.

150. It is highly unlikely that the same policy preferences were held by all Americans in 2003. Different issues resonated more or less with different individuals and constituencies. The "selling" of the war in fall 2002 focused on WMD because this appeared to pull together many of the constituencies, especially after the terrorist attacks of 2001, but this was by no means the primary or only reason for the war. The Bush administration may very well have been more hawkish than the median voter in the United States. This diversity of policy preferences does not, however, undermine the main point here that U.S. policy preferences differed dramatically from those of Iraqis.

151. See Bolger 2014, 160.

The goals of the United States appear quite different from those of the Iraqis. A 2002 poll on "what Arabs want" did not include Iraq but helps nonetheless to paint a general picture.[152] The survey found that respondents from six Arab countries, like people nearly everywhere, ranked family and local issues as their highest priorities, including civil and personal rights, health care, and the economy. Although most identified more strongly as Arabs than as citizens of their own countries, the only international issue that ranked as a relatively high priority was Palestine. Yet the United States was viewed unfavorably by a large majority of respondents; only Israel received fewer positive assessments. This was not necessarily an anti-Western view, as France and Canada were seen quite favorably, as were U.S. freedom and democracy. Rather, it appears that respondents primarily disagreed with U.S. policy in the Middle East. In subsequent polls among Arab countries, Iraq tends to fall in the middle of the range on many similar response categories, so perhaps it is not inappropriate to infer something about prewar attitudes in Iraq even from this survey.

Within Iraq, the first poll after the U.S. invasion found a relatively optimistic population, with a strong majority believing that Iraq would be a better country in five years.[153] At the same time, there was a strong desire to build a new state independently, without the assistance or guidance of the United States; most respondents wanted coalition forces to leave within one year. Although only about a third of the respondents desired an Islamic government, and most had an unfavorable opinion of Osama bin Laden, bare majorities thought that Iran and the United States would hurt Iraq over the next five years even while they believed the United Nations and—surprisingly, given the Shiite-Sunni split in the country—Saudi Arabia would help the new Iraq. Less than 40 percent thought democracy could work in Iraq, and only 23 percent thought the new government should be modeled after that in the United States. Although this survey does not tap into underlying policy preferences, it suggests that Iraqis, at least, saw themselves in 2003 as quite distinct from Americans.

Looking at Iraq's three principal social groups, it seems that all had and continue to possess preferences fairly distant from those of the United States. Although the Kurds were warmly disposed toward the United States for protecting their autonomous region after the Persian Gulf War in 1991 and permitting, if not encouraging, its further autonomy after 2003, the highest aspiration of the community for an independent Kurdistan is strongly opposed by the United States as a threat to its longtime ally Turkey and, more generally, to regional stability. Continued dependence on the United States and on oil

152. Arab American Institute, "Arabs: What They Believe and What They Value Most" (2002), conducted by Zogby, http://b.3cdn.net/aai/15b74344248440f677_xzm6yho0g.pdf.
153. Arab American Institute, "The First Poll of Iraqi Public Opinion," (2003) conducted by Zogby International, https://d3n8a8pro7vhmx.cloudfront.net/aai/pages/9765/attachments/original/1438878480/Iraqi_Public_Opinion_2004.pdf?1438878480.

exports by truck through Turkey keep the Kurds aligned with Washington, and Kurds generally see themselves as better off since the U.S. invasion.[154] This does not, however, necessarily indicate that they share the same policy goals, especially over an independent state.

Conversely, although the Sunni minority in Iraq deeply opposed the U.S. invasion and Washington's role in overturning the regime they previously dominated, with 85 percent supporting "honorable resistance" in attacking the Americans, it shares a strong common identity with other Sunni majority countries closely aligned with the United States.[155] This suggests that there may not be an inherent conflict of interest between the United States and the Sunni minority in Iraq; but their previous support for Saddam, opposition to the United States, and widespread belief that they have suffered economically and politically since the war likely reflect a gap in policy that was impossible to bridge in 2003 and remains so today. As with the Kurds, the support for the United States from traditional tribal leaders in the Sunni heartland starting in 2006 is more an accommodation to the facts on the ground, as it were, than any fundamental consensus on policy goals.

Finally, the Shiites in 2003 appear to have been divided between religious fundamentalists around Sadr and his Mahdi Army, allied with Iran and presumably hostile to the United States from the outset, and less-religious political moderates who, though exiled to Iran or the West under Saddam, were at least in principle open to working with Washington. This group of moderates likely became smaller during the postinvasion civil war, as each group—Shiites included—was driven more deeply into itself as the security dilemma unfolded. As suggested by the strong majorities described above that wanted the United States to leave Iraq as soon as possible, those willing to partner with Washington to help achieve its objectives in the Persian Gulf region were likely a minority that became ever smaller over time.

Although evidence is indirect, it appears reasonable to conclude that the policy preferences of the United States and average Iraqis were quite far apart before and immediately after the invasion, and that these policy preferences grew more distant from one another rather than closer together over time as the deepening U.S. role alienated nearly all factions in the country. There was not a substantial group supporting the United States in Iraq after the invasion. Rather, the United States could rely on only a relatively small cohort of Shiite moderates. Reflecting the basic logic behind figure 3.1b, the gap in policy preferences was large and the "tail" of the distribution favoring the United States was relatively thin.

154. Arab Barometer II, Michael Hoffman, Princeton University, http://www.arabbarometer
    .org/sites/default/files/englishiraqIIreportII.pdf.
155. Bolger 2014, 225.

This interpretation is further supported by the U.S. attempt to lock its policy preferences into the constitution. Even after the supposed return to sovereignty, Iraq was limited by the Transitional Administrative Law written by the CPA before its dissolution, which codified many of the regulations promulgated by the CPA during its period of rule. Specifying that its provisions could be modified only by a supermajority of the National Assembly, this meant that Iraq would continue to be bound by laws and regulations enacted by the CPA. As Undersecretary of State Marc Grossman acknowledged, Iraq would acquire only "limited sovereignty."[156] Had the United States not feared that an independent Iraq would change course, binding the hands of the future Iraqi government would not have been necessary.

Legitimacy and Loyalty

Recognizing the gap in policy preferences, the United States attempted to deal with the trade-off between legitimacy and loyalty central to the statebuilder's dilemma. Nearly all U.S. decision makers recognized that any Iraqi leader needed some substantial support from the population to succeed over the long term. As implied in the liberal model that dominated U.S. policy immediately after the invasion, a democratic regime was understood as absolutely central to the legitimacy of the new state being created in Iraq. COIN sought to win hearts and minds and to legitimate the state by providing security and public goods. Yet, at the same time, the Bush administration also sought to promote leaders loyal to the United States. The administration attempted to balance these goals as best it could, but even so the tension between legitimacy and loyalty was devastating.

The desire for loyalty was apparent from the opening days of the war, especially in the Pentagon's preference for Chalabi, discussed above. Garner brought this same priority into Iraq. During his brief tenure, he moved immediately to appoint an Iraqi Leadership Council (ILC), subsequently known as the G-7, that was reconstituted as the IGC on July 13, 2003. Although the IGC was meant to be a power-sharing institution representative of all factions of Iraqi society, its membership was nonetheless hand-selected by the United States and dominated by individuals from the exile community or the KRG.[157] The Shiite parties were represented by Jaafari, leader of the Islamic Dawa party and later the first prime minister, and Adil Abd al-Aziz al-Hakim, SCIRI's second in command. Both parties they led were formed by exiles in Iran and maintained close ties with the neighboring fundamentalist regime, and

156. MacDonald 2014, 187.
157. The IGC was not representative of the various regions of Iraq nor did it include notable traditional leaders. For a detailed account of the formation of the IGC, see Herring and Rangwala 2006, 107. For an analysis of the IGC composition, see Bremer 2006, chap. 4; Marr 2006.

SCIRI possessed a significant paramilitary wing known as the Badr Brigades. Also included were two "Western" exiles: Chalabi, of course, and Ayad Allawi of the Iraqi National Accord, a secular Shiite with ties to the Sunni community who had close ties to the U.S. and United Kingdom intelligence communities.[158] All four were regarded by Sunnis as "pure *sheruggis*"—Persian pawns— and, even worse, U.S. collaborators.[159] Kurds were represented by Masoud Barzani, of the Kurdistan Democratic Party (KDP), and Jalal Talabani, of the Patriotic Union of Kurdistan (PUK), both secular Sunni Kurds operating out of Kurdistan with large and separate militias (peshmerga) at their command. One U.S. general described Talabani as "the most able and certainly the most pro-American voice in Baghdad."[160] The only Sunni Arab was Naseer al-Chaderchi, whose father had been active in the democracy movement of the 1960s. All of these individuals would play central roles in subsequent Iraqi politics under the guidance of the United States. All were close to the Americans, with the Kurds and Shiites particularly dependent on support from Washington that was expected to make them relatively compliant in the years ahead. As Larry Diamond reports, the ILC "was probably a step on the way toward the administration's original goal of establishing Chalabi as the effective interim head of Iraq."[161]

With Garner's departure and Bremer's arrival as head of the CPA, the same strategy of promoting pro-Western elites continued. Indeed, Herring and Rangwala argue that a key motivation behind the adoption of full-on state-building under the CPA was, in fact, to ensure that only Iraqis approved by Washington would rise to power.[162] The members of the interim government, formed in June 2004, were also handpicked by the White House. When the UN envoy Lakhdar Brahimi, assisting in the political transition, advanced the popular Hussein al-Shahristani as candidate for interim prime minister, for instance, he was vetoed by U.S. officials because of uncertainty over his ties to Iran. Instead, Allawi was forwarded by the United States and approved by the IGC.[163]

In the election of December 2005, the first under the new constitution, the United States was also heavily involved in vetting candidates, negotiating with the parties, and eventually selecting Maliki as the least objectionable alternative, even in the face of British opposition.[164] U.S. ambassador Zalmay Khalil-

---

158. Herring and Rangwala 2006, 16–17. Allawi was a former Ba'athist who resigned from the party in 1975 and was subsequently the target of an assassination attempt in 1978, presumably ordered by Saddam.
159. Bolger 2014, 161.
160. Ibid., 229.
161. Diamond 2005, 40–41. See also Rice 2011, 209; Bremer 2006, 42–46.
162. Herring and Rangwala 2006, 15–17.
163. Gordon and Trainor 2012, 77–88, 142. U.S. officials later became frustrated with Allawi's frequent trips out of the country, which made rapid communications and decision making difficult. Ibid., 109.
164. Ibid., 189, 196–198. On leadership changes in general, see Marr 2006.

zad was deeply involved in the extensive negotiations over the choice of prime minister. Jaafari was quickly rejected as both incompetent and deeply sectarian. Abd al-Mahdi, another popular and leading contender with good executive skills, was struck from the list of candidates by Khalilzad as too deferential to SCIRI leader al-Hakim and too close to Iran. After rejecting several other weak or dark horse candidates, the ambassador finally settled on Maliki, who, although a Shiite who had spent time in Iran during his exile, was a hard-liner on de-Ba'athification and the Sunni insurgency, reportedly had deep concerns about Iranian influence, and had distanced himself from Sadr and the Mahdi Army.[165] Michael Gordon and Bernard Trainor write that "Khalilzad's role in selecting the Iraqi prime minister remained a secret." The notion that he was the American choice would do Maliki no good, and the Bush administration was interested in fostering the belief that the compromise choice was purely the product of the Iraqis' deliberations, but there was no doubt that, "as far as the United States government was concerned, Maliki was fine."[166]

Thus, even within the trappings of democratic elections, the United States was heavily involved in vetting and selecting Iraq's new leaders. Despite a concern with legitimacy, loyalty was still prized. The belief in democracy as a legitimating force, and later COIN, may have blinded Bush and others to the magnitude of the trade-off they faced, but the dilemma remained. Indeed, while many have pointed to failures of implementation in the election process as a cause of the new state's eventual failure, the administration's mucking about and selecting favored leaders would have caused problems for the ultimate legitimacy of the state even in the best of circumstances.

To be clear, however, despite the administration's role in his selection, no one suffered under the illusion that Malaki was an ideal leader or simply a puppet of the United States. Although he was willing to work with the Americans and was elevated above more senior leaders for this reason, his own political and policy preferences were still far from those of the United States. As suggested in figure 3.1b, Malaki might have been in the tail of the distribution closest to the United States, but this did not mean he fully shared the preferences of the administration or the United States more generally. His own preferences were still quite far from those desired by Washington. This was not a case like West Germany or Japan after World War II when policy preferences were sufficiently flexible and close to those of the United States that loyal leaders could also be popular and legitimate leaders. Rather, Malaki was, at most, the best of a bad lot—the best the United States could hope for under the circumstances.

---

165. Gordon and Trainor 2012, 183–189. Subsequent reports indicate that the United States actually knew little about Maliki at the time, with some administration officials consistently getting his given name wrong until Maliki himself corrected them. Baker 2014a.
166. Gordon and Trainor 2012, 197–198.

The Failure of Statebuilding

Once in power, not surprisingly, Maliki turned to consolidating his own political support base in the Shia community. Rather than govern from near the center of the Iraqi political spectrum as a unifier, Maliki quickly emerged as a Shiite partisan.[167] In a 2006 briefing, Celeste Ward, then a political adviser at CENTCOM, argued that Malaki was intent on consolidating his Shiite coalition and appeared to be "an instrument of sectarian warfare" with security forces "dominated by Shia militias, which persistently restrained U.S. forces from going after known Shia terrorists." His government's "economic ministries systematically withheld services from Sunni citizens while lavishing Western aid on programs that benefited only Shiites."[168] Whether this was his intent all along or a circumstance forced on him by the need to solidify his coalition is almost irrelevant.

Upon taking office, Malaki's first move was to gain control over the Islamic Dawa Party, where he had previously been deputy, getting himself elected as general secretary. He then installed a group of loyal supporters, the "Malikiyoun," at the top. Malaki also relied heavily on family members, appointing his son, Ahmed, as deputy chief of staff overseeing all of Iraq's security services and in charge of his personal security detail. The prime minister then set about gaining control over the military, subverting the existing chain of command and promoting those tied to him personally.[169] Given his narrow base of support within the country, this attempt to build a personal support coalition should have been expected.

Most devastating were the alliances with other Shiite leaders that Maliki required to stay in office. As the price for his support for the new prime minister, for instance, Sadr insisted on control of the Interior Ministry, which allowed him to transform the national Iraqi police force into a virtual extension of his Mahdi Army.[170] Sadr also demanded the Transport and Telecommunications Ministry, which controlled major infrastructure projects and the Baghdad airport, and the Health Ministry, which allowed his allies to control access to crucial government services.[171] Through their control of the airport, Sadrists kept track of movements of people and resources in and out of the country, but also smuggled in weapons and explosives. The Health Ministry guards, in turn, were killing Sunnis in the hospitals, soon causing nearly all to avoid the formal health system under any circumstances.[172] Sadr's control extended to some portions of the Iraqi military as well, with the 3-1-6 Battalion, for instance, barely distinguishable from his militia except for the uniforms they

---

167. Herring and Rangwala 2006, 33; Dodge 2012, 2013b.
168. F. Kaplan 2013, 209–210.
169. Dodge 2012, 151–156.
170. Gordon and Trainor 2012, 140–141, 146–148; Cole 2007, 116–117.
171. Herring and Rangwala 2006, 37; Gordon and Trainor 2012, 220–222.
172. F. Kaplan 2013, 180.

wore.[173] Under the joint training rules in effect, this high penetration meant that the insurgents were often tipped off to Coalition operations before they could be carried out.[174] Under Maliki, who needed to build a political coalition to sustain himself in power, the Mahdi Army thus effectively captured key elements of the Iraqi state from within. As explained above, the partisanship of the police and elements of the military played a large role in stimulating the spiral of violence in Iraq, but the point here is that this was the price paid to consolidate power under Malaki.

Seen as politically weak by the United States, Maliki was nonetheless supported almost unconditionally by the Bush administration—despite its knowledge about the partisan political strategy he was pursuing.[175] Without other viable leaders to choose from, the United States was the dog that was wagged by the proverbial Iraqi tail. On the one hand, Maliki was clearly struggling to solidify his position within the Shiite community. This required making peace even with factions that were actively kidnapping and executing Americans.[176] Although Maliki did not seek to undermine the Sunni Awakening happening in Anbar and spreading elsewhere, he was adamant about not allowing similar initiatives by Shiites in the southern provinces, where his own political base was concentrated.[177] Maliki began to distance himself from Sadr and the Mahdi Army as the surge took hold in 2007, but he was simultaneously using Iraqi special operations forces, trained by the United States as an elite team, to target his political opponents directly. In the two weeks before the provincial elections in August 2008, for instance, some six hundred Iraqis were detained, many of whom were members of the Iraqi Islamic Party.[178] U.S. officials had long complained that Maliki was too weak and tentative, but now he was using the instruments of the state quite overtly to consolidate his own political power and moving in an increasingly authoritarian direction. Indeed, General Ray Odierno, commander of U.S. forces in Iraq, feared that Maliki might even refuse to step down in March 2010 if he were not reelected.[179] It became increasingly clear that Maliki was manipulating U.S. assistance, both military and economic, to bolster his narrow support base within the country and becoming increasingly authoritarian.[180]

---

173. Gordon and Trainor 2012, 343. Every ministry was allocated "facilities protection forces," creating over 145,000 officially armed militiamen. Filkins 2008, 322–323.
174. F. Kaplan 2013, 185. Later evidence indicates that operations were sometimes revealed by top aides to Maliki himself.
175. Robinson 2008, 23; on fissures within the Shiite community, see ibid., 145.
176. Gordon and Trainor 2012, 354.
177. Ibid., 443–448. In fact, Maliki was actively working to neutralize Shiite groups that resisted his rule. Ibid., 473; F. Kaplan 2013, 268. Maliki became willing to take greater political risks, however, after a successful Iraqi operation in Basra in spring 2008. Some U.S. officials feared that he was becoming "over-confident." Ricks 2009, 283.
178. Gordon and Trainor 2012, 543–544.
179. Ibid., 614.
180. Ibid., 585. See also Dodge 2013b.

On the other hand, there were few alternative leaders. Frustrated with the lack of political progress, President Bush speculated in an August 8, 2007, National Security Council meeting that "if you dump Maliki, ensure we get someone we can live with," but "definitely not Jaafari but perhaps Adil Abd al-Mahdi," a senior SCIRI politician and former finance minister who was one of the few genuine statesmen in Iraq but, as noted above, was once regarded as too close to Iran.[181] As pressures from within Iraq mounted against Maliki, from both those concerned about his sectarian bent and political rivals seeking to unseat him, Bush repeatedly came back to the same question: "If not Maliki, who?"[182] In the end, there was no Plan B.

Indeed, even in the March 2010 elections, the United States stage-managed Malaki's retention of power. Despite widespread allegations of electoral fraud by Maliki and even though his State of Law Party received two fewer seats in the parliament than his principal rival, Allawi's Iraqiya, Maliki was still asked first to try to form a coalition, in direct violation of the constitution.[183] The United States actually preferred a power-sharing agreement in which Allawi, whom it supported as interim prime minister in 2005, would assume the presidency and Maliki would remain prime minister, a proposal that met stiff resistance from Talabani, who already occupied the president's office. After the United States tested several alternative means of expanding leadership positions to include Allawi, Turkey ultimately helped negotiate a deal in which he would head a National Council for Higher Policies, which was then never formed. Allawi was eventually cast aside. Iran also played a key role in the decision of Sadr and his followers to back Maliki.[184] Nonetheless, lacking better alternatives, the United States was still the prime mover in orchestrating Maliki's reselection as prime minister.

By 2010 the United States as statebuilder clearly knew about the liabilities of the leader it was promoting and the direction in which he was likely to take the country. Indeed, Secretary of State Condoleezza Rice even traveled to Baghdad at one point to tell Maliki to shape up. "You're a terrible prime minister," she supposedly told him. "Without progress and without an agreement [to maintain U.S. forces in Iraq], you'll be on your own, hanging from a lamppost."[185] Yet the United States was trapped by its preference for a leader who would accommodate its interests and work with it when nearly the entire population wanted the statebuilder gone. Without a natural base of support in society, Maliki manipulated U.S. aid and support and then defied Washington to do anything about it. As he well knew, there was nothing the United States could do but support him further. As we shall see below, this U.S. support wavered only as the Iraq state fell again in the summer of 2014.

181. Gordon and Trainor 2012, 187, 431.
182. Ibid., 456.
183. Ibid., 631–636, 642, 650–651; Arraf 2010.
184. Gordon and Trainor 2012, 640.
185. Baker 2014a.

The primary and most devastating consequence of Maliki's political strategy as prime minister was to exacerbate the insurgency already under way when he assumed office. Maliki did not start the violence, which ignited in the security dilemma that exploded immediately after the U.S. invasion, but he did little to stop it. Indeed, his partisanship drove many Sunnis into the insurgency or to support it.[186] Maliki added fuel to the fire already raging. Diverting aid from Sunni to Shiite areas for partisan political purposes was bad enough. But the more serious offense was that by supporting a leader expected to the loyal, the United States had to fight longer and harder and incur more casualties to quell the violence in Iraq. One might blame Maliki for this paradoxical outcome, but it was in the end an inevitable consequence of orchestrating the rise to power of a prime minister who—precisely because he was expected to be the most pro-Western of the alternatives—lacked a natural base of support within the population as a whole. That he would put his own political survival above the interests of Iraqis or the United States should not have been a surprise. This is the tragedy inherent in the statebuilder's dilemma.

As a final blow to U.S. statebuilding efforts, Maliki ultimately exploited his position to demand that U.S. forces leave the country. Recognizing that he did not have the full support of the United States and perhaps wanting a freer hand politically than Washington was willing to give him, Maliki played on the theme of full sovereignty to insist that all U.S. troops be withdrawn from Iraq as soon as possible. This bargaining strategy, in turn, rested on the increasing support from and reliance on military assistance and aid from Iran, which was also eager to see the United States leave the region and to expand its own influence in the country. Rather than agree to a new SOFA that would allow U.S. troops to remain in Iraq to bolster stability, Maliki held out for provisions that he knew the United States would find unacceptable.[187] The Bush administration, in turn, agreed to withdraw U.S. forces when an agreement could not be reached. This resonated with those within the United States, and especially in the military, who still believed that U.S. troops were part of the problem behind the insurgency rather than its solution. Growing dissatisfaction with the war, even after the successes of the surge, meant that its months were limited. President Obama has often been criticized, especially after the Iraqi state failed again in June 2014, for not trying harder to renegotiate the SOFA so that U.S. troops could remain in the country. Having freed himself from his American overseers, however, Maliki had no incentive at that point to make concessions that he was unwilling to make earlier or to use additional political capital to press parliament to approve an agreement acceptable to Obama. Maliki was no neutral statesman, but then again he should not have been expected to be. As this case shows plainly, the statebuilder need

186. Robinson 2008, 17.
187. Bolger 2014, 271.

not emphasize loyalty to the exclusion of all else to produce catastrophic consequences and cause the state it supports to fail again.

The Kurdish Exception

Like Somaliland, described in chapter 5, Iraqi Kurdistan is in many ways the exception that proves the rules of statebuilding—in this instance, highlighting the devastating effects of the statebuilder's dilemma by its absence. Kurds span Turkey, Syria, Iran, and Iraq, forming by some accounts the largest single ethnic group in the world today without a state of their own. The absence of sovereignty has insulated the KRG from the pressures of the statebuilder's dilemma, just as the acknowledged dependence of the region on the United States lessens the effects of the gap in policy preferences that otherwise exists. Without significant external intervention or an acute dilemma, statebuilding has been far more effective in Kurdistan than in the rest of Iraq.

A Kurdish state has long been an aspiration, on the international agenda but thwarted since the League of Nations contemplated the breakup of Ottoman Empire after World War I.[188] The Kurds were promised autonomy when Iraq gained full sovereignty in 1932, and again after the 1958 coup that overthrew the monarchy, but each time the central government in Baghdad has reneged. Continued frustration led to the formation of the KDP by Mullah Mustafa Barzani in 1946 and to open revolt in 1961. A compromise reached with Saddam in March 1970 granting limited autonomy to Iraqi Kurdistan broke down in 1974 over whether Kirkuk, long understood by Kurds as part of their historic homeland, would be part of the autonomous region. In response, Saddam began a massive program to "Arabize" the city.[189] Thinking that he had American support, Barzani launched another revolt in 1975, cut short when the shah of Iran reached an accord with Saddam and closed access to safe havens across the border.[190] This termination of the revolt, much disputed within the Kurdish community, led Jalal Talabani to found the PUK, which fought both the Iraqi regime and the KDP through the late 1970s. The two parties flipped sides in the Iran-Iraq War when the KDP aligned with Iran and the PUK opened negotiations with Saddam. Following the end of the war with Iran, Saddam turned his forces against the Kurds, using chemical weapons in attacks that destroyed more than four thousand villages, created over one million displaced persons, and killed between one hundred thousand and two hundred thousand civilians. This campaign united the KDP and the PUK against their common enemy. Seizing the opportunity during the Persian Gulf War, the KDP and the PUK took control of the newly

188. Galbraith 2006, 149–151.
189. Gordon and Trainor 2012, 34.
190. Galbraith 2006, 152.

liberated Kurdish region in the North to establish the KRG. Protected by a no-fly zone and a safe haven for Kurdish refugees imposed by the U.S.-led coalition, the Kurdish militias, the peshmerga, pushed Iraqi troops out of the area by October 1991. Saddam retaliated by stopping all salaries for Kurdish civil servants, forcing the Kurds to develop a taxation and fiscal system of their own, and imposing an internal embargo on the region, forcing it to develop ties with its neighbors and an independent economy.[191] The net result was a region of de facto political and economic autonomy, although Saddam and the Kurds continued to dispute the boundaries of Kurdistan and especially the status of Kirkuk. In 2003 the peshmerga fought with the coalition to overthrow Saddam. Although they have not given up hope for a sovereign Kurdistan, the relationship with the United States has taken root as a strong marriage of convenience.

As a condition for Kurdish support, the new Iraqi constitution of 2005 defines Iraqi Kurdistan as a federal entity. Kurdistan is permitted to have its own military, the peshmerga; although the federal government is supposed to have exclusive control over foreign affairs and defense, it has no control over the "guards of the region" and cannot deploy the peshmerga outside the region against its will. The Kurdistan constitution is superior to the federal government in the region, and KRG law prevails when there is a conflict with federal law.[192] De facto, the Kurds have not given up control over their borders with Turkey and Iran and have continued to develop their oil resources without concern for Baghdad, though they remain dependent on the federal government for their export.[193] This is less a federal system of government than a confederation between two otherwise sovereign states.

The KRG is a reasonably stable parliamentary democracy, dominated by the KDP and the PUK. Competition between the parties is intense, occasionally breaking down into violence as during the 1990s, but managed through a modus vivendi in which the KDP draws its support from the Kermani-speaking areas along the Turkish border and the PUK from around the eastern city of Suleimania, as well as agreement that Mosoud Barzani, the son of the founder of the KDP, will be the president of the KRG, while Talabani represents the region in Baghdad, including as president of the new regime.[194] Disagreements between the parties have long been sublimated to their common opposition to the central government in Baghdad, regardless of whether it is led by Saddam, Maliki, or any successor. What will happen in the future if the Kurds get an independent state or even more autonomy remains an open question.

191. On Operation Provide Comfort, see Ricks 2006, 8–9. On the repression of the Kurds after 1991, see Freedman and Karsh 1993, chap. 30.
192. Galbraith 2006, 169.
193. Ibid., 168.
194. Ibid., 155.

Barzani and Talabani are, however, legitimate indigenous leaders of Kurdistan who gained their status through decades of leadership in the struggle for regional autonomy.[195] Importantly, they gained office and power prior to the U.S. engagement with the region, and thus were in no way selected by the United States. They were already the leaders within Kurdistan with whom the United States had to work if it was to succeed. Benefiting from U.S. protection after 1991, Barzani and Talabani both aligned with the United States again in 2003, wanting to be firmly on the U.S. side of the war.[196] Though the region as a whole has benefited from U.S. policy, the leaders are not directly beholden to the United States nor necessarily loyal. The Americans have frequently mistaken the support of Barzani and Talabani for an alignment of interests, and then been surprised when the Kurds unsettled the plans of the CPA for a new constitution, for instance, or otherwise pushed hard for their own interests in the new Iraq. The stability of Kurdistan and the successful functioning of the KRG, however, testify to the power of indigenous statebuilding.

Importantly, confronted with established leaders in Kurdistan, the United States would face a significant hurdle to appointing its own, more loyal leaders in the region. Rather than imposing its own policy preferences on the Kurds, the United States accepts the leadership of Barzani and Talabani, indigenous leaders with already strong legitimacy. The case of Kurdistan illustrates forcefully how statebuilding is possible and likely to be more successful when the statebuilder does not demand loyalty but permits legitimate leaders to achieve or retain power.

The Failure of the New Iraqi State

With the departure of the United States in 2011, Maliki became even more partisan. Within days he issued arrest warrants for his Sunni vice president, Tariq al-Hashimi, for running a death squad, as well as for his deputy prime minister and minister of finance, further consolidating his power at the expense of the Sunnis.[197] He also marginalized parliament and politicized the military and the judiciary. He is accused of detaining thousands of Sunnis without trial, pushing leading Sunnis out of the political system by accusing them of terrorism, stopping payments to the members of the Sunni Awakening, refusing to allow constitutionally sanctioned votes on regional autonomy, and suppressing peaceful protests and killing dozens of unarmed protesters.[198]

195. Robinson 2008, 144–145; see also Ricks 2009, 318.
196. Galbraith 2006, 157.
197. Schmidt and Healy 2011; Dodge 2012, 149.
198. Al-Essawi and al-Nujafi 2014. Maliki reportedly refused to step aside in August 2014 without a guarantee of immunity from possible prosecution for war crimes and crimes against humanity. See Arango 2014.

From the viewpoint of the Sunni minority in Iraq, Maliki led a Shiite state that aimed to exclude them from power. Always under the influence of Iran through his alliance with Sadr and perhaps more directly, Malaki grew increasingly close to Tehran as an alternative source of support after the U.S. forces withdrew.

Believing it was time for Iraq to manage its own affairs, the United States, and President Obama in particular, did not at the time offer much public criticism or pushback against the regime. Economic and military aid continued to flow and, in fact, was increased as the regime began to come under pressure from insurgents in 2013.[199] Despite warnings, Iraq began to spin out of control, with civilian deaths increasing from a total of 4,153 in 2011, the last year of the U.S. deployment, to 9,850 in 2013 and 17,166 in 2014. Casualties for the first half of 2015 were running about the same as for the prior year.[200]

The partisanship of the Maliki government created fertile soil for Sunni resentment and opposition. As violence in the country rose, ISIS, led by Abu Bakr al-Baghdadi, began a new insurgency in January 2014 and by June had conquered the Sunni-dominated areas to the west and north of Baghdad. On June 29, it was sufficiently ensconced in the region to publicly announce the founding of a new caliphate. The startling fact of ISIS is not that it challenged the Iraqi state but that the Iraqi armed forces collapsed so quickly when confronted with a few thousand armed militants—literally melting away during the night from lack of provisions.[201] Once challenged, the weakness of the state was only too clear, with renewed sectarian fighting on and off the battlefield beginning almost immediately.[202] With over one-third of the country beyond the control of the central government in Baghdad, both the Iraqi state and the statebuilding enterprise that created it failed in the summer of 2014.

As the Iraqi state collapsed again, the KRG seized Kirkuk, with its substantial oil reserves, and extended the borders of Kurdistan. The regional government also began plans for a referendum on independence.[203] These moves were also rooted in the partisanship of the prime minister. As described by Colin Kahl of the Center for a New American Security, "as Nouri al-Maliki has become more capable and more confident, he's actually become less inclined to reach out to those he most needs to reconcile with," especially the Kurds.[204] Seeing an opportunity to resolve the long-standing dispute with Baghdad over the boundaries of Kurdistan, the KRG seized it even though it might lead to the further dismemberment of the Iraqi state. These moves

199. On increasing violence in 2013, see Arango 2013. See also Baker 2014b.
200. Figures are from Iraq Body Count at https://www.iraqbodycount.org/database/.
201. Chivers 2014; Kirkpatrick 2014.
202. Semple 2014; Hubbard 2014; Fahim 2015.
203. Gordon and Rubin 2014.
204. Quoted in Ricks 2009, 297.

have been resisted by the international community, and even by Turkey, which had previously helped Kurdistan by allowing it to transport oil by truck to its ports on the Mediterranean coast.[205] Yet the reality of the informal dissolution of the country has put the question of formal partition on the table once again.[206] As ISIS turned its sights on parts of Kurdistan, however, the peshmerga was reinforced with Iraqi troops and assistance, and some foundation for national unity was apparent. The future of Iraqi Kurdistan remains open.

With the second failure of the Iraqi state, the Obama administration considered a range of options, from letting Iraq handle its own problems to launching air strikes on ISIS forces. Resisting calls to "leap before we look," President Obama first chose a "70 percent" option of sending special operations forces to help the Iraqi government and stepping up surveillance flights—both prerequisites to more aggressive steps—and deploying an aircraft carrier to the Persian Gulf capable of delivering air strikes.[207] At the same time, the president initially rejected a full-scale return—even if requested by the Iraqis.[208] In announcing his position, the president declared, "We do not have the ability to simply solve this problem by sending in tens of thousands of troops and committing the kinds of blood and treasure that has already been expended in Iraq. Ultimately, this is something that is going to have to be solved by the Iraqis." Still proclaiming that the United States would not become the "Iraqi air force," only days later the president nonetheless authorized air attacks on ISIS forces gathering near Kurdistan and began air relief operations for stranded refugees. In early 2015, U.S. troops returned to the country to begin retraining the Iraqi military, sometimes accompanying Iraqi units to the front lines. Slowly escalating troop numbers to 4,500, the Obama administration is trying to shore up the crumbling foundations of the Iraqi state while avoiding direct involvement and responsibility for the fight against ISIS.

Most important, it appears that the administration is seeking to avoid worsening the statebuilder's dilemma. The ISIS attacks and the failure of the Iraqi state followed the extended negotiations over a new government after the April 2014 elections, in which Maliki's party received the largest vote share but far from a majority (89 of 328 seats in parliament). Although extended negotiations have been necessary after every Iraqi election, they were especially troubling in the midst of the war with ISIS. Maliki insisted on standing

205. Arango and Krauss 2014.
206. Worth 2014.
207. Once these troops arrived, moreover, they found the Iraqi forces so deeply infiltrated by either Sunni extremist informants or Shiite personnel backed by Iran that only half of the units were capable enough for American commandos to even advise them. Schmitt and Gordon 2014.
208. Baker 2014b.

for a third term as prime minister despite pressure from nearly all factions within the country for him to step aside.

Indicating some degree of learning and certainly a sensitivity to the state-builder's dilemma, however, President Obama declared:

> Now, it's not the place for the United States to choose Iraq's leaders. It is clear, though, that only leaders that can govern with an inclusive agenda are going to be able to truly bring the Iraqi people together and help them through this crisis. Meanwhile, the United States will not pursue military options that support one sect inside of Iraq at the expense of another. There's no military solution inside of Iraq, certainly not one that is led by the United States. But there is an urgent need for an inclusive political process, a more capable Iraqi security force, and counterterrorism efforts that deny groups like ISIL a safe haven.[209]

Ironically, given Maliki's partisanship and the failure of the Iraqi state, the United States ended up in 2014 advocating for a less extreme and more broad-based government than the prime minister whom, at one time, it had selected as its loyal agent in Baghdad.

Yet there may be limits to the lessons learned by the administration. Once again, the United States stage-managed the selection of a new Iraqi leader, Haider al-Abadi, as prime minister in September 2014.[210] The set of alternatives is still vanishingly small. Although Abadi spent his exile in the West rather than Iran, he comes from the same political party and has a support coalition similar to that of the former prime minister. Although he initially reached out to the Sunnis and broadened their role in the cabinet, that Abadi had to call upon the Shiite militias to lead the war against ISIS is a worrisome sign that the state remains very weak and that partisanship still reigns. Whether the choice of Abadi eventually leads to a more legitimate government in Iraq remains to be seen, but the statebuilder's dilemma suggests that it is highly unlikely. One key question is whether the Sunni tribes that formed the backbone of the original Awakening movement will support Abadi against ISIS or whether they will stand by or even actively assist ISIS against the Shiite-dominated central government.[211] A second is whether Abadi can reach out to successfully share power and govern from "the middle" as the United States has always hoped.[212] Perhaps the only winner from the second failure of Iraq is the United States' longtime regional rival, Iran.[213]

209. Remarks by the President on the Situation in Iraq, June 19, 2014, http://www.whitehouse.gov/the-press-office/2014/06/19/remarks-president-situation-iraq. See also Obama's interview with Friedman (2014).
210. Arango, Rubin, and Gordon 2014.
211. See Lara Jakes, "Haider al-Abadi: Unabashed and Unplugged," *Foreign Policy*, April 15, 2015, http://foreignpolicy.com/2015/04/15/haider-al-abadi-unabashed-and-unplugged/.
212. See Pollack 2015; Arango 2015.
213. Barnard 2015; Cooper 2015.

Lessons from Iraq

The lessons of statebuilding in Iraq will be debated for many years.[214] Those drawn will color whether the United States and others engage in statebuilding in the future and, if so, how it will be done. By way of conclusion, I group the insights from Iraq in three broad categories: ambition, models of statebuilding, and the real dilemma.

Ambition

Regime change requires statebuilding. An external power cannot topple an existing state without replacing it with something else. This is especially true for autocratic states that have, over time, decimated civil society so as to preserve their own power. Although it may be possible for cooperation to emerge spontaneously from the anarchy that is created when political authority is removed, it is by no means guaranteed and is, in fact, rather unlikely. The biggest mistake in the Iraq War was in not anticipating the need for statebuilding after removing Saddam and his regime. Had the likely costs of statebuilding been properly assessed, the United States might not have chosen to go to war on weak evidence of Iraq's supposed weapons programs. David Kilcullen, an Australian military officer, one of the guiding lights behind the new U.S. COIN strategy, and then a special adviser to Secretary of State Rice, drew up a "field manual" in 2008 for civilians involved in postconflict operations that emphasized the difficulties of statebuilding and warned against getting involved in counterinsurgency wars if at all possible. The manual was leaked, and an interview with Kilcullen ran under the headline "Rice Advisor: Iraq Invasion Was 'F*cking Stupid.' "[215]

The failure to anticipate the need for postwar statebuilding was a systemic failure of the U.S. policymaking process. Even if members of the Bush administration were blinded by ideology, the bureaucratic process of vetting proposals and anticipating consequences failed to function. The military, intelligence, and diplomatic communities were either themselves too myopic to see the probable future or, more likely, were cowed into not raising objections by the perceived policy preferences of the president and his closest advisers. The "war gaming" ended too early in the process, even though some critics, such as General Zinni, tried to suggest as much (and were then shut out of the further deliberations). Unfortunately, this systemic failure has not produced any systemic reforms, even under the administration of President Obama, who ran in 2008 against the war.

The limited commitment of the United States to Iraq, almost entirely self-imposed absent the approval of the international community, failed to gener-

214. One early and influential attempt to draw tactical lessons is Diamond 2005.
215. F. Kaplan 2013, 284–293.

ate credibility for the new regime. The Bush administration might have checked itself in deference to international norms of sovereignty, but given its willingness to go to war without the approval of the United Nations and the minor role played by that organization in postwar reconstruction, this is unlikely to have been a significant force. Rather, the United States had a mostly free hand in deciding the extent of its involvement in the statebuilding process. Yet the effect was not entirely different than it would have been if the United Nations had granted the United States only a limited mandate. From the start, the ambition of the United States was to withdraw as quickly as possible—even after it was recognized as early as October 2003 that the emphasis on the "exit strategy" was undercutting the statebuilding project.[216] This was reflected in the absence of any plan for the postwar period, in the military strategy carried out under General Casey through 2006, and even in the surge, which was explicitly billed as a temporary expansion of force levels. Even as the insurgency waned after 2007, President Obama, having run against the Iraq War, was eager to withdraw. Overriding all other aspects of political and military strategy, the United States' commitment to Iraq was always to be of limited depth and duration.

This lack of U.S. commitment produced few incentives for societal actors in Iraq to vest themselves in the new order. Sunnis hoped to reverse the direction of political change. Shiites hoped to consolidate their new domination and, perhaps, to create a new Islamic republic modeled on Iran next door. Iraqi businesses failed to invest and focused mostly on moving their assets out of the country as quickly as possible. No one anywhere in Iraq knew what to expect of the future nor appears to have expected the new regime to last in its current form. Fighters kept fighting, stepping up attacks after U.S. forces left. Political opponents continued to oppose, even at the risk of toppling the new regime—as did Sadr on the eve of the U.S. withdrawal. The state that the United States left in Iraq was not legitimate, or, to say the same thing, society was not sufficiently vested in the new regime to defend it against challenges. This contributed to the subsequent failure of the state in 2014.

Models of Statebuilding

It is now clear that liberal statebuilding is a failed paradigm. The failure goes beyond simply the timing of elections or whether power should be divided or shared in a new regime. These are important questions of tactics, but the problem goes deeper, and so should the lesson. Democracy and free markets are laudable goals, but, as shown clearly in the case of Iraq, they necessarily alter the balance of political power within societies and challenge interests vested in the ancien régime. All political institutions privilege some social interests over others. In autocratic regimes, the elite, the military, or sectors of the

216. Bremer 2006, 216.

economy that share their rents with politicians tend to have influence disproportionate to the number of votes they control, as did the Sunnis under Saddam. Democracy shifts political power from these interests toward the majority of a country's citizens. In Iraq, this necessarily meant a massive shift in
power from Sunnis to Shiites and Kurds. Though this is one of democracy's key
benefits, leveling the political playing field and disrupting the political equipoise, democracy can be extremely destabilizing.[217] This was a significant
factor driving many Sunnis into the insurgency. Economic reform has a similar effect and was devastating for many Sunnis after 2003. Again, liberals see
this process of economic and political change as one of the benefits of market
reform. Yet these economic reforms also disrupt existing interests and, in
Iraq, served to deepen the insurgency. Oil wealth remains a tremendous source
of contention within Iraq.

Statebuilding via COIN has potential. The surge, coupled with COIN, succeeded in reducing violence in Iraq to a level at which the United States could
withdraw, the constant ambition of leaders in Washington from the earliest
days of the war. The relevant counterfactual, of course, is what might have
happened in Iraq had adequate troops been provided and COIN implemented immediately after the fall of Saddam's regime. The security dilemma
described above would likely have been moderated. There still would have
been insurgents within the Sunni community willing to fight to reverse their
political and economic losses under any new regime, but this might have
been limited to the fringe of "dead-enders" the United States thought it was
actually fighting in 2003–2004. Had the United States not rushed to elections
that allowed the Shiites to claim their majority and twist the ministries into
private militias, a more neutral state organized from above might have reduced
the ability of extremists on both sides to pull on the social fabric. Providing a
secure environment, in turn, might also have legitimated the U.S. role in
Iraq, buying it more time to ensure a smoother transition. Whether COIN
could have succeeded as a statebuilding strategy remains open, of course,
with even Petraeus noting that there is always a shelf life after which "every
army of liberation . . . becomes an army of occupation."[218]

The Real Dilemma

Neither liberal statebuilding nor COIN as implemented in Iraq obviated the
statebuilder's dilemma. The trade-off between building a legitimate state and
a loyal state was acute. The United States did desire a legitimate government
in Iraq. Indeed, in consistently pushing for a government of national inclu-
sion, it clearly put greater emphasis on legitimacy than did Maliki and his
Shiite supporters. Yet, throughout its involvement with Iraq, the United States

217. Mansfield and Snyder 2007.
218. F. Kaplan 2013, 163–164.

intervened deeply to shape the political structure and politics of the new regime to ensure that it was dominated by leaders loyal to the United States. Whether it was handpicking the members of the IGC or managing the strained negotiations over who would become prime minister in 2005, 2010, or 2014, the United States attempted to ensure that relatively pro-Western leaders sympathetic to its interests always rose to the top. As Herring and Rangwala note, "when the U.S. has had to choose between trying to build a state and trying to retain control, it has mostly chosen the latter."[219] This pro-American tilt rendered many factions in Iraq skeptical of Maliki. Indeed, as evidence of his unpopularity, Maliki and his supporters were accused of fraud in the 2010 election, and even then his party failed to earn a majority; yet he was offered the first chance to form a coalition only by a twisted reading of the constitution. In part because of his association with the United States, Maliki managed to stay in power—ironically, given initial U.S. aspirations—only through means of dubious democratic legitimacy. This was, however, entirely predictable if we understand the political incentives of both the statebuilder—the United States in this case—and the loyal leader.

At the same time, the limited number of potential leaders acceptable to Washington allowed Maliki to escape the control of his U.S. benefactors. Choosing a loyal leader does not necessarily mean that the statebuilder is entirely pleased with its options. Malaki's views as prime minister were hardly aligned with Washington's. Rather, he was simply the best available in an otherwise small set of candidates. Malaki cut deals with extremists in his Shiite coalition, notably giving Sadr and his Mahdi Army control of the Interior Ministry, that deepened the security dilemma driving the conflict. Once in office, he surprised the United States by pursuing closer ties to Iran and accepted its influence over Iraqi politics. Over time, he became at least publicly more critical of the U.S. presence in Iraq and eventually held out for terms in the SOFA that were well known to be unacceptable to the United States, leading to the complete withdrawal of U.S. forces in December 2011. Recognizing Maliki's precarious political position and his need to solidify his own coalition to sustain himself in power, neither Bush nor Obama was able to push Maliki "too hard." In the end, despite its desire to control the political evolution of Iraq, the ability of the United States to influence events was limited indeed.

In trying to balance between legitimacy and loyalty, it appears that the United States succeeded in getting neither. There was no George Washington in Iraq in 2003, no high-minded leader who might have put national stability and success over personal ambition. Given thirty years of repressive autocratic rule that destroyed civil society, it is not at all clear where such a leader might have been found. Only Sistani or Abd al-Mahdi might have had some of the necessary qualities, but the first was the highest-ranking Shiite cleric in the country and consistently advocated for his sect's interests, and the second was

219. Herring and Rangwala 2006, 161.

deemed too close to Iran. The many competitors for power from within the exile community were far too self-aggrandizing to put country first. Nonetheless, had the United States not cared about loyalty, a leader with broader public support might have emerged. But here is the dilemma. If the United States had not cared about who ruled Iraq, it would not have invaded in the first place. Any country concerned enough to bear the costs of statebuilding will inevitably care about the nature and political orientation of the new state.

5

Statebuilding in Somalia

Somalia is one of the longest-festering cases of state failure in modern history. Since independence in 1960, the Somali state has failed twice, once in 1969, when General Mohammed Siad Barre seized power in a coup amid widespread social unrest, and again in 1991, when Siad Barre himself fell from office in the midst of widespread famine. After the second failure, the United Nations, supported by the United States, undertook a largely humanitarian mission that later evolved into an effort to rebuild the fractured state. A second major statebuilding attempt began in 2002, with the foreign-brokered creation of the Transitional Federal Government (TFG), recognized by the international community as the Federal Republic of Somalia (FRS) in 2012.[1] Despite these efforts, Somalia remains a failed state unable to extend its writ much beyond the presidential palace in Mogadishu.

There are two phases of statebuilding in Somalia, each illustrating one side or horn of the statebuilder's dilemma. Somalia in 1991 was an almost ideal test bed for statebuilding. One of the first major humanitarian crises after the end of the Cold War liberated the United Nations to pursue a more active role in international affairs, and soon after its victory in the Persian Gulf War gave the United States new confidence in the uses of military force, Somalia was a near-perfect opportunity to solidify the foundations of the New World Order. The effort embodied both the euphoria of the post–Cold War era and the triumph of liberalism and the supposed end of history. Although the United States had an existential interest in stability in the Horn of Africa, a region of strategic importance largely for its proximity to the oil fields and

---

1. Pham (2011, 133–134) observes that there have been no fewer than fourteen attempts to reconstitute a federal government. The creation of the TFG was the fifteenth. For my purposes, it is more appropriate to divide the statebuilding effort into two phases, one which began in the early 1990s under United Nations and U.S. leadership, and a second that began in 2002 under Ethiopian and Kenyan leadership.

shipping routes around the Arabian Peninsula and the Persian Gulf, Washington did not have a history of deep involvement in Somali politics or any apparent bias toward any group or leader within the country. Thus, the United States promised to be a neutral statebuilder, a commitment made credible by its insistence that the United Nations take the lead role in political reconstruction. The United Nations, in turn, sought to implement faithfully the model of liberal statebuilding in which it would create a new, more legitimate state through "bottom-up" democratization. Yet in trying to reconfigure the basis of political power in Somalia, the UN effort ended, if not in disaster, then at least in a whimper of despair. At the first sign of significant resistance, the United States withdrew its forces from the war-torn country, leaving the society stateless and propelling a further descent into anarchy. The United States simply did not care enough about the future of Somalia to pay the necessary costs, and the United Nations could not sustain the statebuilding mission alone. This phase affirms that only countries concerned deeply about the future policies of a failed state will volunteer to pay the price of rebuilding that state.

By 2002 or so, in turn, a promising social movement appeared to be gaining momentum in building a new governance structure in Somalia. The Union of Islamic Courts (UIC) grew from a coalition of local religious bodies that had emerged to fill the judicial vacuum left by the collapse of the central government into a national political movement with its own militia, al-Shabab (the Youth).[2] As it rose to prominence within Somalia, however, it became increasingly radical in its religious orientation and vociferous in its nationalism, especially in its calls to unify the Somali population spread across four different states in the Horn of Africa.

Irredentism has long dominated Somalia's foreign policy.[3] The increasingly forceful irredentism of the UIC, in turn, opened old wounds with Somalia's neighbors. Ethiopia, having fought wars with Somalia in the 1960s and again in 1977–1978 over the Ogaden, and another war with Somali separatists in Eritrea, was deeply worried by the emerging regime. The threat to its still unconsolidated border regions was real and credible. In concert with Kenya, which possessed its own substantial Somali population in the North, the United Nations, and other regional states, Ethiopia created a government-in-exile in Nairobi—the TFG—in 2004. After the UIC conquered Mogadishu in June 2006 and began to establish control over the South, Ethiopia launched a major military intervention in December 2006 and installed the TFG in the capital. This foreign-imposed and decidedly pro-Ethiopian regime, however, has not succeeded in gaining legitimacy within the country or extending its reach beyond the major cities. This second phase of statebuilding in Somalia illus-

---

2. Also known as the Islamic Courts Union (ICU) and, later, renamed the Council of Somali Islamic Courts (COSIC). I use the most common appellation, UIC, throughout.
3. Lewis 2008, 36.

trates the opposite end of the statebuilder's dilemma. Creating a loyal regime—this time, one responsive to the policy preferences of Ethiopia—undermines its legitimacy in the eyes of those it would rule. Although the TFG and its successor have sustained their tenuous hold on power, Somalia as a whole remains largely ungoverned and, perhaps, ungovernable. Ethiopia's intervention into Somalia demonstrates clearly that the statebuilder's dilemma is not restricted to the United States or other great powers but is a universal problem inherent in all statebuilding efforts.

This chapter begins with a brief overview of state failure in Somalia. The second section examines statebuilding efforts after 1991, and the third section focuses on the exception of Somaliland, which broke off from the rest of the country in the 1990s, built its own autonomous governance structure, and, though not recognized as a sovereign state by the international community, is one of the few autonomous democratic regimes in Africa. As with the case of Iraqi Kurdistan, examined in chapter 4, this indigenous statebuilding success provides a useful contrast to the rest of the country and the efforts of the international community. The fourth section surveys statebuilding efforts after 2001, and especially the competition between the UIC and the TFG and the role of outside powers in both creating and coping with the statebuilder's dilemma. The chapter concludes by examining the lessons from statebuilding in Somalia.

State Failure in Somalia

The history of Somalia is complex, though at a general level the main narrative is simple enough. Somalis are often understood to be a relatively homogeneous people, sharing a common heritage, language, and culture.[4] European colonialism divided the Somali people among British Somaliland, Italian Somalia, Djibouti, the Ogaden region of Ethiopia, and Kenya's North-Eastern Province.[5] This division has left Somalia with persistent social pressures for national unification and irredentist claims against its neighbors that have contributed to its difficulties, especially in the statebuilding efforts of the new century.[6] On independence in 1960, British Somaliland and Italian Somalia were unified in the present state of Somalia—albeit against the wishes of the northerners in Somaliland, who were outvoted on the referendum by the more numerous southerners.[7]

Though not the only traditional, nonstate authorities, clans are the dominant force in people's everyday lives.[8] According to David Laitin, the inevitable

4. Laitin 1976, 449. For a skeptical view of Somalia's homogeneity, see Hesse 2010a.
5. Bryden 1995, 146.
6. Laitin 1976, 455.
7. Lewis 2008, 35.
8. Bradbury 2008, 15–19.

first question that Somalis ask of one another when they first meet is, "What is your clan?"[9] All Somalis are organized into clans, subclans, and dia-paying groups. The last is the basic unit of Somali society and consists of groups of two hundred to two thousand related families "whose members are unified by virtue of the collective obligation to pay or receive compensation or blood money for homicide and other injuries."[10] The dia-paying groups also recognize an obligation to support their members in times of emergency.[11] Dia-paying groups rarely have single leaders but are egalitarian and led by a council of elders. Strong clan identity provides the glue that holds the groups together and limits free riding. Though highly fluid in the level at which members are mobilized—sometimes at the clan level (for example, Darod) and sometimes at the subclan level (for example, Majerteen)—the clans are the primary vehicles for making political demands on the state. In turn, the state, by funneling resources through the clans, has strengthened their hold on Somali society, even in urban areas.[12] As Laitin and Said Samatar summarize their role, "the clan is the only reliable welfare system in Somali society."[13]

Divisions among clans, however, are riven by race, with most minorities being descendants of slaves from elsewhere in Africa; class, especially with the rise of a state bourgeoisie (see below); and regional identities. One of the deepest divides—interpretable either in clan, class, race, or regional terms—is between the Samaale and the Sab. The former is constituted by the so-called noble clans of the Dir, Darod, Isaq, and Hawiye, mainly nomadic pastoralists. The latter is composed of the Digil and Rahanweyn clans, primarily agro-pastoralists located mainly in the South and who speak a Somali-related but distinct Af-Maymay language.[14] Although the debate among scholars of Somalia has devolved into an argument about whether clans or race/class divisions are more important in explaining state failure, it is entirely possible that both sets of cleavages can exist simultaneously.[15] As discussed in chapter 1, such combinations of horizontal and vertical segmentation make for a particularly volatile mix, of which the sad experience of recent Somalia is a telling example.

The period after independence saw a rapid rise in centrifugal forces in Somalia. British Somaliland never accepted its integration into Somalia and remains opposed to a strong centralized state.[16] Indeed, as discussed later in the chapter, (formerly British, now just) Somaliland used the second failure of the state in 1991 to set up an autonomous and de facto sovereign govern-

9. Laitin 1976, 456.
10. Laitin and Samatar 1987, 30.
11. Ahmed and Green 1999, 114.
12. Laitin and Samatar 1987, 46.
13. Ibid., 47.
14. Lewis 2004, 495.
15. On alternative social cleavages, see Besteman 1996, 1998; Helander 1998; Lewis 2004, 2008, 6–11.
16. Ahmed and Green 1999, 115–116.

ment. The highly segmented structure of Somali society also led to a prolif-
eration of political parties, with more than sixty contesting the last democratic
election in March 1969—meaning that Somalia had more political parties
per capita than any democratic state except Israel.[17] Corruption was rampant.

As the political system was spinning out of control after the election in
1969, Siad Barre, then the highest-ranking officer in the army, seized power,
leading to the first failure of the state just nine years after its birth. Demonstrating that irregular transfers of power can be legitimate, the coup was greeted
with joy by many Somalis.[18] Siad Barre's rule demonstrates how, in the face of
strong but in this case multiple traditional authorities vying for dominance,
leaders willing to use enough coercion can stay in power for a substantial period of time. His doing so, however, distorted the economy, gutting farming
and other private economic activities, and actually served to reinforce the
role of clans in social and political life.[19]

Allying with the Soviet Union soon after the coup, Siad Barre promoted a
form of scientific socialism that promised to reduce corruption and increase
equality for Somalis, with some initial success.[20] Siad Barre subsequently na-
tionalized most sectors of the economy and prohibited traders from importing, storing, or purchasing food items, severely disrupting both the nomadic
pastoralists in the North and the agro-pastoralists in the South.[21] His na-
tionalization of the banking sector also drove borrowers to rely even more
heavily on their fellow clan members, reinforcing the hold of these traditional
authorities.

Siad Barre did attempt to reduce the salience of clans in Somali society.
One of his first moves after seizing power was to outlaw clans and all references
to them in public life; Somalis then greeted one another by asking, "What is
your ex-clan"? Despite this move, Siad Barre nonetheless played divide and
conquer with the clans quite effectively.[22] Over time, the southern clans, from
where Siad Barre hailed, came to dominate the government.[23] Although they
could not be publicly named, the special trinity of clans under Siad Barre was
widely known as MOD, after the initial letters of the corresponding names of
Marrehan, the president's own clan, Ogaadeen, that of his mother, and Dulb-
hante, that of his son-in-law, who served as head of the secret police.[24] In an
early version of the statebuilder's dilemma, massive military aid to Siad Barre,
first from the Soviet Union and later from the United States, supported his
repressive apparatus. Economic aid, funneled by donors through the state,

17. Laitin and Samatar 1987, 69.
18. Ibid., 77; Bradbury 2008, 36.
19. See Bradbury 2008, 35–45.
20. Laitin 1976.
21. Ahmed and Green 1999, 116–117.
22. Leeson 2007, 694.
23. Huliaras 2002, 159.
24. Lewis 2004, 501.

accounted for 50 percent of government spending in the mid-1980s.[25] Military and economic assistance made the state a rich prize for those who might control it and an object of competition between clans, but also allowed Siad Barre to consolidate his political support coalition—despite criticism of his human rights record from Western donors.[26]

Over time, Siad Barre became increasingly autocratic and predatory. Rather than providing public services, the "state took on the character of a privatized enterprise managed for the running elite," creating the state bourgeoisie noted above.[27] In the aftermath of the Ogaden War with Ethiopia (1977–1978), opposition groups began to organize. The war created huge refugee flows into Somalia, especially in the North. Resentment among Somalilanders intensified, as the refugees placed enormous pressure on already stressed resources and received special treatment by the government, which was actively recruiting refugees into the military.[28] The Somali National Movement (SNM) was formed in 1981 by business and religious leaders, intellectuals, and former army officers drawn from the Isaq clan, dominant in the North. When Siad Barre signed a peace accord with Ethiopia, the SNM assaulted military installations in northern Somalia, which, according to I. M. Lewis, "quickly led to the all-out civil war in 1988–91 between the regime and Somaliland's Isaq clansmen."[29] The United Somali Congress (USC) was formed in 1989. Drawn largely from the Hawiye clan in the South, the USC immediately split into two wings, with an armed militia led by Mohamed Farah Aidid and a political wing led by Mohamed Ali Mahdi, Aidid's principal rival.[30]

When a major drought swept the region and famine again struck in 1990, the clans proved their resilience as they endeavored to protect their members. Escalating pressure from the SNM and the USC and growing clan violence eventually led Siad Barre to flee Mogadishu in January 1991. With the SNM hegemonic in the North, conflict was primarily limited to the southern half of the country and the capital, where three main coalitions struggled for power. In the southernmost areas, along the border with Kenya, troops and political leaders loyal to Siad Barre's Somalia National Front fought to remain a viable political force. The remainder of the region was controlled by the USC militia. Controlling large swaths of the South, Aidid was regarded by many, himself included, as a national hero for leading the victorious fight against Siad Barre and as the rightful heir to the presidency. The area north of Mogadishu was dominated by groups loyal to Ali Mahdi, who after the fall of Siad Barre had been proclaimed interim president by his supporters at a UN-sponsored conference in Djibouti in July 1991, a conference to which Aidid

25. Leeson 2007, 694; Bryden 1995, 146.
26. See Lewis 2010, 135.
27. Bradbury 2003, 13.
28. Ahmed and Green 1999, 118; Huliaras 2002, 157–182.
29. Lewis 2008, 71.
30. Ahmed and Green 1999, 118–119.

was not invited.[31] Amid this escalating violence, the northern region of Somaliland declared its independence, an act still not recognized by the international community.

By late 1991, Somalia had clearly failed as a state—for the second time in its short history.[32] There was no central government. The clan—always a potent force in Somalia—reemerged as the primary political unit. Once Siad Barre was deposed, the opposition fragmented and interclan warfare gave way to intraclan fighting.[33] Militias competed for power across the South, using food as a weapon to gain and solidify control over their supporters. As anarchy spread, crops were destroyed by the fighting, and drought and relief aid was bottled up in the ports or stolen by the militias. Widespread famine and human suffering ensued. In 1992 alone, over three hundred thousand people died from starvation.[34] As is usual in famines, the problem was not a lack of food but its distribution—an eminently political phenomenon.[35] As the state failed, a humanitarian crisis of massive proportions ensued.

Statebuilding in Somalia, 1991–2001

After the second failure, the United Nations, with the armed support of the United States, intervened to quell the violence and deliver food to the hardest-hit areas through UNOSOM I (United Nations Operation in Somalia, April 1992–March 1992) and UNITAF (United Task Force, December 1992–May 1993). Beginning under UNOSOM II (March 1992–March 1995), the mission gradually evolved into a statebuilding effort. The statebuilder's dilemma was not acute in this first phase because the United States, in particular, did not have deep interests in Somalia. But precisely because of this lack of interests, Washington was also not willing to bear any substantial cost to help rebuild the failed state—nor did any other states step forward to volunteer.

UNOSOM I

Stepping into the maelstrom that followed the fall of Siad Barre, the United Nations first sought to mediate between the rival factions and, eventually, to rebuild the state itself. In January 1992, Under Secretary-General James Jonah first visited Mogadishu to assess the willingness of the various parties to accept UN assistance.[36] Secretary-General Boutros Boutros-Ghali then invited Ali Mahdi and Aidid to New York for negotiations, which were also attended

31. Doyle and Sambanis 2006, 147.
32. Bradbury 2008, 45–49.
33. Menkhaus 2003, 410.
34. Patman 1997, 509.
35. Sen 1981.
36. Hirsch and Oakley 1995, 17–21.

by representatives from the League of Arab States (LAS), the Organization of African Unity (OAU), and the Organization of Islamic Cooperation (OIC). A formal cease-fire was successfully negotiated and was signed on March 3. Shortly thereafter, the United Nations Security Council (UNSC) adopted Resolution 746 (1992), which dispatched a technical team to Somalia to prepare a cease-fire monitoring mechanism, approved by Aidid and Ali Mahdi.[37] On April 24, the UNSC adopted Resolution 741 (1992), establishing UNOSOM[38] to monitor the cease-fire agreement and cooperate with all Somali parties and the LAS, OAU, and OIC on national reconciliation. Although there was no state from which to gain approval, the United Nations followed standard peacekeeping practice in securing the agreement of the major warring parties prior to the deployment of UN forces.

With a force comprising up to 54 military observers, 3,500 security personnel, and 719 military support personnel and more civilian and local support staff,[39] UNOSOM's mandate was to ameliorate famine in Somalia, monitor the newly negotiated cease-fire, provide security for UN personnel and humanitarian aid workers, and reconcile the warring parties. With the possible exception of the last, none of these goals envisioned significant statebuilding or implied any obvious political role. Of these tasks, the highest priority was given to protecting food shipments and relief workers as they sought to deliver aid. Accordingly, UNOSOM focused its efforts on the more violent southern regions of Somalia, virtually ignoring the northern areas, including Somaliland. Given the negotiated nature of the UN mission, this first phase of UNOSOM was similar to previous UN peacekeeping operations, even though it involved mediating and monitoring a cease-fire within a single country.[40] If the effort had stopped or succeeded at this stage, we would regard UNOSOM as just another case of UN peacekeeping, not statebuilding.

UNOSOM's unarmed observers were initially deployed to Mogadishu, the capital, and other smaller ports to secure the delivery of relief supplies. The mission was unable to extend its reach very far into the southern countryside, where the famine was most severe. Under increasing pressure from bandits and feuding militias, several NGOs withdrew from Somalia over the summer of 1992.[41] Those that remained typically hired private security firms and sometimes the Somalia warlords themselves for protection: Save the Children spent nearly $10,000 per week hiring local gunmen to provide "security,"[42] while CARE spent $100,000 per month on bodyguards, and the International

---

37. United Nations 1996, 137.
38. The roman numeral I was added only later, once UNOSOM II was initiated.
39. Contributing countries were Australia, Austria, Bangladesh, Belgium, Canada, Czechoslovakia, Egypt, Fiji, Finland, Indonesia, Jordan, Morocco, New Zealand, Norway, Pakistan, and Zimbabwe. Total direct costs were $42.9 million.
40. Patman 1997, 510.
41. George 2005, 161.
42. Patman 1997, 515–516.

Committee of the Red Cross spent $100,000 per week.[43] This comparatively huge inflow of resources and cash into the Somali economy reinforced the power of the warlords.[44] Yet neither UNOSOM nor the private efforts of the aid community were sufficient. Food from international donors was getting to the ports but not to the people in need.

Under mounting pressure from the NGO community, the United States began Operation Provide Relief starting in August 1992.[45] This was primarily an airlift operation to support UNOSOM by dropping food supplies in southern Somalia and refugee camps in northern Kenya. The United States also transported five hundred Pakistani peacekeepers to Somalia. In late August, UNOSOM expanded its activities to include protecting humanitarian convoys and distribution centers outside the cities, but still to little effect.

The role of the United Nations was initially greeted with skepticism by at least some Somalis. Then secretary-general of the United Nations Boutros-Ghali was previously foreign minister of Egypt and had long been seen as a supporter of Siad Barre. Despite his initial cooperation, Aidid was opposed to the United Nations, and especially Boutros-Ghali, maintaining that the mission was prejudiced against him and biased in favor of Ali Mahdi, a not unreasonable impression given Aidid's exclusion from the Djibouti conference.[46] A carefully brokered deal between the special representative of the secretary-general, Mohamed Sahnoun, and Aidid was later overturned by the UN headquarters, reinforcing the warlord's beliefs.[47] The role of the United Nations, especially the deployment of peacekeepers, was also opposed by secessionist Somaliland, which feared efforts to reunite the country.[48]

UNOSOM was quickly regarded as a failure.[49] The limited humanitarian effort was not able to return the country to stability. Although negotiating a cease-fire was a significant accomplishment, this did not lead to a substantial reduction in violence or to the delivery of enough aid to the areas most affected by the drought and war. By mid-November 1992, a consensus emerged within

43. Ahmed and Green 1999, 121. Trocaire, an Irish relief agency working in Gedo near the Kenyan border, refused to pay for protection and thereby avoided some of the extortions to which other NGOs were subjected. It made clear that if threatened, it would withdraw and cease operations, and in one case it actually did retreat to Kenya and discontinue aid. This gave local elders and clan leaders incentives to protect the aid workers. See Anderson 1999, chap. 11. ACTIONAID, working in Somaliland, operated in a similar fashion. See Bradbury 1994.
44. Bradbury, Abokor, and Yusuf 2003, 462.
45. Hirsch and Oakley 1995, 39–40.
46. Ibid., 19.
47. Ibid., 26.
48. Pouligny 2006, 105.
49. There is, to be sure, some debate on this point. Several analysts believe that the famine had already been essentially overcome and that the country was thrown back into chaos by the intervention later in December. See Bryden 1995. Others argue that the first United Nations envoy, Sahnoun, had made significant progress and that if he had not been forced to resign, continuing negotiations might have rendered Operation Restore Hope unnecessary. See Stevenson 1993, 151. On his early efforts, see Sahnoun 1994.

the U.S. government at least that UNOSOM was on the wrong track, with most of the supplies falling into the wrong hands and reinforcing rather than diminishing the political power of the warlords. This spurred new action.

UNITAF

As UNOSOM was unraveling, the NGO community working in Somalia lobbied the United States for direct military engagement.[50] During Thanksgiving week, the Deputies Committee of the National Security Council developed a set of options for the president, which included the following: (1) augment the current UNOSOM peacekeepers; (2) sponsor a UN "peacemaking" force to provide security and deliver aid, and bolster it with an American quick-reaction force for armed support; and (3) lead a large-scale military effort to fix the problem aggressively.[51] To the surprise of many, President George H. W. Bush opted for the third and most forceful option. On November 24, the secretary-general issued a pessimistic report to the UNSC; one day later, President Bush offered the United Nations a U.S. force to stabilize Somalia sufficiently for stalled food and relief shipments to resume. On December 3, the UNSC passed Resolution 794 (1992) approving "all necessary means to establish as soon as possible a security environment for humanitarian relief operations."[52] The first elements of UNITAF were deployed in Somalia six days later.[53] UNITAF eventually fielded thirty-seven thousand troops from twenty-one countries, including a peak of twenty-eight thousand soldiers from the United States.[54] This was the largest external military operation in Africa since 1945.[55]

This U.S.-led multilateral force was a compromise. Although the United States made clear that it was willing to lead an official UN peacekeeping operation, the secretary-general and key members of the UNSC believed that a U.S.-led mission endorsed by the United Nations would be preferable, as "the forceful approach envisaged by the United States did not fit UN peacekeeping practice or theory at that time."[56] Thus, although UNITAF was composed of troops from many countries, it was under the command of U.S. lieutenant general Robert Johnson, who reported to General Joseph P. Hoar,

---

50. Although this was controversial, as some NGOs resisted the idea of a unilateral U.S. intervention, senior executives of the NGOs were unanimous in their support for a multilateral armed intervention with the United States at its core. Hirsch and Oakley 1995, 40.
51. Woods 1997. On the motivations of the president, see also Hesse 2014, 5–6.
52. United Nations 1996, 214–216.
53. Ibid., 34.
54. Contributors included Australia, Belgium, Botswana, Canada, Egypt, France, India, Italy, Kuwait, Morocco, New Zealand, Nigeria, Pakistan, Saudi Arabia, Sweden, Tunisia, Turkey, the United Arab Emirates, and Zimbabwe. Hirsch and Oakley 1995, 64. Net cost of UNITAF was $42.9 million.
55. Freeman, Lambert, and Mims 1993.
56. Hirsch and Oakley 1995, 45.

commander in chief of CENTCOM. Mission command and control was always entirely under the U.S. military.[57]

UNITAF was designed as a strictly humanitarian and short-term operation. The mission statement of the U.S. forces, and by implication the rest of the coalition as well, was "to secure the major air and sea ports, key installations and food distributional points, to provide open and free passage of relief supplies, to provide security for convoys and relief organization operations and assist UN/NGOs in providing humanitarian relief under UN auspices."[58] Intentionally omitted from the mission statement were a general disarming of the militias, the reviving or training of police and other local security forces, mine clearing, and the rebuilding of the country's fractured physical infrastructure. Most important, UNITAF eschewed any mandate to reconstruct Somalia's political or social systems. Indeed, plans for an extensive team of civil affairs officers and military police trainers were rejected by CENTCOM, which wanted to ensure that it was not saddled with responsibility for any statebuilding tasks.[59] Originally intended to last only six weeks, a fiction driven more by the U.S. presidential calendar than any realistic plan, UNITAF was to stabilize the humanitarian situation and build the foundation for a follow-on UN force that would seek to restore political and social order. In short, the U.S.-led rescue was to be followed by a UN-led rehabilitation. Although the United Nations always wished for a more extensive UNITAF operation—one that would cover the entire country and include disarmament—this two-phase plan was clear from the beginning and confirmed in an exchange of letters between Secretary-General Boutros-Ghali and President Bush in December.[60] Wrapping the U.S. mission in an explicit UN mandate made credible both the limited nature of its role and its commitment to neutrality in Somali politics.

UNITAF has to be regarded as a relative success, at least within its highly circumscribed mandate. Its limited humanitarian and military objectives were rapidly and successfully met.[61] As Michael Doyle and Nicholas Sambanis write, "In December 1992 the U.S.-led UNITAF temporarily became the Somali

---

57. Ibid., 49.
58. The mission statement is quoted in Freeman et al. (1993, 64). See also Kennedy (1997, 100) and Woods (1997, 159). The Bush administration adopted rules of engagement that were little more than those provided for in UN peacekeeping (UN Charter, chapter 6) operations, rather than exercising the "all necessary means" of a peacemaking (UN Charter, chapter 7) operation. Clarke 1997, 10.
59. Doyle and Sambanis 2006, 149.
60. On the differing views of the United States and the United Nations over the mission of UNITAF, see Drysdale 1997, 128. Patman (1997, 511) claims that Boutros-Ghali had a private understanding with the Bush administration for disarmament under UNITAF. See also Lewis 2010, 128.
61. Clarke and Herbst (1996, 76) argue instead that UNITAF should be regarded as a failure; having made the short-term nature of their intervention clear, the U.S.-led forces did not deter the warlords and their violence but merely created an incentive for them to lie low pending the arrival of the weaker UN forces.

Leviathan, and the roads were opened and the famine broken."[62] By mid-
January, mere weeks after the initial deployment of UNITAF troops, there
were almost no light weapons visible on the streets of Mogadishu, casualty
figures at hospitals dropped, deaths by gunshot wounds plummeted, and
shops and street booths reopened. People even returned to the streets after
dark, and schools and clinics began to reopen. By February, relatively normal
life resumed in the towns and secure sectors of the countryside.[63] Within
ninety days, according to James Woods, deputy assistant secretary of state for
African affairs during Operation Restore Hope, "UNITAF had accomplished
its mandate and was ready to withdraw. . . . The famine in Somalia had been
brought under control, a measure of tranquility restored, and some important first steps taken to start the process of reconciliation."[64] Perhaps most
important, the U.S. troops were welcomed in Somalia and earned a measure
of popular support because, as one Somali said, "we trust the Americans . . .
because they don't want anything from us."[65] Yet this same lack of interest in
Somalia would eventually be the statebuilding effort's undoing. On April 29,
1993, the United States officially notified the United Nations that it had accomplished its mission and was ready to transfer control of the operation to
the international organization.[66]

UNOSOM II

On March 3, 1993, with the active support of the new administration of President Bill Clinton, the UNSC adopted Resolution 814 (1993), which called
upon the United Nations, as before, "to assume responsibility for the consolidation, expansion, and maintenance of a secure environment throughout
Somalia" and, in new authority, requested the secretary-general to provide
"assistance to the people of Somalia in rehabilitating their political institutions and economy and promoting political settlement and national recon-

62. Doyle and Sambanis 2006, 153.
63. Hirsch and Oakley 1995, 83. The "secure" areas were somewhat limited. According to
    ibid., 81–83, in the large areas between Kismayo and the Kenyan border, and west of
    Bardera to the Kenyan border and north to the Ethiopian border, there were no UNITAF
    forces. As a result, several large militias and a large number of bandits still operated.
    Doyle and Sambanis (2006, 155) note, however, that within the first three months of UNI-
    TAF's relief operations, more aid workers were killed than in the previous two years. This
    was likely not a function of inadequate security, but rather better security that allowed aid
    workers to venture further into the famine-stricken countryside. Patman (1997, 515) ar-
    gues that the failure of UNITAF to disarm and suppress the warlords emboldened them
    to attack NGOs.
64. Woods 1997, 160.
65. Peterson 2000, 56.
66. Freeman, Lambert, and Mims 1993, 71.

ciliation." With the passage of Resolution 814, the transition from UNITAF to UNOSOM II officially began and was completed on May 4, 1993.[67]

UNOSOM II's mandate was considerably enlarged from that of UNITAF. In addition to providing security for the provision of humanitarian aid, it was now charged with installing civilian institutions, building an effective state, and ultimately transferring control to a Somali government. Moreover, it was expected to operate over the country as a whole rather than just in the South, as had UNITAF (although it never ventured into Somaliland), and do all this with fewer troops and resources. UNOSOM II was a peacemaking (UN Charter, chapter VII) rather than a peacekeeping operation. In this effort, the United Nations clearly claimed for itself responsibility as the primary state-builder in Somalia.

With the creation of UNOSOM II, the American force in Somalia was greatly scaled back, falling to fewer than five thousand troops. UNOSOM II was headed by Admiral Jonathan T. Howe (Retired), the U.S. special envoy to Somalia.[68] The overall military commander of the UN forces in Somalia was a former NATO commander, Lieutenant General Cevik Dir from Turkey (replaced in January 1994 by General Aboo Samah Bin-Aboo Bakar from Malaysia). The deputy commander was U.S. general Thomas Montgomery, who simultaneously served as commander of all American forces in Somalia. Of the U.S. troops in Somalia, approximately three thousand served in logistics, communications, and intelligence positions and reported directly to Montgomery in his capacity as UN deputy commander. None of these "logistics" forces were deployed for combat. Another eleven hundred troops were stationed on ships off the Somali coast in a quick reaction force (QRF) intended to support UN troops in emergencies. The QRF reported not to the UN command but to the U.S. Central Command (CENTCOM) in Tampa, Florida. Tactical control over the QRF was delegated in specific instances to Montgomery in his role as commander of all U.S. forces in Somalia.[69] Finally, in August 1993, a unit of U.S. Army Rangers was added to the American contingent. This unit

67. United Nations 1996, 262–263.
68. The appointment of a retired American admiral as the United Nations special envoy is now seen, at least by some in the U.S. diplomatic community, as a mistake. Although the United Nations wanted an American to head the operation to keep the United States involved and to reassure other countries of this fact, Howe's military background introduced an unfortunate degree of ambiguity into the lines of authority. Given his background, Howe felt competent to get involved in military operations and planning and exercised his ties to the Pentagon directly rather than going through more traditional diplomatic channels. His presence also served to make UNOSOM II more of a U.S. operation than was intended. Interviews with Herman J. Cohen, then assistant secretary of state for African affairs, November 13, 1996; Robert Houdek, then deputy assistant secretary of state for African affairs, November 13, 1996; and an anonymous Department of Defense official, November 12, 1996.
69. United States, Senate, 1993, 70–75, 94–104.

reported not to Montgomery but directly to CENTCOM.[70] In UNOSOM II as well as UNITAF, all American combat forces remained entirely under U.S. command. Nonetheless, demonstrating the United States' lack of interest in statebuilding in Somalia, the responsibility for everything from political reconciliation to designing new state institutions remained with the United Nations.

With the withdrawal of the UNITAF forces, UNOSOM II was greatly weakened, with only seventeen thousand troops (excluding the QRF) remaining in Somalia in early May 1993.[71] This was far less than the authorized troop strength of twenty-eight thousand, and nearly twenty thousand less than the peak deployment in UNITAF. Moreover, many of the replacement forces were just arriving, often unprepared, and UNOSOM II was only beginning the difficult task of forging a unified command.[72] Rather than being the hoped-for seamless web, the transition from UNITAF to UNOSOM II left the United Nations in a precarious position and the forces themselves in a situation of maximum vulnerability. UNOSOM's ability to protect relief shipments necessarily suffered under these reduced forces, as did efforts to enforce its now broader mandate.

Following the script of liberal statebuilding described in chapter 3, UNOSOM's statebuilding efforts revolved around a system of district, regional, and national councils that was developed at a national reconciliation conference in Addis Ababa in January 1993.[73] The accord reached at that meeting outlined a two-year process intended to transfer authority from the United Nations to representative institutions developed by the Somalis. The first district councils were created in spring 1993, about the time of the transition from UNITAF to UNOSOM II.

The councils were intended to be a bottom-up institution with three primary layers of organization.[74] District councils were to be created and twenty-one members appointed through election or consensus in accordance with Somali custom. The councils were responsible for public health, education, and safety. Regional councils were to be composed of three members from each district council, and were responsible for police and judicial functions, a census, and humanitarian, social, and economic programs delegated by the national

70. Clarke and Herbst 1996, 73.
71. Contributors included Australia, Bangladesh, Belgium, Botswana, Canada, Egypt, France, Germany, Ghana, Greece, India, Indonesia, Ireland, Italy, Kuwait, Malaysia, Morocco, Nepal, the Netherlands, New Zealand, Nigeria, Norway, Pakistan, the Philippines, Republic of Korea, Romania, Saudi Arabia, Sweden, Tunisia, Turkey, United Arab Emirates, United States, Zambia, and Zimbabwe. Net cost was $1.6 billion.
72. United Nations 1996, 50.
73. Note that this effort began, then, under UNITAF. In fact, UNOSOM continued to function through the UNITAF period. Although its role in protecting relief efforts was superseded by UNITAF, it continued to monitor the cease-fire and to develop a plan for national reconciliation.
74. United Nations n.d.

council. At the highest level, a body known as the Transitional National Council (TNC) was established with seventy-four members. Each regional council appointed three members to the TNC, one of which was reserved for a woman—a marked departure from Somali tradition.[75] Each of the fifteen major factions in Somalia also had one representative, and Mogadishu received five additional seats in recognition of its large population.

In actuality, however, the councils were largely a top-down initiative. The architecture was designed by UNOSOM with little local input. In turn, the councils themselves were formed with substantial guidance from UNOSOM's political division, and especially its head, Dr. Leonard Kapungo. Visiting each district, Kapungo asked the residents to compile a list of members, but also insisted on a fair division of seats among the various constituent groups of each district.[76] Although clan leaders played an important role in assembling the lists, UNOSOM demanded a more representative membership (including women) than would have arisen from traditional processes alone. In this way, the district councils were intended to create a more democratic or at least more broadly representative system than Somalia had previously experienced.

This statebuilding effort was, at most, a mixed success. Within the United Nations, statebuilding progress came to be measured by the number of district and regional councils formed rather than by how self-sustaining or effective these entities were. A field study of the first district councils, carried out one year after they were created, found that "there existed widespread feelings, both among ordinary people and among council members, that the councils had been too much a creation by UNOSOM and that the councils would vanish when UNOSOM pulled out." The study also determined that the councils did not have many tasks, that many met only infrequently, and that few constituents could actually name their councilors. Nor could constituents point to actual concrete accomplishments. For example, "in one district (Baydhabo) it was claimed by one of the council members that the council had constructed some wells. These wells were, however, never pointed out and it remains unclear whether they were not in reality the private property of that councilor." The study concludes that while many councils enjoyed local goodwill, they had limited ability to act. Most of their activities focused on certifying applications for UNOSOM funds.

The council system, in turn, engendered considerable opposition, especially from the warlords and Aidid in particular. This focus on the councils was a sharp break from practice under UNOSOM I and UNITAF. The earlier missions had chosen to work through rather than around the warlords in order to secure the delivery of humanitarian aid. This implied that, by the time

75. Hirsch and Oakley 1995, 98. Since the TNC was composed of representatives from the regional councils, which in turn were composed of members of the district councils, this required that lower levels include some women members as well.
76. The material in this paragraph and the next is based on Helander, Mukhtar, and Lewis 1995.

of UNOSOM II, the warlords were the real power brokers in the country. The councils, on the other hand, sought to empower a new, more broadly representative set of interests. This hardened the warlords, and especially Aidid, against the councils. Aidid argued somewhat disingenuously that under the Addis Ababa Accords, UNOSOM had no right to interfere with or be involved in creating local government structures. His real objection, however, was that he controlled few of the councils and therefore viewed them as a direct challenge to his aspirations.[77] As the strongest military leader in Somalia, Aidid correctly recognized that any attempt to build order on principles other than force would leave him at a political disadvantage. As a result, Aidid actively worked to undermine the councils and retain his role as intermediary between local supporters and the United Nations and the United States.

UNOSOM's efforts under the guise of national reconciliation make clear that statebuilding remained a priority throughout, that it began early in the mission, and that it emphasized an inclusionary model of participatory institutions designed from the top and imposed on local actors. With relatively few resources and little apparent oversight from UNOSOM, the councils were neither able to restore order themselves nor to provide the public goods for which they were formed. Actively opposed by some, they did not succeed in establishing themselves as important local institutions upon which their constituents could or should depend. In short, contrary to the conditions for success discussed in chapter 1, they failed to create expectations of stability, vested interests, and thus the legitimacy they would need to survive over the longer run.

Over the spring of 1993, relations between Aidid and the United Nations deteriorated, especially as UNOSOM began an inconsistent and incoherent effort to disarm various factions.[78] This was easily interpreted as an effort targeted at Aidid, and indeed he was singled out by many within the United Nations as the single largest source of opposition to their statebuilding efforts. Rather than accept defeat, Aidid decided to challenge the United Nations while it was still weak and potentially vulnerable, launching a major assault against a contingent of Pakistani peacekeepers on June 5 and provoking an all-out war between himself and the UNOSOM II forces.[79] In response, the UNSC passed Resolution 837 (1993), which encouraged the secretary-general to "take all necessary measures against all those responsible for the armed attacks . . . including against those responsible for publicly inciting such attacks, to establish the effective authority of UNOSOM II throughout Somalia, including to secure the investigation of their actions and their arrest and detention for prosecution, trial, and punishment." Although the resolution did

---

77. Hirsch and Oakley 1995, 135–136.
78. Pouligny 2006, 118.
79. According to Woods (1997, 169), "from Aidid's perspective, the UN had invaded Somalia, had sought by innumerable actions to diminish his stature and power, and in June had declared war on him." See also Patman 1997, 519.

not identify Aidid by name, it did single out his organization, and there was no doubt who was in the crosshairs.

Another turning point was the "Bloody Monday" attack on July 12 by UN forces on a meeting in Mogadishu of the elders of the Habr Gedir clan, later described by Admiral Howe as a terrorist planning cell but which was in reality a follow-up meeting to one he held with the same elders only days before. In a scene of startling brutality, U.S. Cobra gunships decimated the compound where the meeting was taking place with sixteen TOW missiles and 2,020 rounds of 20 mm cannon fire. The Somalis interpreted the killing as a deliberate signal of UN resolve, a message that was underscored in Howe's public remarks on the attack. Scott Peterson, a journalist who was nearly killed by a Somali mob after the attack, concludes that this was "the day that Somalis turned almost unanimously against the U.N."[80] With the United Nations eager to match Aidid's June 5 challenge, the statebuilder lost "any moral high ground" and, more important, became an explicit partisan in the internal power struggle in Somalia.

As the violence escalated over the summer, the United States joined in the "hunt" for Aidid.[81] After four U.S. soldiers were killed by a land mine on August 8, President Bill Clinton ordered the Rangers to Somalia with the explicit task of capturing Aidid.[82] The conflict culminated in the ill-fated raid on Aidid's headquarters in southern Mogadishu on October 3, 1993, immortalized in the movie *Black Hawk Down*. This raid was planned, approved, and executed entirely by U.S. forces and CENTCOM, which, fearing leaks (of which there appeared to be many), notified Howe, Montgomery, and UNOSOM of the operation only as it was beginning.[83] In a heavy battle, two U.S. helicopters were shot down and eighteen Rangers were killed, seventy-five were wounded, and one was taken hostage. The body of an American serviceman was dragged through the streets of Mogadishu past a jeering crowd of Aidid's

---

80. Peterson 2000, 127.
81. At the time, and in many postmortems since, much emphasis was placed on "mission creep" or the expansion of the mission under the Clinton administration. As the above makes clear, UNOSOM II's mandate was carefully crafted and adhered to by all parties. The expanded mission of the United Nations, and in turn of the United States in its supporting role, was laid out at the beginning. In this sense, there was no mission creep. Where policy did go off the rails was in the ill-fated hunt for Aidid. This was, in part, structural, a response to Aidid's understandable if unfortunate attempt to block the United Nations' statebuilding effort. It was also a matter of policy and vision, however. Sahnoun, from the United Nations, and Oakley, the American intermediary, both viewed Aidid as central to the peace process and sought to ensure that he was involved and respected. The United Nations and Howe, in turn, tended to regard Aidid as a troublemaker who could and should be politically marginalized. The latter view eventually took hold in the U.S. government as well. Interviews with anonymous Department of Defense official, November 12, 1996, and Cohen, November 13, 1996.
82. Hirsch and Oakley 1995, 122.
83. United Nations 1996, 55, 331.

supporters. Ill-prepared UN troops eventually had to be mobilized quickly to rescue the U.S. forces.

The hunt for Aidid had serious consequences for statebuilding. Not only did outright violence between UN peacekeepers and Aidid's forces increase, but UNOSOM II's tactics began to produce heavy collateral damage and drew "increasing criticism from the media, NGOs, and even anti-Aidid Somalis."[84] In a series of incidents in September, hundreds of Somalis were killed and dozens of UNOSOM peacekeepers were wounded. As American troops pursued Aidid's forces, they arrested scores of Somalis, including some peaceful bystanders and aid workers, thereby alienating the population. As ever more military resources were absorbed into the fight with Aidid, humanitarian operations were neglected and reduced by two-thirds in Mogadishu and by half in the interior.[85] Where UNITAF had previously succeeded in the foundational role of delivering essential relief to starving peoples, UNOSOM II now abandoned that goal in an elusive quest to arrest a power broker who would not consent to its vision of a new, more democratic Somali state.

As UNOSOM II's legitimacy eroded, in turn, opinion in Somalia and elsewhere turned against the mission. The UN compound was referred to by Somalis with disgust as the "Camp of the Murderers."[86] Retaliations against aid workers, journalists, and troops rose. As a result, many NGOs fled Mogadishu for Nairobi, as did the UNOSOM humanitarian coordinator.[87] The growing hostility of the population was now returned by UNOSOM II staff. "Among members of UNOSOM the feeling spread very rapidly that the population was 'entirely hostile' to them. Typically, gatherings of crowds and assemblages are greatly feared in such contexts . . . social and community actors frequently spoke of their impression that members of missions . . . seemed, in fact, 'to be afraid of the people.' "[88] By the latter part of 1993, the United Nations could not even count on support from Aidid's opponents. In the minds of many Somalis, the UNOSOM troops and the U.S. QRF had become "forces of oppression."[89] Whatever fragile support UNOSOM II might have inherited from UNITAF quickly dissipated, and along with it societal backing for the council system it was trying to erect. The tragedy is that of the $1.6 billion allocated to UNOSOM through the end of 1993, only about 4 percent was expected to enter the Somali economy, and most of this went to the warlords for "protection."[90] A surprising amount went to constructing the UN compound in Mogadishu (with a 9 percent profit for Brown & Root, the U.S. contractor building the camp) and a $9 million sewer system, which itself totaled more

84. Hirsch and Oakley 1995, 125.
85. Ibid., 123.
86. Peterson 2000, 79.
87. Hirsch and Oakley 1995, 123.
88. Pouligny 2006, 146.
89. Ibid., 175–179.
90. Lewis 2002, 280.

than that spent outside the compound on "infrastructure repairs" in the same period.[91] While seeking greater democracy, the legacy of UNOSOM may well have been the entrenching of the political power of the warlords.

The End of Phase 1 Statebuilding

Following the firefight between the Rangers and Aidid's forces on October 3, 1993, the United States reversed course and began to withdraw from Somalia. Although the public pulled back in horror from a humanitarian mission gone awry, the actual loss of life in Somalia was roughly equivalent to that in the earlier and "successful" interventions in Grenada and Panama.[92] Nonetheless, public support within the United States quickly evaporated, and the deaths crystallized growing doubts within the Clinton administration about statebuilding. While announcing that additional reinforcements would be sent to Somalia, President Clinton pledged on October 7 that all U.S. troops would be out of the country by March 31, 1994.

The U.S. retreat signaled the end of the UN mission. On February 4, 1994, the UNSC passed Resolution 897 (1994) revising UNOSOM's mandate to exclude coercive actions. After the U.S. withdrawal, twenty thousand UN troops remained behind to keep the peace and facilitate statebuilding. By March 2, 1995, all these UN troops had been withdrawn as well. With this final evacuation, the involvement of both the United States and the United Nations in Somalia was terminated, leaving a bitter legacy.

Despite propitious circumstances, statebuilding failed in Somalia. First, Somali experience, especially under Siad Barre, has been that the state is a predatory entity, legitimate perhaps only to those clans and elites that control its coercive apparatus. Conversely, historically, balances of power between traditional clans and intraclan policing have been effective in restraining conflict—even though the equilibria in this balance-of-power system were fragile and often broke down into sporadic violence. Whereas the international community clearly prefers that a "state" govern Somalia, local sentiment is, at best, ambivalent, and sees greater potential for more traditional forms of governance.[93] This resistance to any form of political centralization creates an immediate hurdle for any would-be statebuilder.

Second, Siad Barre's demise and the ensuing violence reinforced the clans as central providers of public goods to their members. Acutely insecure, members retreated into their clans for protection and basic necessities, invoking the emergency provisions of their dia-paying groups—although pretty much

91. Peterson 2000, 165.
92. In eighteen months in Somalia, an estimated thirty American soldiers were killed. In Grenada, nineteen were killed in a few days, and in Panama, twenty-three were killed in the attempt to arrest General Manuel Noriega on drug charges. Johnston and Dagne 1997, 202.
93. Menkhaus 2003, 408.

everyone faced the same extreme conditions. In the absence of a state, the clans have provided whatever public goods and services are available. As their role has expanded to fill the vacuum created by the state's failure, any new public authority would undermine the renewed and expanded authority of these traditional political actors. Preserving the structure that had rendered Somalia a highly fractionalized state in the first place, as explained in chapter 1, the clans blocked any new state from emerging.

Third, the humanitarian assistance and the way it was distributed elevated the power of warlords who rely on violence. The tremendous influx of resources into Somalia, and especially the "protection" payments made to the warlords by the NGOs and the United Nations, shifted the balance of power toward the militias and created new vested interests in rule by the gun. Indeed, the most active area of the economy today is transshipment, not because Somalia is naturally advantaged with ports but because the absence of effective government allows the smuggling of goods into the country and then on to others in the region. This activity has arisen precisely because the state is unable to police its borders; but the interests vested in transshipment, along with the warlords—often one and the same—now conspire to keep the state weak.[94] Any consolidation of public authority would greatly weaken the warlords, who not only gain authority from protecting their followers but also benefit from numerous "illegal" activities like piracy that flourish in the absence of public authority.

Fourth, the attempt to reconstruct Somalia along more inclusive, democratic lines disrupted society, challenged the role of the clans, threatened the political power of the warlords, and ultimately led to significant resistance to the United Nations and, in turn, the United States. Mistaking the liberal model for reality, statebuilders in Somalia failed to recognize that democracy is not, itself, inherently legitimate or legitimizing.

Finally, and perhaps most important, the explicitly temporary and short-term nature of the international intervention—especially that by the United States, the only power with substantial combat resources on the ground in Somalia—undermined the credibility of the UN statebuilding effort and failed to encourage any of the vesting that would have been necessary for success. The warlords in particular chose to stand and fight rather than accept the new world being built around them. As UNITAF indicated, more force was not necessary. Rather, what was needed was the resolve to endure challenges, and this was distinctly lacking.

Altogether, the failure of statebuilding in Somalia, and especially the liberal model of statebuilding as described in chapter 3, was obvious by the time the United States withdrew its forces in 1993–1994. Surprisingly, this failure did not lead to substantial rethinking of the liberal model, nor did it change the practice of statebuilding, as we saw in the case of Iraq before 2007. Whatever prom-

94. Bradbury 2003, 20–21; Menkhaus 2003, 417.

ise statebuilding might have had in Somalia was lost by the lack of commitment of the United States.

The Statebuilder's Dilemma, Phase 1

It was precisely this lack of will, however, that both obviated the statebuilder's dilemma during the 1990s and led to the failure of statebuilding. Somalia is a curious anomaly, an exception that affirms the rule, if you will. In Somalia, as in many other failed states around the world today, especially in Africa, the United States or other possible statebuilders lacked any substantial interests in the political future of the country. In most instances, the lack of interests produces "non-cases," countries that fail without any international effort to rebuild them. Perhaps it was the euphoria of the Cold War victory. Perhaps it was the desire to consolidate the New World Order. Perhaps it was an idiosyncratic decision by a lame-duck president looking to burnish his reputation or, more cynically, burden his successor with a new albatross. Whatever the reason, the United States undertook a humanitarian mission in a clearly failed state that eventually grew into a statebuilding effort despite a lack of any real interests in Somalia. Although the United States had general interests in stability in the Horn of Africa, these were not enough to justify any substantial cost in blood and treasure. As analysts observed, once "America was free [after the Cold War] to pursue its own interests in Africa"—that is, once U.S. policymakers could move beyond containing communism—"it found it didn't have any."[95] Rather, in this unusual case, the United States chose to intervene without "good reason." It is the anomalous status of this humanitarian mission, an "out of equilibrium" case, that allows us to observe a statebuilding effort in the absence of interests in the new state. Here we can see clearly the problems created by a lack of interests in the future of the state.

This lack of interests in the country allowed the United Nations and the United States to emphasize the legitimacy of the new state. Indeed, there was no interest in—and early on, an explicit attempt to avoid—any involvement in the internal politics of Somalia. The United States took pains, and worked through the United Nations as a signal of its commitment to neutrality, to avoid partisanship or any appearance of supporting one possible leader over another. This allowed the United Nations to carry out the liberal model of statebuilding in close to pure form and to attempt to create new, more inclusive, and more representative political institutions with the goal of creating a democratic and thereby, it was assumed, a legitimate government in Somalia. The implementation of this model, of course, was carried out without sufficient attention to the realities on the ground or its consequences for existing power brokers within Somalia. This brought the United Nations into conflict with Aidid, setting off a chain reaction that culminated in withdrawal. But

95. Hesse 2014, 3.

this was different from the other horn of the statebuilder's dilemma where the statebuilder promotes a leader loyal to its interests in the country. The problem in this first phase, at least, was not the inevitable trade-off between legitimacy and loyalty but rather the lack of interest that led to an ephemeral commitment to statebuilding.

The Somaliland Exception

Somaliland shares many features with the rest of Somalia, including a common culture, extreme poverty, and a clan-based social structure.[96] It also experienced intense violence both under Siad Barre, who sought to destroy the region in response to the growing rebellion in the 1980s, and from the subsequent civil war to remove the dictator from power. As the War-torn Societies Project described it:

> Somaliland in 1991 was a scene of awesome devastation. Those who chose to struggle back from the refugee camps in neighboring Ethiopia found their homes demolished, their belongings looted, their land sown with mines and unexploded munitions. In Hargeysa, a town of nearly 300,000 people, barely 10% of the structures remained intact, leaving only a vast field of blasted rubble strewn with explosives. Less than 1% of its prewar population lived there. Burco, to the east, had suffered roughly 70% destruction, and countless villages in the interior had been razed to the ground. Hospitals, schools, clinics and wells had all been destroyed, government offices ransacked, bridges blown up, and roads mined and made impassable. Mines lay so thick across the country (the exact number is not known, but is estimated at nearly one million) that many towns and rural areas had become uninhabitable.[97]

Yet by 1997 the region was relatively peaceful and had begun the slow process of rebuilding itself without any significant international aid or assistance. After two "false starts" of renewed violence in the early and mid-1990s, it has enjoyed uninterrupted peace;[98] demobilized thousands of young gunmen and melded them into a national army;[99] restarted its economy; restored public services, including police, education, and health; and nearly doubled public revenues.[100] Although denied international recognition as an independent country, Somaliland has clearly emerged as an effective state within a failed

---

96. Bradbury 2008, 9. Others argue that Somaliland was nomadic pastoralist, whereas the South was agro-pastoralist, and that they differ in culture, language, and social structures. Ahmed and Green 1999, 115.
97. WSP 2005, 24; Ahmed and Green 1999, 115.
98. Bradbury, Abokor, and Yusuf 2003, 462.
99. Gettleman 2007e.
100. WSP 2005, 18.

state—"the most positive political achievement" within Somalia since its collapse.[101]

The Somaliland exception, if you will, begins with its differing colonial experience.[102] In the scramble for Africa in the late nineteenth century, Britain seized Somaliland, whereas the South was colonized by Italy. Britain governed lightly, largely using the region as a source of fresh meat for its garrison across the Red Sea in Aden. Critically, it ruled through the existing clan elders, keeping this traditional governance mechanism alive and preserving the historic skepticism of Somalis toward centralized government. Italy governed the South more directly, importing an army of Italian bureaucrats, encouraging Italian investment and plantation agriculture, and building Mogadishu into perhaps the most beautiful city in Africa.[103] When decolonization arrived in the Horn of Africa in 1960, the British Somali Protectorate and Somalia Italiana merged in what was then expected to be a larger Somali union (including Djibouti, the Ogaden region of Ethiopia, and the Northern Frontier District of Kenya). Nonetheless, union was controversial.[104] As noted, Somalilanders rejected union in a plebiscite, and were further alienated by the South's push for rapid integration and direct rule.[105] Somaliland existed as an independent country for five days between independence from Britain and the formation of Somalia. It is this brief status as an independent country on which the claim to Somaliland's sovereignty now rests. Recognizing the international norm on territorial integrity, Somaliland claims that it is not seceding from Somalia but revoking a failed federation agreement.[106] So far, such arguments have fallen on deaf ears within the international community.

Unlike the rest of Somalia, which simply disintegrated after the fall of Siad Barre, Somaliland essentially fought its own war of independence against the regime, galvanizing society and forging a more unified identity.[107] The SNM, which led the rebellion, also articulated a vision for the future that blended "traditional Somali egalitarianism" based on clans and traditional institutions of governance and "the requirements of good central government."[108] Nonetheless, the SNM ultimately could not transform itself into an effective government, with its brief period of rule followed by a return to civil war between 1994 and 1996.[109]

Somaliland also possesses a slightly less complex clan structure than does the rest of Somalia.[110] The Isaq clan comprises more than 70 percent of

---

101. Quote from Lewis 2008, ix. See S. Kaplan 2008.
102. Bradbury 2003, 18; Huliaras 2002, 158.
103. Bradbury 2003, 12.
104. Bradbury 2008, 32–35.
105. Ahmed and Green 1999, 116.
106. On the territorial integrity norm, see Zacher 2001.
107. Bradbury 2008, 61, 72.
108. Ibid., 63.
109. Ibid., 73, 88–90, 115–121.
110. Ibid., 91.

Somaliland's 2.5 million inhabitants.[111] This same clan formed the core of the SNM, which led the rebellion against Siad Barre. The peace in Somaliland and rebuilding of an effective state cannot be attributed to this fact, however, as soon after Siad Barre's overthrow the Isaq declined into intraclan violence lasting from 1992 through 1994 and fracturing the SNM. No hegemonic clan or unified party existed to lead the society after the civil war. Somaliland could have spiraled down into chaos as did the rest of Somalia after 1991.

Instead, Somaliland took a different path.[112] Most important, potentially destabilizing conflicts were managed by the traditional councils of elders, representing the various clans and subclan factions.[113] De facto, the councils came to take on many of the responsibilities normally performed by governments. They held numerous conferences that were locally financed and managed, mediated between clans and subclans, persuaded the militiamen to give up their armed pickups (technicals) and heavy guns, and protected the main port at Berbera from falling under the control of any single clan, thereby ensuring that some public assets survived.[114] Between February 1991 and June 1996, there were no fewer than thirty-two major reconciliation conferences in Somaliland.[115] As Asteris Huliaras suggests, "by solving disputes at the level of traditional social organizations . . . the elders were able to deprive the politicians of the possibility of making war, and thus helped to create conditions of peace."[116] The elders succeeded in this role because of their traditional legitimacy and the respect they earned from successful mediation. Where warfare and "protection" payments to the warlords undermined the elders in the rest of Somalia, their role and status were reinforced in Somaliland by their ability to produce and preserve at least a minimalist social order.

Only after laying this foundation and stabilizing the region did Somaliland move toward reconstituting state institutions. The Borama conference (January–May 1993) wrote a new national charter, creating a two-year transitional government under Mohamed Haji Ibrahim Egal, the last prime minister of Somalia before Siad Barre's coup. It also designed a hybrid system of government with a bicameral legislature, including an elected lower house and a Guurti or upper house of clan elders, a president, and an independent judiciary. Importantly, through the Guurti the role of the clan elders was institutionalized within a democratic system of government.[117] Also noteworthy was that the non-Isaq clans received disproportional representation in the

---

111. Huliaras 2002, 158.
112. On politics in Somaliland, see Lewis 2008, chap. 4; Fergusson 2013, chap. 10; Harper 2012, 125–141; and Mills, Pham, and Kilcullen 2013, chap 5.
113. Renders 2007.
114. Gettleman 2007e; Bradbury, Abokor, and Yusuf 2003, 459–460.
115. WSP 2005, 64; Bradbury 2008, 95–105.
116. Huliaras 2002, 160.
117. Bradbury, Abokor, and Yusuf 2003, 460.

lower house.[118] As the transitional government was expiring, however, new violence broke out in November 1994 (lasting until October 1996). This was finally resolved by another elder-led national reconciliation conference that suspended the national charter and extended the term of President Egal for another four years. Although a governmental structure was in place, the councils of elders still played a critical role in mediating conflicts and restoring peace when violence broke out. Government continued to rest on the foundation provided by traditional, nonstate authorities.

A final constitutional crisis was resolved by the fortuitous death of President Egal during surgery in South Africa. As his extended four-year term was again expiring, Egal became increasing autocratic and began arresting his political opponents. Taking Somaliland to the brink of civil conflict, the crisis was finally averted by another reconciliation conference that extended his term for a final year to allow more time for political organizations to form and elections to be organized. During this year, however, Egal died and was immediately succeeded by his vice president, Daahir Rayaale Kaahin, from another clan. Egal's death served to level the playing field and persuaded opposition groups to reenter the political process.[119] Since then, Somaliland has enjoyed three peaceful and successful rounds of multiparty elections.[120] Although the elections originally scheduled for 2008 were postponed several times due to political instability in regions of Somaliland, they were eventually held in 2010. Opposition candidate Ahmed Mahamoud Silanyo won the three-way race with a plurality of the vote (49.6 percent), defeating the incumbent Kaahin (33.3 percent). Although problems with voter registration lists have repeatedly led to postponements of legislative elections, including another postponement in May 2015 for twenty-one months, Somaliland is one of the few functioning democracies in Africa and the only one in the Horn.[121] By comparison, Somalia has not had free elections since 1969.

It is important not to exaggerate the success of Somaliland. Although it is a functioning democracy, many irregularities in elections persist. Its economy now depends heavily on remittances from abroad, and its public health indicators remain as low as those elsewhere in the region.[122] Marked disparities in wealth persist, and the government bureaucracy is ineffective and corrupt.[123] Whether its democratic experiment can be sustained in the face of international resistance and, now, reincorporation within the federal system of the

118. WSP 2005, 64.
119. Bradbury, Abokor, and Yusuf 2003, 464.
120. Gettleman 2007e.
121. Hansen and Bradbury 2007. On the 2015 postponement, see the criticism of the British Foreign Office on May 13, 2015, available at http://www.somalilandpress.com/wp-content/uploads/2015/05/Somaliland-Elections.-Written-Statement-on-Behalf-of-the-International-Community-@-13-May-2015.pdf. On Somaliland as a "hybrid" but not democratic regime, see Hoehne 2013.
122. Huliaras 2002, 163. On improvements in social services, see Bradbury 2008, chap. 7.
123. Bradbury 2008, 5.

FRS established in 2012 (see below) remains an open question. Nonetheless, in a situation of social anarchy, clans reemerged as the dominant actors within society. Although struggles over redistribution and control of the state threatened violence, cooperation among the elders served to limit conflict and create a minimalist social order that protected people, property, and promises. The councils of elders were able to achieve this result because of the legitimacy they retained from tradition and their success in preserving the peace.[124] Only once this social order was in place were new state institutions erected—and their success depended on the continuing stability provided by inter- and intraclan cooperation.

Somaliland has achieved this success almost entirely on its own. Without international recognition, it has received little in the way of aid from the United Nations or even from NGOs, who do not receive significant contracts from governments or international organizations to work in the area.[125] Nor has Somaliland been able to borrow on international financial markets. Political reconstruction has been largely an internal affair, albeit bolstered by substantial remittances from abroad.[126] Indeed, although it may be unique to Somalia and its historic skepticism toward centralized rule, this lack of international recognition and the resources it can provide may have contributed to political stability in Somaliland by keeping the government weak.[127] When society fears centralized and overweening authority, the absence of explicit statebuilding may actually help support effective states.

Most important, its international isolation has protected Somaliland from the statebuilder's dilemma. Not only has it been free from external actors trying to reconstruct a centralized state, but there has been virtually no attention paid to the leadership of this internationally unrecognized state—always assumed by outsiders to be temporary pending reintegration into a unified Somalia.[128] Not without its difficulties, evidenced by delayed elections, the selection of leaders in Somaliland has been an entirely internal affair. Like Iraqi Kurdistan (discussed in the previous chapter), the case of Somaliland suggests that not only are external actors unnecessary for effective statebuilding but that their presence may actually inhibit indigenous political processes from selecting leaders and creating new institutions responsive to local conditions and traditions that can ultimately legitimate the state.

---

124. Ibid., 246.
125. Ahmed and Green 1999, 124; Bradbury 2008, 92, 157. Nonetheless, aid to Somaliland constitutes a substantial fraction of government revenue. In 2002 it received a total of $43 million in aid, which was approximately double the reported government revenue of $20 million.
126. Bradbury, Abokor, and Yusuf 2003, 458. Unusually, the thirty-nine peace conferences in Somaliland held since 1991 have all been managed and financed without external support. Mills, Pham, and Kilcullen 2013, loc. 598.
127. See Bradbury, Abokor, and Yusuf 2003, 462.
128. Bradbury 2008, 106–108.

Statebuilding in Somalia, 2001–Present

Two largely unrelated developments brought Somalia back onto the international statebuilding agenda early in the new century. First, the terrorist attacks on the United States on 9/11 raised the salience of ungoverned spaces from which future strikes might be launched.[129] Although it had no direct connection with the attacks, Somalia was the most visible ungoverned space in the world.[130] In addition, al-Qaeda was reported to have established an early presence in the country, training forces loyal to Aidid and participating in attacks on U.S. forces in UNITAF.[131] By the late 1990s, al-Qaeda had established a substantial presence in East Africa, primarily in Sudan but also in Somalia, and had carried out attacks on the U.S. embassies in Kenya and Tanzania. After 2001 it was not unreasonable to fear that al-Qaeda and other terrorists might flee to the ungoverned spaces of Somalia. By default, the country became implicated in the global war on terror.[132]

Second, after a decade of failed statebuilding attempts, the UIC began to achieve and consolidate some measure of authority over the country. Although this might have been welcomed by the international community, the UIC was immediately worrisome because of its Islamic identity and irredentist program. According to the journalist Mary Harper, "the USA and others seemed incapable of perceiving what was initially a loose alliance of highly localized sharia courts as anything other than an al-Qaeda-linked threat," a perception fed by the warlords supported by the United States.[133] More important, though, was the threat the UIC posed to its neighbors, especially Ethiopia and Kenya, who feared renewed calls for a greater Somalia. As explained below, this fear led to new efforts to build an alternative to the UIC in the form of the TFG, nurtured in Kenya starting in 2002 and brought to power by Ethiopian troops in 2006.

The Union of Islamic Courts

After the withdrawal of UN forces, Somalia reached an uneasy but nonetheless viable equilibrium. In the absence of a state, a variety of indigenous institutions arose that kept violence in check, including the traditional clan structures that served as mutual deterrents to the escalation of disputes. Somewhat more ominously, the warlords became vested in the anarchic system, exerting the political power that flows from the barrels of guns and engaging in the illicit activities of extortion, gunrunning, drug smuggling, and so on that would not be possible under an effective state. Piracy also grew dramatically starting

---

129. Elmi 2010, 74–75.
130. Lewis 2010, 186–188.
131. J. Miller 1999.
132. Ibrahim 2010.
133. Harper 2012, 170. See also Verhoeven 2009.

in the late 1990s, rising to attacks on 237 ships in 2011.[134] Even many in the Somali business community, which would have undoubtedly gained from a well-governed state, preferred the status quo to the uncertainties of a new regime, the likely violence that would be entailed in any transition, and the possibility that any reconstituted state would revert to the predatory behavior of its predecessors.[135] Indeed, with private authorities substituting in part for public authority in large parts of the country, and the otherwise illicit activities that grew outside the eyes of any state, the quality of life was not obviously worse than, and may actually have been improved from, the last years of Barre's rapacious rule.[136] Within Somalia, statebuilding was not necessarily a high priority; at the very least, it was an activity that some significant groups opposed and to which others were merely indifferent.

Local Islamic courts—often quite local, sometimes covering only a few city blocks or small villages—have a long history in Somalia of adjudicating disputes. In the failed state, these local courts grew in importance and substituted for state authority, even as their existence and efficacy made it more difficult to consolidate authority at the center. As Somalia descended into anarchy after the fall of Siad Barre and especially after the withdrawal of the UN peacekeepers, the local Islamic courts became ever more important to social and political life and a welcome alternative to the more capricious rule of the warlords.[137]

As they began to expand in the early 2000s, however, the local courts immediately fell afoul of a "ragtag coalition of warlords," recently organized by the United States into an Alliance for the Restoration of Peace and Counter-Terrorism (ARPCT) and funded by the CIA to combat extremist groups in Somalia.[138] Facing this armed opposition, the courts unified into a single entity with a clearer authority structure—the UIC—and quickly formed an alliance with al-Shabab (the "youth"), originally a militant club of about three dozen Islamic fundamentalist teenagers that later grew into a full-fledged militia.[139] Although clearly Islamist and favoring a harsh form of Sharia law in areas they controlled, the UIC and al-Shabab at this stage were still relatively moderate.

By June 2006, after intense fighting with ARPCT, the UIC seized Mogadishu. After many years of violence and extortion by the warlord militias, the group finally brought a measure of peace and stability to the capital. Over the second half of 2006, the UIC spread throughout the southern half of Soma-

134. ICC 2014. On the political context of piracy, see Pham 2010.
135. See Hesse 2010b. On the resilience of the informal economy, see Mills, Pham, and Kilcullen 2013, chap 4. On the fear of predation by the state, see ICG 2011, i.
136. Menkhaus 2003, 2006/2007; Leeson 2007; Powell et al. 2008.
137. Barnes and Hassan 2007, 152; Verhoeven 2009; Elmi 2010, 63; ICC 2014.
138. Lewis 2008, 85–86; Pham 2013, loc, 249. See also Shabazz 2006; Fergusson 2013, 63. The CIA apparently funded the ARPCT at the level of $150,000 per month.
139. Barnes and Hassan 2007, 154.

lia, taking the port of Kismayo in September. Despite their demands for the veiling of women, prohibitions on musical entertainment and the chewing of qat (a mild stimulant widely used by Somalis), and harsh punishments for law-breakers, the UIC grew in popularity because it established a degree of security in the areas it controlled, cleared trash and provided other public services, reopened the airport, and began the process of figuring out the competing property claims that had exploded during the previous years of anarchy.[140] "Because the courts emerged from a grassroots level to perform some of the key functions of government in a stateless society," Mary Harper concludes, "they were increasingly viewed as legitimate authorities by the communities they served."[141] Indeed, as the International Crisis Group reports, the UIC's "imposition of public order and basic government services promised an end to long years of state collapse and earned it 'performance legitimacy' among Somalis."[142]

Although perhaps the last best hope for indigenous statebuilding in Somalia, the UIC gradually became more radical. A critical figure in this process was Sheikh Hassan Dahir Aweys, a former leader of al-Itihaad al-Islamiya, a far more extremist group that adhered to the Wahhabi strain of Islam found in Saudi Arabia, and considered a terrorist organization by the United States.[143] Aiming to establish an Islamic theocracy in Somalia, Aweys and others in his "indigenous" faction of the UIC, as it was first known, were fundamentally nationalists focused primarily on domestic affairs.[144] Aweys transformed al-Shabab into a significant fighting force and promoted the interests of his Ayr subclan within the organization, causing moderates to defect, including Sheikh Sharif Sheikh Ahmed, who later became president of the TFG.[145]

Beyond the pursuit of an Islamic state in Somalia, which alienated the United States, the UIC also drew support from Eritrea, Ethiopia's longtime enemy, and promoted Somali irredentism as a theme to rally nationalists. Igniting old fears, this renewed irredentism worried all the neighboring states with significant Somali populations.[146] As Ken Menkhaus describes the situation:

> The ICU [UIC] declared jihad against Ethiopia, hosted two armed insurgencies opposed to the Ethiopian government, made irredentist claims on Ethiopian territory, and enjoyed extensive support from Ethiopia's enemy, Eritrea, which was eager to use the ICU to wage a proxy war against Ethiopia. In short, the

140. Ibid.
141. Harper 2012. See also Gettleman 2006.
142. ICG 2008, 33. See also Mills, Pham, and Kilcullen 2013, loc. 180.
143. Elmi 2010, 75.
144. This faction is distinguished from the "international" faction, dominated by foreign jihadi fighters. Fergusson 2013, 102.
145. Ibid., 65 and 107. The rise of former UIC moderates within the TFG raises the interesting question of why earlier compromises with the UIC were impossible.
146. Barnes and Hassan 2007, 155.

hardliners in the ICU did everything they could to provoke a war against Ethiopia, and in late December (2006) they got their wish.[147]

Thus, the initial success of UIC suggests that the difficulties of statebuilding in the face of domestic interests entrenched in violence can be overcome. Although the international community might have otherwise welcomed an indigenous statebuilding effort in the failed state that was Somalia, it was the Islamist and irredentist nature of that state that provoked widespread concern. In the end, Somalia's neighbors, backed by the United States and allied with domestic forces opposed to the UIC and state consolidation more generally, decided to replace this organically developed, indigenous, and potentially legitimate state with a more loyal one that would not threaten their interests.

External Statebuilding Efforts, Phase 2

After the withdrawal of U.S. and UN forces in the mid-1990s, periodic efforts were made to form a national government for Somalia. One promising effort was the Transitional National Government established in May 2000 at the Somalia National Peace Conference held in Djibouti, but which failed to gain support of important warlords, including Aidid, and was opposed by Somaliland and Puntland.[148] Continuing negotiations, held in Kenya under the auspices of the Intergovernmental Authority on Development (IGAD) and supported by the United Nations, the European Union, the African Union, and the League of Arab States, produced agreement on the TFG in November 2004.[149]

Departing from the liberal statebuilding script that insisted on a rapid return to elections, the TFG contained a unicameral parliament with 275 appointed members, "endorsed" by traditional clan elders and vetted by the IGAD facilitation committee. Membership was allocated on a "4.5 formula," in which the four major clans (Darod, Hawiye, Dir, and Digil-Mirifle) received sixty-one parliamentary seats each and the remaining clans together received a total of thirty-one seats. The parliament then selected the president, who appointed the prime minister, who in turn selected the council of ministers. The first president of the TFG was Abdillahi Yusef Ahmed, a founder of the Somali Salvation Democratic Front, which had fought against Siad Barre and—important for the statebuilder's dilemma explained below—was closely allied with Ethiopia.[150]

147. Menkhaus 2009, 225. See also Lewis 2008, 88–89.
148. Lewis 2010, 183–184.
149. Somaliland refused to participate. Bradbury 2008, 200.
150. See Hanson and Kaplan 2008.

In a hopeful sign, the TFG began negotiations with the UIC in June 2006 for a power-sharing agreement, including joint army and police forces. These talks ultimately failed. After the UIC succeeded in taking Mogadishu that same month against intense fighting with ARPCT forces, the TFG called upon its ally, Ethiopia, for assistance. Ethiopia responded by sending fourteen thousand troops to help retake the capital and the southern parts of Somalia. In the midst of a complex power struggle within the UIC, the TFG-Ethiopian forces in late December captured Mogadishu in a rout and retook the strategic city of Kismayo on January 1, 2007. Al-Shabab fighters fled into the "impenetrable bush" at the Kenyan border, and UIC leaders escaped to Eritrea.[151]

Plagued by internal divisions, once installed in power the TFG proved unable to pacify Mogadishu or even extend its control beyond the few blocks of the capital area.[152] According to James Fergusson, "the TFG's 'army' is actually an uncertain alliance of clan militias" prone to desertion and as likely to shoot one another as al-Shabab.[153] Facing their historic enemy, Ethiopia, a complex insurgency of al-Shabab, clan militias, and other armed groups fought back viciously and effectively.[154] Continuing violence forced over seven hundred thousand refugees to flee Mogadishu alone and transformed the city, once again, into an "urban battleground."[155]

Confronting renewed civil war, the African Union Mission in Somalia (AMISOM) was finally deployed in late 2007, a long-delayed peacekeeping mission with troops originally from nonneighboring states, primarily Uganda and Burundi, but later expanded to include Kenya and Ethiopia.[156] Although the AMISOM force is supposed to support the TFG (later FRS) army, in actuality it still takes the lead in the continuing fight against al-Shabab.[157] Despite hundreds of casualties, however, AMISOM also failed to establish control over even the central district of Mogadishu.[158] Unable to win on the battlefield, the TFG formed an alliance in June 2008, brokered by the United Nations in Djibouti, with moderates formerly associated with the UIC, now within the Alliance for the Re-liberation of Somalia (ARS). In addition to an agreement

---

151. On infighting in the UIC, see Menkhaus 2009, 225. On the flight to Kenya, see Harper 2012, 83.
152. The grim headlines from the era tell the story. See the titles of four articles filed in a little over one month by Gettleman (2007a, 2007b, 2007c, 2007d). See also Menkhaus 2009, 226.
153. Fergusson 2013, 15.
154. Menkhaus 2009, 226; Moller 2009, 17.
155. Harper 2012, 173.
156. AMISOM replaced the long planned but never fielded IGASOM peacekeepers, first proposed in March 2005. In January 2007, the African Union proposed to create AMISOM, which was approved by the UNSC in February.
157. Fergusson 2013, 14–15.
158. Ibid., 17.

on the withdrawal of Ethiopian troops, replaced by augmented forces in AMISOM, the parliament was extended by two years and expanded to 550 seats to accommodate new ARS members. The new parliament then appointed Sheikh Ahmed, a former UIC leader and chair of ARS, as the second president of the TFG.

After 2007 the UIC—now dominated by al-Shabab—grew rapidly to over five thousand fighters, including some Americans from the Somali diaspora. Having driven out the remaining moderates and killed others, the Ethiopian invasion of 2006 had the unintended consequence of further radicalizing the UIC, consolidating the control of its most violent faction. Significantly weakened, it has still managed to make the country "virtually ungovernable." Though formed to lead a counteroffensive against al-Shabab in the South, the new TFG coalition government, led by Sheikh Ahmed, steadily lost ground. From controlling about 70 percent of south-central Somalia in 2008, inherited from the Yusef Ahmed government, the TFG area of control fell to only about 20 percent of the region by early 2011.[159] Publicly joining al-Qaeda in February 2010, al-Shabab was the only affiliate of the global jihadist network to control large territories.[160] Intense fighting in the region forced many to flee to Kenya, creating a refugee crisis at the border.

In October 2011, Kenya invaded southern Somalia in a long-planned operation to suppress al-Shabab fighters and establish a buffer zone at the border, the troops from which were later incorporated into AMISOM.[161] Although Ethiopia had withdrawn its forces in 2009, its army rejoined the fight against al-Shabab in November as well. These efforts, in the view of James Fergusson, "surely finished" al-Shabab "as an occupying military force, let alone as a viable alternative system of government for Somalia."[162] This judgment was, perhaps, premature. Al-Shabab subsequently announced in August 2011 that it was withdrawing from Mogadishu. Called a "victory" by the TFG, it appears that this move was more a reversal of tactics by al-Shabab rather than a visible sign of success by TFG forces and AMISOM.[163] Al-Shabab has subsequently focused on terrorist attacks in Kenya, largely intended to force that country to withdraw its forces from Somalia so as to level the playing field in its war against the central government.

With its mandate extended twice, the TFG met in Garowe, Somalia, in February 2012, in association with IGAD to begin negotiations on a new constitution and a permanent government, ultimately producing agreement on the

159. Garowe online 2011.
160. On relationship with al-Qaeda, see Shinn 2011. Affiliation with al-Qaeda was pushed by the so-called internationalist faction within al-Shabab, led by Sheikh Moktar Ali Zubeyr. Fergusson 2013, 102.
161. Fergusson 2013, 368–369. On Kenya's motivations, see Hesse 2014, 11–12.
162. Fergusson 2013, 381.
163. Harper 2012, 87.

new FRS in June, with the new constitution coming into effect on August 20. The basic structure of the government remains the same as under the TFG, although the legislature is now bicameral, with a lower house of 275 representatives and an upper house limited to 54 members. Deviating from the liberal playbook for statebuilding, members of both houses are nominated by a National Constituent Assembly of clan elders and then vetted by a Technical Selection Committee. The new parliament chose Hassan Sheikh Mohamud as president on the second round of voting; he then appointed the defeated incumbent president as prime minister. On the one hand, Sheikh Ahmed's acceptance of the parliamentary election result, as well as that of the other power brokers in Somalia, suggests a new era in Somali politics. On the other hand, that the president, prime minister, and parliamentary Speaker colluded to pack the Constituent Assembly with Sheikh Ahmed's supporters and that election fraud was also rampant suggest stronger continuities.[164]

Despite continued limits on the reach of the FRS's authority, the United States recognized the new government in January 2013, appointing its first ambassador to Somalia in twenty years in June 2014. Recognition by the United States and others then allowed Somalia to rejoin the IMF and the World Bank and begin new borrowing. Yet even with international recognition and the inflow of new resources, Somalia remains a failed state.[165] The FRS cannot broadcast power even to all neighborhoods in Mogadishu, and piracy remains a significant if somewhat attenuated problem.[166] Al-Shabab remains a potent force in much of the country, able to carry out attacks against the government and neighboring countries, including one in Kampala, Uganda, in July 2010 that killed seventy-four people, and a second in Nairobi, Kenya, in September 2013 that killed sixty. In July 2014, al-Shabab was still strong enough to attack the presidential palace in Mogadishu.[167] Even after the formation of the new government, Somalia remains number two on *Foreign Policy*'s Failed State Index for 2015, surpassed only by South Sudan.[168] Most discouragingly, famine once again returned to Somalia in 2014.[169]

164. Seats in parliament were reportedly selling for as much as $25,000. The Persian Gulf states apparently gave Sheikh Ahmed $7 million for bribes. Seeking to keep most of the money for himself, Sheikh Ahmed apparently offered smaller bribes than his competitors and thus lost the election. Pham 2013, loc. 700–711.
165. On the continuing weakness of Somali political institutions, see Bryden 2013; Dias 2013; and ICG 2008, 7–9.
166. Incidents of piracy have fallen from a high of 237 in 2011 to 15 in 2013. On piracy in Somalia more generally, see Harper 2012, chap. 5.
167. On the continued weakness of the Somali state, especially in relation to al-Shabab, see ICG 2014.
168. See http://foreignpolicy.com/fragile-states-2014/.
169. Agence France-Presse 2014. On the 2011 famine, see Fergusson 2013, 132.

The Statebuilder's Dilemma

After 2001, Ethiopia took the lead in statebuilding in Somalia by creating and supporting the TFG, along with support from the international community, the United States, and other neighboring states.[170] It is here, for Ethiopia and, to a lesser extent, Kenya, that the statebuilder's dilemma took hold. Accused by many of actually preferring a weak and internally divided Somalia, Ethiopia was primarily concerned with Somali irredentism, especially once it became a key plank of the UIC platform under Aweys.[171]

Territorial disputes have long existed between Ethiopia and Somalia. Lewis grounds such tensions in the "protracted 'holy wars' (jihads), which raged in the Middle Ages between Christian Ethiopia and the surrounding Islamic sultanates" in what is today's Somalia, as well as the expansion of the Ethiopian Empire into the region in the nineteenth century.[172] More proximately, as explained above, Somalia's border was somewhat arbitrarily drawn by European imperialists in ways that left substantial Somali populations in all the neighboring states. Ethiopia and Somalia have long clashed over the Ogaden, inhabited primarily by Somalis but part of Ethiopia, fighting major wars in 1964 and 1977–1978 over the region.[173] Over the years, Somalia had also been an active promoter and supporter of secessionist groups in neighboring countries, especially Eritrea.[174] On the key issue of the Ogaden and greater Somalia more generally, Ethiopian and Somali preferences are diametrically opposed and quite distant from one another, resembling the extreme version of figure 3.1b.

The UIC played to Somali nationalism by reasserting rights to all territory inhabited by Somalis, including a threat by Aweys to seize the Ogaden.[175] While a decade and a half of anarchy had put Somali irredentism on hold, the consolidation of a new Islamic-nationalist state threatened Ethiopia's core territorial interests. Although Kenya was more concerned with trying to insulate itself from the growth of al-Shabab, which threatened to spill over onto its territory, especially its Swahili coast, Ethiopia's primary goal was ensuring that a moderate government would come to power in Somalia that would not challenge the territorial status quo.[176] According to the International Crisis Group, Ethiopia's "principal fear" is the "rise of a strong, centralist, nationalist or Islamist state . . . that would revive irredentist claims on Ethiopian terri-

---

170. Ethiopia's involvement through IGAD began soon after the collapse of Somalia. Elmi 2010, 102. On Kenya, see ibid., 97–98; ICG 2012a, 2012b.
171. On Ethiopia's preferences, see Elmi 2010, 96–97; Aime 2013, 33–35; Hagmann 2014, 29; Hesse 2014, 9–10.
172. Lewis 2008, 2, 28–29.
173. On the Ogaden, see Hagmann 2014.
174. Lewis 2008, chap. 2.
175. Harper 2012, 33.
176. Elmi 2010, 103.

tory and, like Eritrea, sponsor armed insurgencies inside the country."[177] Along with the international community, this overriding aspiration was central to the formation of the TFG in Kenya and Ethiopia's propelling it to power with armed force in 2006.

The TFG, as well as its successor, the FRS, was and largely remains a creation of Ethiopia. Described as the "Ethiopian candidate," the TFG's first president, Yusef Ahmed, appointed as his prime minister Ali Geedi, a politically inexperienced veterinary professor who nonetheless had direct ties to Ethiopian prime minister Meles Zenawi.[178] The rest of the cabinet was carefully selected from different clans but consisted entirely of members who nonetheless shared the president's pro-Ethiopian views.[179] According to Afyare Abdi Elmi, Ethiopia under the guise of IGAD imposed "a charter, parliament, and government on Somalia" and subsumed the sovereignty of the state.[180] Subsequent leaders have been less blatantly pro-Ethiopian, including Sheikh Ahmed, who, as a former leader of the UIC, criticized Ethiopia's involvement in Somali affairs. Nonetheless, Ethiopia remains the power behind the throne, with its forces, though now integrated into AMISOM, still central to the stability of the FRS.

As predicted by the statebuilder's dilemma when policy preferences are far apart, Ethiopia has been successful in getting the loyal government it sought but not in securing legitimacy for that regime. Derided by critics as "being a puppet of neighbouring Ethiopia," Somalis nicknamed the TFG *daba dhilif*, which roughly translates as a government set up for a foreign purpose, or a satellite government.[181] Widely understood to be an Ethiopian proxy opposed to Somali territorial claims and unable to quell the violence—indeed, blamed by many for fomenting the violence when Ethiopia drove the UIC out of Mogadishu—the TFG failed to achieve legitimacy from virtually any corner of Somali society.[182] Although the TFG has been widely proclaimed by the United Nations and the European Union as the sole "legitimate" governing power in Somalia, Lewis writes that "this was definitely not the view of the general Somali public" and that the "TFG soon found itself confronting growing public hostility to its claimed status."[183] In emphasizing loyalty, Ethiopia fatally undermined the legitimacy of the new state it helped create.

---

177. ICG 2008, 1–2. The combination of Islam and irredentism was feared by Ethiopia given its prior experience with al-Itihaad al-Islamiya, a group established in the 1990s by Aweys that sought a union of all Muslins in the Horn of Africa. Pham 2013, loc. 260.
178. Lewis 2008, 84.
179. On Yusuf's status as an "ally" of Ethiopia, see Moller 2009, 20. On this cabinet, see Hanson and Kaplan 2008.
180. Elmi 2010, quote on 94; see also 105.
181. Quote from Menkhaus 2009, 224. Nickname from Harper 2012, 177, 188–196.
182. As Harper (2012, 177) again notes, "the USA, the U.N. and others failed to recognize that, for a government to be considered legitimate by Somalis, it cannot be associated with foreigners."
183. Lewis 2008, 84–85.

Although it remains concerned with instability in the Horn of Africa, the United States was a crucial but secondary actor in this second phase of statebuilding in Somalia.[184] Already engaged in two land wars, in Afghanistan and Iraq, where casualties were rapidly mounting, the United States was unwilling and unable to engage in any new statebuilding effort. As earlier, U.S. interests were not implicated deeply enough to compel an already stretched nation to deploy troops to yet another conflict. Beyond its existential interest in stability in the Horn, the United States was now mostly concerned with preventing the radicalized UIC from consolidating its authority within Somalia.[185] Ungoverned space, worrisome though it might be, was less threatening than a fundamentalist Islamic regime allied with al-Qaeda. U.S. officials tried not to "Americanize" the conflict and consistently depicted statebuilding as a Somali or regional problem.[186] Recognizing that it shared interests with states in the region, the United States essentially transferred responsibility for statebuilding to Ethiopia. As then acting assistant secretary of state Charles Snyder phrased it, the United States does not "want to be the bus driver. We'd like to sit in the third row on the bus. We don't want to sit all the way in the back of the bus, but we don't want to be the bus driver."[187] The United States limited its role to advising the TFG forces, sharing intelligence, deploying the navy to suppress piracy off the coast, sending special forces teams after January 2007 to hunt down suspected al-Qaeda operatives, and providing ninety-four tons of arms and ammunition in May and June 2009. It has also carried out several drone strikes against suspected terrorists within Somalia. Overall, its role is to support Ethiopia and, when necessary, identify and kill suspected terrorists, but not to fight al-Shabab directly or build a new Somali state.[188] In this sense, the role of the United States in Somalia has remained broadly similar before and after 2001. The statebuilder's dilemma has been felt mostly in Ethiopia, though the United States also suffers from the trade-off between the desire for a legitimate government in Somalia able to govern its territory effectively and the need for an acceptable regime.

The continuing failure of the Somali state cannot be blamed on a misguided liberal strategy of statebuilding. The TFG and FRS are power-sharing agreements in which leadership is established through elite negotiations brokered by external mediators. The 4.5 formula and clan-appointed representatives in parliament created a power-sharing system that has yet to hold national elections or build other institutions associated with liberal democracy. Similarly, neither the TFG nor FRS has sought to win or buy hearts and minds. With official international recognition came new international aid,

184. For a plea for less U.S. engagement, see Samatar 2010.
185. Barnes and Hassan 2007, 151.
186. Fergusson 2013, 30.
187. Elmi 2010, 82.
188. Menkhaus 2009, 231; Elmi 2010, 62, 84.

the lifting of the arms embargo, and resuscitated trade relations. This was not enough, however, to provide many public services to the population given the continuing lack of security throughout the capital and southern regions of the country.

This lack of state capacity, however, is rooted in the lack of social support for the state and its leaders, which in turn is founded in the statebuilder's dilemma. The externally sponsored state, seen by many as a proxy for Somalia's longtime regional nemesis, Ethiopia, has yet to gain the legitimacy necessary to tip society in its direction. Indeed, the government remains dependent on what Lewis calls the "Ethiopian occupation."[189] According to the International Crisis Group, "far from shoring up the government's shaky legitimacy," the Ethiopian intervention "has deepened public disaffection, inflamed Somali nationalism, and intensified the pace of religious extremism and radicalization."[190]

As the statebuilder's dilemma implies, the presidents of the TFG and FRS, as foreign-backed leaders, have focused on creating narrow political coalitions to support themselves in office. Yusef Ahmed, for instance, was criticized as "unwilling to create a genuinely broad-based government, forming instead a factional coalition that exacerbated divisions and rendered the TFG non-functional, incapable of delivering the bare minimum of the transitional agenda." Accordingly, he "built a largely subservient and loyal apparatus by putting his fellow Majerteen clansmen in strategic positions," including in the National Security Agency and so-called Majerteen militias within the army that have been accused of operating "above the law" and carrying out human rights abuses.[191] Sheikh Ahmed's administration did not fare much better.[192] When al-Shabab attempted to encircle the TFG in Mogadishu in the summer of 2009, the president's own Harti subclan clan was reluctant to defend him, taken by Peter Pham as "a strong indicator of his near total lack of legitimacy."[193] As expected in a narrow coalition with access to foreign aid, corruption is also rampant. Indeed, though he has denied it, Sheikh Ahmed is accused of diverting 70–90 percent of Somalia's $1.5 billion in foreign aid; of the $75.6 million in bilateral aid received between 2009 and 2010, only roughly $2.9 million (3.8 percent) can be accounted for.[194] Much of the foreign aid, it appears, has not been used to build a new state but has been directed to building a narrow support coalition and the personal finances of regime insiders.

Whether the FRS will be able to shed its ties to Ethiopia, earn legitimacy, and consolidate its authority remains to be seen. Political opponents of the

189. Lewis 2008, 90.
190. ICG 2008, 1.
191. Ibid., 4–5.
192. ICG 2011.
193. Pham 2013, loc. 282.
194. Mills, Pham, and Kilcullen 2013, loc. 49–54; Pham 2013, loc. 317.

FRS have continued to portray the regime as a puppet of Ethiopia and seek to rally support through explicitly anti-Ethiopian appeals and anti-American propaganda. They have successfully cast themselves as the "true Somali patriots."[195] If the opposition ever comes to power, the external statebuilders know that it will be extremely hostile to their interests, causing Ethiopia and, to a lesser extent, the United States to support even more fully the loyal regime they have decided to back. According to Lewis, the Somali government is likely to obtain legitimacy if and only if it sheds its ties to Ethiopia.[196] As Greg Mills, Peter Pham, and David Kilcullen conclude: "A solution to Somalia's challenges or, for that matter, those of any other failed state, will not ultimately come from a person more acceptable to foreigners. Although that will help spin the international aid faucet open, a form of governance can be constructed only by allowing locals to build it from the base themselves, however precarious and chaotic this may be."[197]

Lessons from Somalia

The failure of statebuilding in Somalia over the past two decades follows from a lack of interest and commitment by the United States and the international community more generally in the 1990s, and from too much interest and meddling from regional states in the new century. This sad experience yields important insights and implications, which, as in the previous chapter, I group under the headings of ambition, strategy, and the statebuilder's dilemma.

Ambition

The first phase of statebuilding in Somalia demonstrates the problem of too few interests. The U.S. role in Somalia was in many ways a fluke, an anomaly, begun perhaps on a whim by a lame-duck president caught up in the euphoria of the New World Order. Without significant interests in Somalia, the United States was an almost ideal statebuilder, playing a relatively neutral role under UNITAF in the internal affairs of the country, and pulled into a more partisan role only as UNOSOM II began a larger statebuilding program. After the deaths of eighteen servicemen, however, the United States bolted, reflecting its lack of commitment to the statebuilding mission. Without the United States, the United Nations lacked the resources to sustain its operations, and it too soon withdrew. Humanitarianism can, in principle, be

195. ICG 2008, 14.
196. Lewis 2008, x.
197. Mills, Pham, and Kilcullen 2013, loc. 810.

a sufficient motivation. But in practice statebuilding is a very costly undertaking. Without specific interests in the future policies of the country, external powers will not intervene to assist or, if they do, will withdraw as soon as the costs become evident.

This "statebuilding lite" mission of the early 1990s was doomed to fail. The limited ambition of the United States meant that its commitment to statebuilding in Somalia was also limited. This was immediately recognized by all parties in the country, who conditioned their behavior on expectations of rapid withdrawal. Few expected the new regime promoted by the United Nations to "stick," and even fewer invested assets on this basis. The warlords were happy to take money from the United Nations, NGOs, and the United States, but they invested not in running for office or building political constituencies but in more weapons. These expectations were confirmed when the increasingly violent "war" on Aidid led the United States to withdraw after October 1993. If the statebuilder lacks commitment, so will local leaders who might otherwise be encouraged to accept and work within new institutions.

In this way, a critical mistake by the United States and the United Nations was the explicitly limited and short-term nature of their mission to reestablish order in Somalia. From the first days of UNITAF, it was clear that the United States would act only to reestablish a measure of order to facilitate the delivery of humanitarian aid; it would quickly devolve responsibility for statebuilding to the United Nations, and even then the collective commitment to statebuilding would be of limited duration and magnitude. This time-delimited commitment did not encourage Somalis to invest in a new order. Instead, it created perverse incentives for those actors who would lose under a new regime to wait out the United Nations and continue to threaten and use violence to block the emergence of a stable system of governance. Isolated internationally, Somalilanders took a longer-term view and actively sought to resolve their conflicts and build peace in their war-torn region. Statebuilding is an all or nothing undertaking. Those without the commitment to go all in will have little effect on the game.

This all changed in the second phase of statebuilding in Somalia, creating at least a chance for success. The TFG had no right to succeed. It was not remarkably different from prior attempts by the international community to stop the violence and form the rudiments of a new Somali state. The TFG held together because of the commitment of Ethiopia, and to a lesser extent other regional states, to make it work. There was little doubt that Ethiopia was committed to the proxy regime it was supporting and continues to support with the assistance of the African Union forces. The emphasis on loyalty has created real problems of legitimacy for the TFG and its successor. Yet the FRS is now, with external support, a fact on the ground to which Somali society is beginning accommodate itself. As society adjusts itself to the FRS, new interests may eventually vest themselves in the regime and develop legitimacy over time—but "may" is by no means a certainty. If the FRS succeeds, it will largely be because of the open-ended commitment of the regional states.

Strategy

Despite initial optimism, Somalia was a statebuilding failure for the international community. Although tragic, this record of failure gives us some empirical leverage on different strategies of statebuilding. First, after the initial humanitarian phase, statebuilders in Somalia, led by the United Nations, sought to implement a liberal theory of statebuilding premised on constructing more representative and participatory institutions from the bottom up. Yet, as became all too evident, more participatory institutions do not by themselves legitimate a new state. Starting under UNITAF, but developed more fully under UNOSOM II, the district councils became an end in themselves for the United Nations and an institution that had to be defended against the warlords they were designed to sideline. With few powers and fewer resources, the councils never became important actors in community development and, likewise, failed to gain support and legitimacy. Without legitimacy at the local level, where their contributions to stabilizing the country might have been most evident, the district councils could not then legitimate the regional or national-level councils. In the end, the councils were a top-down United Nations creation that, while more representative, failed to gain acceptance by the only group that really counted, the Somalis themselves. By the same token, the attempt to impose more representative institutions on Somalia may have actually disrupted domestic politics and worsened the crisis. As the UN statebuilding effort was expanded and based on more inclusive principles, Aidid, who had the "best" claim on the presidency due to his role in overthrowing Siad Barre, reacted in what should have been predictable ways by declaring war on the UN peacekeepers. In this case, democratization likely made the situation worse rather than better. Conversely, traditional institutions in Somaliland eventually spawned a quasi-state that is increasingly recognized as one of the most democratic in Africa. Yet one must be cautious in recommending indigenous rather than liberal, top-down institutions. The TFG and subsequently the FRS are more clearly premised on local traditions of clan leadership but have still failed to acquire broad legitimacy. Institutions of whatever form are insufficient to produce legitimate states.

Second, as is central to the current model of counterinsurgency as statebuilding, providing public services, especially security, appears a more solid basis for legitimacy. In the first phase, UNITAF was able to gain some measure of legitimacy because it was understood as central to quelling the violence and restarting aid deliveries, something that UNOSOM I had been unable to accomplish. This may have been a product of the heavier weapons and reputation of the United States and coalition forces, which deterred challengers within Somalia, but the important point is that UNITAF was respected and appreciated by the Somalis because it broke the violence and famine that were destroying their country. Unfortunately, UNITAF's mandate was too limited and its tenure too brief to create the expectations of continuing order that might have induced the investments necessary to vest interests in a new regime. Anticipating that it would soon be followed by a less effective UN force, the Somalis failed to alter their pessimistic expectations of future disorder. As a result, UNITAF never created sufficient legitimacy to bequeath to the weaker UNOSOM II. Once UNOSOM II turned to statebuilding and the partisan hunt for Aidid, the mission came to be seen as imperialist, oppressive, and illegitimate. In Somaliland, by contrast, the legitimacy of the councils of elders continues to rest on their ability to keep the peace among potentially volatile clans and subclans.

Similarly, a significant impediment to legitimacy for the TFG and the FRS has been their inability to stop the violence that continues to plague Somalia or to provide other public services, despite now large aid inflows. This is evidence by absence for a hearts and mind strategy. There are many reasons why the FRS has not yet developed any significant legitimacy, the statebuilder's dilemma being foremost among them. But its lack of capacity is surely one reason why it cannot build support among the population.

The Statebuilder's Dilemma

The lack of legitimacy for the Somali state—and, as a by-product, the lack of capacity that follows from a lack of popular support—is ultimately rooted in the statebuilder's dilemma. The United States initially promised to be a nearly ideal statebuilder, an external power with the ability to impose credibly an impartial solution on the political turmoil. In the first phase of statebuilding, it had strictly humanitarian goals. At the same time, it had limited ambition and a very low threshold for the costs it was willing to bear. Neutral statebuilders may not seek to install loyal leaders, but they are also unwilling to pay the enormous costs of rebuilding a failed state.

Ethiopia and other regional states, on the other hand, have been willing to bear some significant costs to build a new state in Somalia. This case demonstrates the universality of the statebuilder's dilemma. A statebuilder like Ethiopia need not be a superpower to suffer from the same trade-off between building a legitimate government and installing a loyal leader. Concerned about Somali irredentism, and perhaps about the spread of Islamic fundamentalism as al-Shabab has spread into Kenya, the neighboring states have supported what is, from their point of view, a moderate regime that, most importantly, has sworn off nationalist appeals to greater Somalia. Yet, understood as a puppet of the hated Ethiopians, the TFG especially and the FRS, as its successor, are despised at worst and tolerated at best by many Somalis. This lack of legitimacy both inhibits state capacity and creates fertile ground from which al-Shabab and other opposition groups can recruit fighters and support. The net result is a vicious cycle in which a lack of legitimacy prevents building state capacity, despite the inflow of external resources; this lack of capacity precludes the state from stopping the violence and creating social order; and this lack of social order inhibits society from supporting the state; ad infinitum. Despite new statebuilding efforts in the early decades of the twenty-first century, the emphasis on ensuring that Somali's leaders are at least acceptable to its neighbors means that the tragedy continues.

Conclusion

The purpose of statebuilding, as well as the outcome against which it must be judged, is to restore—or, in the extreme, to create for the first time—a monopoly of the legitimate use of violence in a given territory. That is, the object is to rebuild a state that can use force rightfully or with the support of the community against which that coercion might be directed. In the political chaos of ungoverned spaces, where prior authority and institutions have dissolved, the statebuilder must establish a social order and guarantee it into the indefinite future. If the statebuilder is sufficiently credible, social actors will accommodate themselves to this new order; invest resources, time, and effort according to the new rules of politics; and become vested in its success. In this way, statebuilding carries the promise of creating durable, self-enforcing social orders.

To achieve legitimacy, the statebuilder's task is most easily accomplished by establishing and guaranteeing an order with broad social support. In the simplified schema of chapter 1, this order would lie near the political preferences of the median citizen, if one exists, or within the set of policies that leave all members of society as satisfied as possible without harming the welfare of any (the Pareto set). By locating the new social order and accompanying state institutions near the center of the political spectrum, the statebuilder is likely to maximize political support for its creation. Conversely, the further away the new social order is from the preferences of the society, the harder it will be to establish a legitimate state.

At the same time, statebuilding is an enormously costly undertaking of often great risk and uncertain outcome. Any state willing to bear the cost to build a state in some foreign land will have interests of its own in that territory that it wants to protect. At a minimum, the would-be statebuilder will be concerned with the foreign policies that the new state may adopt in the future, but this often extends into policies toward trade and investment, the treatment of minorities that may become refugees, and other issues of national or transnational concern. Statebuilders are not altruists but must satisfy their own constituencies at home who are reluctant to expend blood and treasure without return. In Somalia, Ethiopia wants a state that will forswear irredentist claims against the Ogaden—a key issue of its own territorial integrity. In Iraq, the United States desired a state that would accept the regional status quo, defer to U.S. leadership within the Gulf, liberalize its economic and political systems, and be an ally in the global war on terror. The more intense these interests, the greater the costs the statebuilder is willing to bear and the more likely it will be to undertake a statebuilding effort. Yet in the pursuit of these interests, the statebuilder inevitably promotes a leader who shares its policy preferences or is willing to do its bidding. It will, in short, promote a loyal leader.

This is the statebuilder's dilemma. Statebuilders want a state that is legitimate in the eyes of the people it will govern. This is a necessary condition for success over the long run. At the same time, statebuilders want leaders who will protect their interests in the countries into which they are pouring so much effort. The greater the interests of the statebuilder, or the further apart the policy preferences of the statebuilder and the local society, the more acute is the dilemma. In short, the more the policies of the failed state matter to the statebuilder, the deeper is the statebuilder's dilemma.

This dilemma inhibits and undermines effective statebuilding. Early on, the United States did not have sufficient interests in Somalia to pay the costs of such a mission once they became manifest. Later, Ethiopia backed a regime that met its essential interests in Somalia but could not gain legitimacy from Somali society. In Iraq, the United States built a regime and supported a leader who it appeared would protect its interests but who then used that support to pursue a highly partisan, pro-Shiite agenda that failed to legitimate the new state and has led to continued violence and ultimately a second failure of the state. The United States, in turn, continued to back that leader long after his partisanship was revealed because it believed he would be the most loyal out of a likely disloyal lot. As the case of Iraq demonstrates, the more intense the interests of the statebuilder, the more it will emphasize loyalty, the fewer alternative leaders there will be, and the more easily the leader can exploit the statebuilder and escape its control. President Nouri al-Maliki's highly partisan defiance—as well as President Hamid Karzai's in Afghanistan—was a predictable consequence of attempting to support loyal leaders in countries far different from the statebuilder.

While the case of Ethiopia in Somalia demonstrates the universality of the statebuilder's dilemma, in practice the states most likely to have the capacity and will to engage in statebuilding in the foreseeable future will be from the developed world. Given its global interests, the United States will likely play a lead role in any statebuilding effort, at least in the medium term. The great irony is that, today, the ungoverned spaces and the states most likely to fail are those in which the interests of Western states and the local populations are furthest apart. The Middle East, where the United States is attempting to extend the Pax Americana, has not welcomed the liberal principles of that international political order and their implications for domestic societies. Thus, even as they know they must build legitimate states, the United States and its allies will be constantly tempted to install leaders who support their preferred policies. It took many repeated interventions and decades of highly repressive, autocratic rule to build states in Central America that the United States could find acceptable. The proxy war against Nicaragua in the 1980s and the continuing instability in Haiti, which has required two interventions in as many decades, are testimony to the still ongoing process of U.S. statebuilding in that region. There is little reason to expect that today's statebuilding interventions in the Middle East, Central Asia, or Africa will be any easier. Given the threat of ungoverned spaces and the greater technological capacity that allows small organizations to wreak enormous destruction across national borders, the stakes are also likely greater. The statebuilder's dilemma will both remain central to international politics into the decades ahead and thwart efforts to build stable, legitimate states able to stand on their own and govern their territories effectively.

Alternative Explanations for Statebuilding Failure

Statebuilding can fail for many reasons. Any failure of a social project the magnitude of modern statebuilding is likely to be overdetermined, with too many possible causes and too few cases—fortunately—to sort through properly. Though I cannot demonstrate that the statebuilder's dilemma is *the* cause of any particular statebuilding failure, it does appear to be *a fundamental* cause that underlies many more proximate and frequently examined reasons offered for the lack of success.

Statebuilding may fail simply because it is an impossible task. If we look to the European experience that originally produced consolidated, prosperous, and ultimately democratic regimes, it is obvious that the process unfolded over centuries. Although the external pressures of war and competition drove the process, actual statebuilding itself was both undirected and largely internal. No actor had any conscious intention to build an entity such as the state we know today. Statebuilding was instead a struggle between different groups and factions, pushed forward by thinkers and leaders able to assemble the pieces of politics in new ways through serendipitous institutional innovations. The conceit that, today, some foreign country could almost literally parachute in, establish a social order, assemble self-sustaining states, and then withdraw in a matter of months or years is, frankly, astounding in its audacity. Seldom have we seen modern hubris of such a high order.[1] That the concentrated, time-delimited intervention we call statebuilding should fail is hardly surprising.

Yet statebuilding sometimes succeeds. West Germany and Japan, of course, are the exemplars. For reasons discussed above, the statebuilder's dilemma was not especially acute in these instances. In Iraqi Kurdistan and Somaliland, examined in chapters 4 and 5, respectively, indigenous statebuilding also appears to have been relatively successful. Precisely because these autonomous regions were isolated from the international community and external statebuilders, they were allowed to choose their own leaders by their own mechanisms to reflect their internal priorities. Though admittedly far from definitive, these anomalies suggest that when the dilemma is not deep or can be avoided, as in the autonomous regions, statebuilding can be successful or, at least, started on a positive trajectory.

If statebuilding is not doomed to fail from the start, it can also fail due to inappropriate strategies, based perhaps on flawed theories of legitimation. Given the enormity of the task, it is quite possible that we—the international community in general, scholars in particular—do not actually know *how* to build states. The liberal model of statebuilding so widely applied in the post–Cold War period was not selected because it was a tried and true method. Rather, it was an ideology that fit an emerging academic paradigm on the positive role of limited political institutions that, in turn, reflected the euphoria of the "end of history" moment. Contrary to the prevailing wisdom, however, legitimacy is not inherent in institutions in general nor only in institutions with representative qualities. Institutions are not "strong" or accepted by society simply because they are institutions. This puts the proverbial cart before the horse. Rather, as I have argued here, institutions are strong when it is in the self-interest of individuals and groups in society to defend those institutions against challengers. This is the mistake of nearly all statebuilders in recent decades, and of all institutionalist scholars, who have placed inordinate faith in the legitimating power of democratic institutions. Legitimacy does not exist of its own accord, nor can it be claimed by leaders. Legitimacy exists only when it is conferred by society on leaders and states they regard as rightful and worthy of respect.

The arrogance behind this particular theory of politics, however, grew out of our own time. Given the world in 1991, as history was just ending, how could democracy, free markets, and limited but effective states not be "good things"—and why should all good things not go together?[2] In the end, the model said more about the statebuilders than about statebuilding. That rapid elections and market liberalization reified divisions and disrupted society while failing to legitimate new states was apparent early on, even in Somalia,

1. On the hubris of statebuilding in general, see Scott 1999.
2. Fukuyama 1992.

but the international community persisted with the model at least through the debacle in Iraq.[3] Even today, after Iraq, it appears to be the default strategy of the international community as it attempts to deal with the changes brought about by the Arab Spring, the war in Syria, and Russia's expansion into Ukraine. So pervasive is the model of liberal statebuilding in North America and Europe, from where most statebuilding emanates, it is as if no one can imagine any other strategy, despites its dismal track record.

Nonetheless, it is important not to attribute too much responsibility for the failure of statebuilding to the choice of strategy, liberal or otherwise. By 2007, other strategies were being tried without notably greater success. During the second phase of statebuilding in Somalia, for instance, the Transitional Federal Government and the Federal Republic of Somalia were founded on, at best, modified liberal foundations with appointed legislatures that then elect the president. Direct national elections have not been held, nor are any anticipated. This is a significant change in strategy from the 1990s and other similar cases, but the Somali state remains unconsolidated, a near-empty shell. Similarly, in Iraq, the United States changed strategy dramatically to COIN, with its focus on winning hearts and minds. As explained in chapter 3, this is likely to be better strategy because it aims to meet the basic needs of society first and then earn legitimacy by success, rather than expecting legitimacy to follow naturally from democratic institutions and processes. But even here, though the change in strategy produced enough stability for the United States to withdraw its forces from Iraq, it did not succeed in building a capable state, as the subsequent failure of the state in summer 2014 amply demonstrates. It remains possible that the outcome might have been different had something like the TFG in Somalia or COIN in Iraq been tried from the outset. Liberal statebuilding may have fatally undermined the prospects for success before the alternative strategies could work. But variation in strategy without variation in success suggests that the choice of strategy by itself is not decisive. Even though strategy matters, with COIN being preferred to the alternative, the larger problem in both Somalia and Iraq was foreign-supported regimes that were unable to achieve legitimacy in the eyes of their people.

Finally, statebuilding can also fail because of poor tactics. In this view, liberal statebuilding may still be the correct model, but it has not succeeded, or not succeeded as well as it could have, because of poor implementation. Elections are still necessary but perhaps should not be rushed. Power-sharing institutions should be developed rather than power-dividing institutions, or vice versa. More resources should be put into disarmament, demobilization, and reintegration (DDR), security sector reform (SSR), and transitional justice programs. Combinations of tactics should be fit more carefully to varying local circumstances.[4] It is hard to refute the argument that if only we had employed tactics differently,

3. See especially Paris 2004.
4. P. Miller 2013.

outcomes would have been different. Different tactics in different degrees and mixtures deployed in different circumstances might always work better. Nor have I examined here low-cost statebuilding options like DDR and SSR, focusing instead on armed efforts. However, we would need many more cases of statebuilding to understand which tactics, in what order, degree, and amalgamations, are optimal under what conditions. My hope is that we will never experience enough state failures and statebuilding interventions to ever figure out the "best" mix and sequence of policies from the nearly infinite number of possible combinations. However, as with the choice of strategy, there has been a great deal of heterogeneity already in the tactics of statebuilding. Variation in tactics with uniformity in outcomes again suggests that something deeper is going on. The evidence presented here, at least, suggests that the something deeper is the statebuilder's dilemma.

At the level of both strategy and tactics, as long as the statebuilder intervenes in elections to rig who wins, as the United States did in Iraq, the timing of those elections, for instance, will not matter. If DDR and SSR are employed to bolster the position of a partisan leader, those efforts will ultimately fail. Training the police to be better enforcers of a repressive leader's foreign-inspired policy agenda is not a recipe for building a legitimate state. The greater the interests of the statebuilder in the failed state, or the further apart the policy preferences of the statebuilder and the target society, the more likely the statebuilder will install a loyal leader who will reflect and pursue its interests—and the less legitimate the leader and the new state will be. No strategy or set of tactics can alleviate this fundamental dilemma.

What Is to Be Done?

There are many fragile states in the world today rent by deep class or sectarian fissures, and sometimes both. When these fissures grow too wide, or the state itself becomes a partisan in social conflicts, states fail and their territories become "ungoverned" and a possible threat to the decentralized international order that relies on effective domestic policing. Equally, the people living in these ungoverned areas suffer tremendously from violence and the deprivation of basic public services and often even food. Aside from the existential threat of ungoverned spaces, there is sometimes a humanitarian rationale to "do something" to stop the suffering, often pushed by aid organizations which, as in Somalia, need statebuilders to provide a safer environment in which they can do their work.

One implication of the statebuilder's dilemma is that "outsiders" should not seek to build states, but rather let indigenous leaders build their own systems of governance according to their own lights—regardless of how long this might take. But the existential problem of ungoverned spaces and the particular interests that now drive statebuilders to pay the costs in blood and treasure suggest that states will continue to intervene in their failed cousins, even if legitimacy is not the ultimate goal or ever realized. While the physician's adage of "do no harm" is easy to recommend, it flies in the face of the interests that lead statebuilders to intervene in the first place. Although recognizing the dilemma may temper the advocacy of some statebuilding enthusiasts, the interests that propel the process are still real.

The statebuilder's dilemma is a true dilemma, not some artificial choice designed to incline opinion toward some preferred policy. Rather, it is a real and inescapable trade-off between mutually inconsistent goals. Without strong interests in failed states, would-be statebuilders have no incentive to bear of the costs of statebuilding. The stronger the interests of the statebuilders in the failed states, however, the more likely they will be to select leaders who promise to promote their interests, undermining the legitimacy leaders need to rule successfully. Confronted by this inherent trade-off, what can be done to govern the world's ungoverned spaces more effectively? The lessons from this dilemma are, I admit, extremely pessimistic. As with any true dilemma, there are no good solutions; we can only seek to mitigate its effects.

Good Enough Governance

One possible direction is to recognize the limits of external intervention and accept that building liberal, democratic states with free markets is an overly ambitious goal. On this path, according to Stephen Krasner, statebuilders and the international community should aim only for "good enough governance" with the following core attributes: (1) the physical integrity rights of individuals must be respected, but not necessarily civil and political rights; (2) public authorities would provide order, especially the protection of property rights; (3) transnational threats would be contained either by the state or in association with the United States; (4) corruption by the leader would be accepted but contained; and (5) the state itself or some external actor would provide some basic social services, especially public health. At the same time, mechanisms of political accountability, though desirable, should not be a high priority, and elections would be useful only if they ratified agreements already reached by political leaders.[5]

In essence, good enough governance deemphasizes the legitimacy of the state, expecting perhaps a minimal level to follow from the provision of order and essential services. Seen through the lens of the statebuilder's dilemma, it permits a greater emphasis on loyal leaders willing to work with external powers in exchange for support and aid. In practice, this suggests that statebuilding in the future be modeled after U.S. efforts in the early twentieth century in

5. Krasner 2013. See also Risse 2011.

Central America, where stability was prized over democracy, with the additional aim of curbing some of the more egregious aspects of authoritarian rule. This is the direction in which U.S. policy, at least since Iraq, has been trending under President Obama: target individual terrorists and organizations but avoid large-scale interventions, even into such clearly failed states as Libya, and tolerate authoritarian leaders who promise stability, as with the military in Egypt after the coup against President Mohamed Morsi.

There is much to recommend a less ambitious statebuilding agenda. I reach this conclusion reluctantly. Although I have criticized liberal statebuilding heavily above, I nonetheless share fully in the liberalism of our contemporary era and believe with Winston Churchill that "democracy is the worst form of government, except for all others."[6] Democracy is also a positive good in and of itself. Yet it may be, as Krasner claims, a "bridge too far." There is little evidence that democracy can be imposed on societies from the outside.[7] If our concern is to govern spaces effectively, good enough governance may have to be, well, good enough.

As argued throughout this book, however, to govern effectively over the long run, states must possess at least a degree of legitimacy. Although good enough governance may satisfy the demands of statebuilders and the international community for control over territory, it is not at all clear that building legitimacy through the provision of a minimalist order will satisfy the demands of local populations for improving their quality of life or mitigate redistributive conflicts between competing social factions that threaten to escalate to violence and state failure. As noted in chapter 3, even as COIN works at the local level, it still has not been shown to scale up to the national level in failed states with deep social cleavages. In turn, some measure of democracy or other mechanisms of accountability are likely necessary to constrain leaders, even in the minimalist fashion envisioned in good enough governance. The problem lies in Madison's dilemma that a state strong enough to provide social order is also strong enough to violate the rule of law. Less hubris and the lower ambition envisioned in good enough governance are a step in the right direction but this does not resolve the statebuilder's dilemma or guarantee success in the long run.

Good enough states are also likely to require external assistance into the foreseeable future. Precisely because they lack broad-based legitimacy and are governed by leaders sympathetic to external powers, good enough states cannot stand on their own. This has two likely consequences that, even if good enough governance succeeds in creating stability, are likely to make it unsustainable over the long run.

---

6. For empirical evidence on the efficacy of democracies, see Lake and Baum 2001; Baum and Lake 2003.
7. Paris 2004; Owen 2002; Pevehouse 2005.

First, external support for leaders who govern autocratically will likely create a domestic backlash against those states that sustain unpopular leaders in office. U.S. support for various autocrats in Central America produced decades of anti-Americanism in the region. When opposition movements—Castro's communists in Cuba, the Sandinistas in Nicaragua—eventually succeeded in overthrowing these U.S.-backed tyrants, they inevitably rejected subsequent U.S. influence. We see a similar phenomenon in the Middle East today. U.S. backing for the shah of Iran eventually led the revolutionary regime to define the United States as the "Great Satan." Similar support for Saudi Arabia and other monarchies in the Gulf has spurred terrorist organizations to attack the United States as the "far enemy." Sufficient repression may sustain an autocrat in power for decades, but this only worsens the backlash against the external patron when it comes.

Second, and related, it is not clear today that publics in established liberal democracies will allow their governments to support autocratic, repressive governments abroad over the long term. Although the U.S. public tolerated support for authoritarian leaders in Central America during the early twentieth century and elsewhere during the Cold War, it is not obvious that current voters will back similarly authoritarian leaders into the future. To sustain their role in fragile states over time, would-be statebuilders need the support of their own populations. Yet, as the economic historian Niall Ferguson has written, Americans, in particular, lack the necessary "imperial cast of mind."[8] This reluctance to support authoritarian rule may be even stronger in Europe, where other possible statebuilders are likely to originate. Good enough governance may succeed in creating a measure of stability in otherwise ungoverned spaces, but it appears to lack political constituencies within both fragile states and those statebuilders who must support "good enough" regimes.

Multilateral Statebuilding

A second path is to expand multilateral statebuilding efforts. In multilateral statebuilding, some collective entity authorizes a statebuilding mission and, in some organizations, assesses member states for the costs according to some prenegotiated formula. In theory, this might permit relatively "neutral" statebuilding—statebuilding that emphasizes the legitimacy of the new state rather than the loyal of its leader—without engaging or relying on the interests of particular states. The more countries that are more involved in overseeing the effort, the less partisan the statebuilder can be and the less likely it will be to favor a loyal leader. This is, at least, the hope of multilateral statebuilding.

8. Ferguson 2004, 29.

Multilateral statebuilding has its own problems, discussed in chapter 2. In an uneasy compromise between the principle of sovereignty and the norm of nonintervention, on the one hand, and the responsibility to protect, on the other, multilaterally approved statebuilding efforts are limited in depth and duration. This makes it harder for the statebuilder to commit credibly to sustaining a particular social order and to ignite a process of vesting social interests in that order that might make it self-sustaining.

Under present institutions, all founded on the principle of state sovereignty, multilateralism does not obviate the statebuilder's dilemma. In extant multilateral bodies, statebuilding can be approved only with the active engagement of a state (or states) that pushes for the mission, usually a great power, and with the acquiescence of the other members, especially those with veto rights. Although multilateral statebuilding may be somewhat more neutral in its role in failed states and place greater emphasis on legitimacy, if only to gain the consent of the majority, the fact remains that some "interested" state (or states) must champion and lead the mission. Thus, with states as sovereign entities, multilateral efforts remain dependent on largely voluntary financial assessments, subject to the veto of the great powers. This is even more true for states willing to deploy peacekeepers to violent failed states. Despite international oversight and approval, the most interested states remain the ones who are likely to step forward to lead statebuilding operations in any particular instance.[9]

Reflecting one horn of the statebuilder's dilemma, lacking any significant interests in Somalia, the United States withdrew from the failed state at the first sign of trouble. Today, by contrast, although the African Union ostensibly fields the peacekeepers in Somalia, the key drivers of that effort remain Ethiopia and Kenya—the countries with the greatest interests in the future policies of any reconstituted state. As the case of Somalia makes clear, multilateralism has been tried but still suffers from the statebuilder's dilemma. Conversely, were a multilateral body to insist on a strictly neutral statebuilder concerned only with the legitimacy of the rebuilt state—a public good for the regional or international community—it might well lack any states willing to participate in or pay for the effort. Statebuilding is still dependent on "coalitions of the willing"—and the willing will be those states that have some strong interest in the failed state. Multilateralism does not obviate the statebuilder's dilemma, even though it may soften it around the edges. The real dilemma remains.

---

9. One could, of course, imagine a supranational statebuilding entity with independent powers to decide when a state has failed, tax states for the necessary resources, and deploy its own military forces to quell violence and build order in ungoverned spaces. This would, however, require such fundamental changes in the principles and practices of sovereignty that it remains unrealistic for the foreseeable future. Only if the problem of ungoverned spaces becomes even more severe than at present would such a supranational force be considered.

Creating Conducive Environments for Domestic Statebuilding

Since the statebuilder's dilemma cannot be overcome, the most viable alternative course is for the international community, and the advanced industrialized democracies specifically, to create incentives for fragile and failed states to solve their internal problems on their own. The anomalies of Iraqi Kurdistan and Somaliland, discussed in chapters 4 and 5, respectively, suggest that autonomous statebuilding is possible, even in the contemporary era. Indeed, at least one plausible reason for success in these cases is that they have been largely insulated from foreign meddling in their politics and leadership choices. In both cases, fear of what the collapse of the social order might mean has spurred all parties to manage if not resolve their differences sufficiently to avoid widespread and persistent violence. The object of the international community should be to facilitate similar domestic compromises that can lead to greater state consolidation.

The international community can do this best by creating incentives for domestic groups in fragile states to settle their political differences, establish effective domestic orders and institutions, and govern their territories effectively. Even though statebuilding is most effective as an internal and indigenous process, the international community can still engage in a form of indirect statebuilding by rewarding those states that do it well and successfully. Central to the use of incentives, however, is making the rewards for effective statebuilding *contingent* on success. Other states must be willing to turn off the spigot of benefits as well as turn it on.[10] To date, the international community has been unwilling to manipulate aid and access to international institutions in this way. Fearful of undermining state capacity or weakening loyal leaders further, external supporters rule out manipulating the flow of resources to induce behaviors likely to create greater legitimacy. In doing so, they tie both hands behind their backs in the struggle against transnational insurgents.

Once upon a time, to be recognized by the international community, states needed to demonstrate effective sovereignty, defined as the exercise of actual authority over political space. States were recognized by others as sovereign only after they had reached an appropriate degree of consolidation, judged in major part by whether they could control private actors projecting violence across their borders. As discussed in chapter 2, following the creation of the United Nations—which confers recognition on all members—and the postcolonial struggle that permitted all nominally sovereign states to claim membership, states acquired juridical sovereignty even if they remained only "quasi-states," as Robert Jackson has called them, without effective sovereignty.[11] This looser standard might remain acceptable for membership in the

10. Kapstein 2014.
11. Jackson 1990.

United Nations, but there is no reason that access to the other benefits provided by the international community must follow the same rules.

The best and likely most effective incentives available to the industrialized democracies today are access to the international political and economic order they have constructed over the past seven decades. Making access to this order contingent on building effective states could help push domestic groups in productive directions. Even more, economic integration promises to realign the interests of domestic groups in ways that are consistent with Western and especially U.S. interests, much as happened in Central America and in West Germany and Japan. As policy preferences converge, the intensity of the statebuilder's dilemma will diminish, the trade-off between legitimacy and loyalty will become less acute, and democracy may blossom.

The benefits of joining the Pax Americana, with its security guarantees and free trade, or the European Union (EU) and its Common Market, have in the past created incentives for states to establish effective governance in ways that are also compatible with the interests of the United States and its European partners. Although easy cases, for reasons explained in chapter 3, West Germany and Japan were certainly pulled along the path to stable democracy by the promise of integration into the Pax Americana.[12] These former fascist and militarist states, which could have fallen into internal political conflict over responsibility for the war and the prospects for economic and political change, nonetheless avoided domestic disputes not only as a result of the occupation but also because of the prospects of moving under the U.S. security umbrella and exporting their way to prosperity in an open international economy. These inducements, moreover, pulled both societies toward the more capitalist and open economies desired by the United States. In these cases, integration into the U.S.-led international order induced a reconfiguration of domestic interests in ways that were favorable to U.S. interests, attenuating the statebuilder's dilemma.

More recently, and perhaps even more clearly, the chance to join the EU exerted an enormously positive effect on politics within the former communist states in Eastern Europe. Immediately after the fall of the Soviet Union, many worried that ethnic revanchism and the settling of old scores left festering under communist rule might produce weak states that would fall prey to transnational conflict.[13] Nonetheless, the criteria for joining the EU were sufficiently clear, and the potential gains so large, that internal dissention was sublimated, the rule of law was secured, and markets were freed. Applying for membership starting in the early 1990s, and placing themselves under even stricter scrutiny, eight former communist countries finally joined the EU as full members in May 2004. The process of enlargement created, if not necessarily a race to the top, at least a race to reach "European" standards of state-

---

12. Ikenberry 2001, 2011.
13. On the feared spread of ethnic conflict, see Lake and Rothchild 1998.

hood and political stability. It is true, of course, that the promise of European integration also created new tensions within states, as in the former Yugoslavia, where Slovenia was economically competitive and eager to join the EU, while Serbia was less competitive and vulnerable to ethnic mobilization around underlying economic differences.[14] But we need only compare the political success of the former communist states in Eastern Europe that could join the EU with those in southeastern Europe or Central Asia that could not for geopolitical reasons to see the long-term effects of Europe's incentives for effective statehood. Once again, the promise of integration into a larger and economically open regional order induced an alignment of policy preferences within the potentially failed states of Eastern Europe that was favored by the consolidated states of the West, greatly mitigating the statebuilder's dilemma.

In similar ways, the prospects for integration into a vibrant, economically open, and politically secure international order could potentially induce other fragile states to overcome their domestic political divisions. Today, much foreign aid goes to the poorest of the poor, often fragile states that lack capacity. This is appropriate on humanitarian grounds, but the aid flows may reinforce domestic divisions and conflicts and be used by leaders for their own political purposes. Were access to bilateral and multilateral aid instead made contingent on progress toward resolving domestic political and economic cleavages, it might spur greater statebuilding efforts.[15] Similarly, access to the World Trade Organization and its enormous benefits, now granted to the least capable states on a privileged basis, could be made contingent on domestic progress toward political accommodations. Importantly, as in the post–World War II and post–Cold War cases, integration into a liberal, capitalist, and open international order could promote domestic coalitions that share policy preferences with likely statebuilders. Integration promises to alleviate the trade-off between legitimacy and loyalty, at least with the West, even if it cannot erase the dilemma entirely. Such incentives can work, however, only when the benefits of integration are contingent on explicit criteria such that all domestic actors know the stakes involved.

This strategy of indirect statebuilding is likely to have only a limited impact in the short term on ungoverned spaces. U.S. statebuilding efforts in the Caribbean basin, in many ways more direct and heavy-handed than the strategy proposed here, took almost a century to realign the domestic political economies of the once fragile states in this region. In today's failed states, policy preferences are likely less pliable than in West Germany and Japan in 1945 or in Eastern Europe after the fall of communism, and more distant from those of the industrialized democracies. Incentives might, in some cases, need to

14. On economic origins of ethnic competition in Yugoslavia, see Woodward 1995.
15. The Millennium Challenge Corporation is one such innovative program, but it remains a relatively small player in the aid industry. See http://www.mcc.gov/pages/about.

be combined with armed statebuilding to ensure minimal standards of governance. Statebuilders then risk falling into the dilemma between legitimacy and loyalty. As always, statebuilders are trapped by their own interests. Nonetheless, as the past successes suggest, creating incentives for domestic groups to build their own states can be a force for progress and stability over time.

There is no easy solution to the statebuilder's dilemma. States have little incentive to expend blood and treasure in distant lands in which they have few policy interests. States willing to bear the costs will support loyal rather than legitimate leaders, undermining the chances for long-term success. The best we can do, like it or not, is to create incentives for societies in ungoverned spaces to build their own states.

References

Acemoglu, Daron, and James Robinson. 2012. *Why Nations Fail: The Origins of Power, Prosperity, and Poverty.* New York: Crown Business.

Adam, Herbert. 1998. Corporatism as Ethnic Compromise: Labour Relations in Post-Apartheid South Africa. *Nations and Nationalism* 4 (3), 347–362.

Agence France-Presse. 2014, July 27. U.N. Warns of a Food Shortage 3 Years after Somalia's Famine. *New York Times,* p. A7.

Ahmed, Ismail I., and Reginald Herbold Green. 1999. The Heritage of War and State Collapse in Somalia and Somaliland: Local-Level Effects, External Interventions and Reconstruction. *Third World Quarterly* 20 (1), 113–127.

Aime, Elsa Gonzalez. 2013. The Security Issues behind the Ethiopian Intervention in Somalia (2006–2009). In *State and Societal Challenges in the Horn of Africa: Conflict and Processes of State Formation, Reconfiguration and Disintegration,* edited by A. M. Dias, 32–47. Lisbon: Center of African Studies, University Institute of Lisbon.

Allawi, Ali A. 2007. *The Occupation of Iraq: Winning the War, Losing the Peace.* New Haven, CT: Yale University Press.

Almond, Gabriel A., Scott C. Flanagan, and Robert J. Mundt, eds. 1973. *Crisis, Choice, and Change: Historical Studies of Political Development.* Boston: Little, Brown.

Anderson, Mary B. 1999. *Do No Harm: How Aid Can Support Peace—or War.* Boulder, CO: Lynne Rienner.

Arango, Tim. 2013, August 18. Sectarian Attacks Return with a Roar, Rattling a Capital Already on Edge. *New York Times,* p. A6.

——. 2014, August 8. Islamist Fighters Rout Kurds in Northern Iraq and Seize Dam. *New York Times,* pp. A1, A8.

——. 2015, May 19. Fall of Ramadi Weakens Rule of Iraq Premier. *New York Times,* pp. A1, A10.

Arango, Tim, and Clifford Krauss. 2014, July 5. Poised to Gain in Iraq Crisis, Kurds Face New Barriers to Autonomy. *New York Times,* pp. A4, A8.

Arango, Tim, Alissa J. Rubin, and Michael R. Gordon. 2014, August 12. Iraqis Nominate Maliki Successor, Causing Standoff. *New York Times,* pp. A1, A6.

Arango, Tim, and Eric Schmitt. 2014, August 11. U.S. Actions in Iraq Fueled Rise of a Rebel. *New York Times,* pp. A1, A6.

Arraf, Jane. 2010, March 11. Allegations of Fraud as Iraq Election Results Trickle In. *Christian Science Monitor,* http://www.csmonitor.com/World/Middle-East/2010/0311/Allegations-of-fraud-as-Iraq-election-results-trickle-in.

Autesserre, Severine. 2014. *Peaceland: Conflict Resolution and the Everyday Politics of International Intervention*. New York: Cambridge University Press.

Avant, Deborah D. 2005. *The Market for Force: The Consequences of Privatizing Security*. New York: Cambridge University Press.

Bain, William. 2003. *Between Anarchy and Society: Trusteeship and the Obligations of Power*. New York: Oxford University Press.

Baker, Peter. 2014a, August 12. For 2 U.S. Presidents, Iraqi Leader Proved a Source of Frustration. *New York Times*, p. A6.

——. 2014b, June 23. Relief over U.S. Exit from Iraq Fades as Reality Overtakes Hope. *New York Times*, pp. A1, A8.

Barbara, Julien. 2008. Rethinking Neo-liberal State Building: Building Post-Conflict Development States. *Development in Practice* 18 (3), 307–318.

Barnard, Anne. 2015, March 6. Iran Gains Clout in Fighting ISIS. *New York Times*, pp. A1, A10.

Barnes, Cedric, and Harun Hassan. 2007. The Rise and Fall of Mogadishu's Islamic Courts. *Journal of East African Studies* 1 (2): 151–160.

Barnett, Michael, Songying Fang, and Christoph Zurcher. 2014. Compromised Peacebuilding. *International Studies Quarterly* 58 (3): 608–620.

Barnett, Michael, and Christoph Zurcher. 2009. The Peacebuilder's Contract: How External Statebuilding Reinforces Weak Statehood. In *The Dilemmas of Statebuilding: Confronting the Contradictions of Postwar Peace Operations*, edited by R. Paris and T. D. Sisk, 23–52. New York: Routledge.

Barzel, Yoram. 2002. *A Theory of the State: Economic Rights, Legal Rights, and the Scope of the State*. New York: Cambridge University Press.

Bates, Robert H. 1981. *Markets and States in Tropical Africa: The Political Basis of Agricultural Policies*. Berkeley: University of California Press.

Baum, Matthew A., and David A. Lake. 2003. The Political Economy of Growth: Democracy and Human Capital. *American Journal of Political Science* 47 (2): 333–347.

Beate, Jahn. 2007. The Tragedy of Liberal Diplomacy: Democratization, Intervention, Statebuilding (Part 2). *Journal of Intervention and Statebuilding* 1 (2): 211–229.

Becker, Gary S. 1983. A Theory of Competition among Pressure Groups for Political Influence. *Quarterly Journal of Economics* 98 (3): 371–400.

Benjamin, Daniel J., David Cesarini, Mathijis J. H. M. van der Loos, Christopher T. Dawes, Philipp D. Koelinger, Patrik K. E. Magnusson, . . . Peter M. Visscher. 2012. The Genetic Architecture of Economic and Political Preferences. *Proceedings of the National Academy of Sciences* 109 (21): 8026–8031.

Berman, Eli, Joseph H. Felter, Jacob N. Shapiro, and Erin Troland. 2013. Modest, Secure and Informed: Successful Development in Conflict Zones. National Bureau of Economic Research Working Paper 18674.

Berman, Eli, Jacob N. Shapiro, and Joseph H. Felter. 2011. Can Hearts and Minds Be Bought? The Economics of Counterinsurgency in Iraq. *Journal of Political Economy* 119 (4): 766–819.

Bernard, Chester I. 1962. *The Functions of the Executive*. Cambridge, MA: Harvard University Press.

Bhagwati, Jagdish N. 1982. Directly Unproductive, Profit-Seeking (DUP) Activities. *Journal of Political Economy* 90 (5): 988–1002.

Biddle, Stephen, Jeffrey A. Friedman, and Jacob N. Shapiro. 2012. Testing the Surge: Why Did Violence Decline in Iraq in 2007? *International Security* 37 (1): 7–40.

Billet, Bret L. 1993. *Modernization Theory and Economic Development: Discontent in the Developing World*. Westport, CT: Praeger.

Binder, Leonard. 1971. *Crises and Sequences in Political Development*. Princeton, NJ: Princeton University Press.

Bisson, Thomas N. 2009. *The Crisis of the Twelfth Century: Power, Lordship, and the Origins of European Government*. Princeton, NJ: Princeton University Press.

Black, Duncan. 1948. On the Rationale of Group Decision-Making. *Journal of Political Economy* 56 (1): 23–34.

Blau, Peter M. 1963. Critical Remarks on Weber's Theory of Authority. *American Political Science Review* 57 (2): 305–316.

Bolger, Daniel P. 2014. *Why We Lost: A General's Inside Account of the Iraq and Afghanistan Wars*. Boston: Houghton Mifflin Harcourt.

Boone, Catherine. 2003. *Political Topographies of the African State: Territorial Authority and Institutional Choice*. New York: Cambridge University Press.

———. 2014. *Property and Political Order in Africa: Land Rights and the Structure of Politics*. New York: Cambridge University Press.

Boraine, Alex. 2005. Transitional Justice. In *Making States Work: State Failure and the Crisis of Governance*, edited by S. Chesterman, M. Ignatieff, and R. Thakur, 318–338. New York: United Nations University Press.

Bouillon, Markus E. 2012. Iraq's State-Building Enterprise: State Fragility, State Failure and a New Social Contract. *International Journal of Contemporary Iraqi Studies* 6 (3): 281–297.

Bradbury, Mark. 1994. The Case of the Yellow Settee: Experiences of Doing Development in Postwar Somaliland. *Community Development Journal* 29 (2): 113–122.

———. 2003. Living with Statelessness: The Somali Road to Development. *Conflict, Security and Development* 3 (1): 7–25.

———. 2008. *Becoming Somaliland*. Bloomington: Indiana University Press.

Bradbury, Mark, Adan Yusuf Abokor, and Haroon Ahmed Yusuf. 2003. Somaliland: Choosing Politics over Violence. *Review of African Political Economy* 30 (97): 455–478.

Brancati, Dawn, and Jack Snyder. 2011. Rushing to the Polls: The Causes of Premature Postconflict Elections. *Journal of Conflict Resolution* 55 (3): 469–492.

———. 2013. Time to Kill: The Impact of Election Timing and Sequencing on Post-Conflict Stability. *Journal of Conflict Resolution* 57 (5): 822–853.

Bremer, Paul. 2006. *My Year in Iraq: The Struggle to Build a Future of Hope*. New York: Simon and Schuster.

Brown, Chris, Terry Nardin, and Nicholas Rengger, eds. 2002. *International Relations in Political Thought: Texts from the Ancient Greeks to the First World War*. New York: Cambridge University Press.

Broz, J. Lawrence, and Daniel Maliniak. 2010. *Malapportionment, Gasoline Taxes and Climate Change*. Paper presented at the annual meeting of the American Political Science Association, Washington, DC.

Bryden, Matthew. 1995. Somalia: The Wages of Failure. *Current History* 94 (591): 145–151.

———. 2013. *Somalia Redux? Assessing the New Somali Federal Government*. Washington, DC: Center for Strategic and International Studies.

Bueno de Mesquita, Bruce, and Alastair Smith. 2011. *The Dictator's Handbook: Why Bad Behavior Is Almost Always Good Politics*. New York: PublicAffairs.

Bueno de Mesquita, Bruce, Alastair Smith, Randolph M. Siverson, and James D. Morrow. 2003. *The Logic of Political Survival*. Cambridge, MA: MIT Press.

Bull, Hedley. 1977. *The Anarchical Society: A Study of Order in World Politics*. New York: Columbia University Press.

Bush, George W. 2010. *Decision Points*. New York: Crown.

CFM. *See* United States, Department of the Army

Chandrasekaran, Rajiv. 2006. *Imperial Life in the Emerald City: Inside Iraq's Green Zone*. New York: Vintage Books.

Cheney, Dick. 2011. *In My Time: A Personal and Political Memoir*. New York: Simon and Schuster.

Chesterman, Simon. 2004. *You, the People: The United Nations, Transitional Administration, and State-Building.* New York: Oxford University Press.

Chiozza, Giacomo. 2013. Managing Difficult Allies: Domestic Institutions and Cooperation under Hierarchy. Paper presented at the annual meeting of the American Political Science Association, Chicago, IL.

Chivers, C. J. 2014, July 1. After Retreat, Iraqi Soldiers Fault Officers. *New York Times.* http://www.nytimes.com/2014/07/02/world/middleeast/after-retreat-iraqi-soldiers -fault-officers.html?_r=2.

Clarke, Walter. 1997. Failed Visions and Uncertain Mandates in Somalia. In *Learning from Somalia: The Lessons of Armed Humanitarian Intervention,* edited by W. Clarke and J. Herbst, 3–19. Boulder, CO: Westview Press.

Clarke, Walter, and Jeffrey Herbst. 1996. Somalia and the Future of Humanitarian Intervention. *Foreign Affairs* 75 (2): 70–85.

Clunan, Anne L., and Harold A. Trinkunas, eds. 2010. *Ungoverned Spaces: Alternatives to State Authority in an Era of Softened Sovereignty.* Stanford, CA: Stanford University Press.

Cockburn, Patrick. 2007. *The Occupation: War and Resistance in Iraq.* New York: Verso.

Cohen, Joshua. 1989. Deliberation and Democratic Legitimacy. In *The Good Polity: Normative Analysis of the State,* edited by A. Hamlin and P. Pettit, 17–34. Oxford: Basil Blackwell.

Colas, Alejandro. 2008. Open Doors and Closed Frontiers: The Limits of American Empire. *European Journal of International Relations* 14 (4): 619–643.

Cole, Juan. 2007. Shia Militias in Iraqi Politics. In *Iraq: Preventing a New Generation of Conflict,* edited by M. E. Bouillon, D. M. Malone, and B. Rowswell, 109–123. Boulder, CO: Lynne Rienner.

Collier, Paul. 2009. *Wars, Guns, and Votes: Democracy in Dangerous Places.* New York: Harper.

Collier, Paul, Anke Hoeffler, and Mans Soderbom. 2008. Post-Conflict Risks. *Journal of Peace Research* 45 (4): 461–478.

Cooper, Helene. 2015, March 6. Iran as Unlikely Ally. *New York Times,* pp. A1, A13.

Cox, Gary W. 2005. The Organization of Democratic Legislatures. In *The Oxford Handbook of Political Economy,* edited by B. R. Weingast and D. Wittman, 141–161. New York: Oxford University Press.

Cox, Gary W., and Mathew D. McCubbins. 2005. *Setting the Agenda: Responsible Party Government in the U.S. House of Representatives.* New York: Cambridge University Press.

Cox, Gary W., and Kenneth A. Shepsle. 2007. Majority Cycling and Agenda Manipulation: Richard McKelvey's Contributions and Legacy. In *Positive Changes in Political Science,* J. H. Aldrich, J. Alt, and A. Lupia, 19–40. Ann Arbor: University of Michigan Press.

Coyne, Christopher J. 2008. *After War: The Political Economy of Exporting Democracy.* Stanford, CA: Stanford University Press.

Crawford, Neta C. 2013. *Accountability for Killing: Moral Responsibility for Collateral Damage in America's Post-9/11 Wars.* New York: Oxford University Press.

Daalder, Ivo H., and James M. Lindsay. 2003. *America Unbound: The Bush Revolution in Foreign Policy.* Washington, DC: Brookings Institution Press.

Day, John. 1963. Authority. *Political Studies* 11 (3): 257–271.

Debs, Alexandre, and Nuno P. Monteiro. 2014. Known Unknowns: Power Shifts, Uncertainty, and War. *International Oganizaiton* 68 (1): 1–31.

Diamond, Larry. 2005. *Squandered Victory: The American Occupation and the Bungled Effort to Bring Democracy to Iraq.* New York: Times Books.

———. 2006. Promoting Democracy in Post-Conflict and Failed States: Lessons and Challenges. *Taiwan Journal of Democracy* 2 (2): 93–116.

Dias, Alexandra Magnolia. 2013. International Intervention and Engagement in Somalia (2006–2013): Yet Another External State Reconstruction Project? In *State and Societal Challenges in the Horn of Africa: Conflict and Processes of State Formation, Reconfiguration and Disintegration*, edited by A. M. Dias, 90–107. Lisbon: Center of African Studies, University Institute of Lisbon.

Dobbins, James, Seth G. Jones, Keith Crane, and Beth Cole DeGrasse. 2007. *The Beginner's Guide to Nation-Building.* Santa Monica, CA: RAND Corporation.

Dobbins, James, John G. McGinn, Keith Crane, Seth G. Jones, Rollie Lal, Andrew Rathmell, . . . Anga Timilsina. 2003. *America's Role in Nation-Building: From Germany to Iraq.* Santa Monica, CA: RAND.

Dobbins, James, Michele A. Poole, Austin Long, and Benjamin Runkle. 2008. *After the War: Nation-Building from FDR to George W. Bush.* Santa Monica, CA: RAND.

Dodge, Toby. 2003. *Inventing Iraq: The Failure of Nation Building and a History Denied.* London: Hurst.

——. 2005. Iraqi Transitions: From Regime Change to State Collapse. *Third World Quarterly* 26 (4–5): 705–721.

——. 2007a. The Causes of US Failure in Iraq. *Survival: Global Politics and Strategy* 49 (1): 85–106.

——. 2007b. State Collapse and the Rise of Identity Politics. In *Iraq: Preventing a New Generation of Conflict*, edited by M. E. Bouillon, D. M. Malone, and B. Rowswell, 23–39. Boulder, CO: Lynne Rienner.

——. 2012. Iraq's Road Back to Dictatorship. *Survival* 54 (3): 147–168.

——. 2013a. Intervention and Dreams of Exogenous Statebuilding: The Application of Liberal Peacebuilding in Afghanistan and Iraq. *Review of International Studies* 39 (5): 1189–1212.

——. 2013b. State and Society in Iraq Ten Years after Regime Change: The Rise of a New Authoritarianism. *International Affairs* 89 (2): 241–237.

Dower, John W. 1999. *Embracing Defeat: Japan in the Wake of World War II.* New York: W. W. Norton.

——. 2003, February 1. A Warning from History. *Boston Review: A Political and Literary Forum*, http://www.bostonreview.net/world/john-w-dower-warning-history.

Downing, Brian M. 1992. *The Military Revolution and Political Change: Origins of Democracy and Autocracy in Early Modern Europe.* Princeton, NJ: Princeton University Press.

Downs, Anthony. 1957. *An Economic Theory of Democracy.* New York: Harper and Row.

Doyle, Michael W. 1986. *Empires.* Ithaca, NY: Cornell University Press.

Doyle, Michael W., and Nicholas Sambanis. 2006. *Making War and Building Peace: United Nations Peace Operations.* Princeton, NJ: Princeton University Press.

Drysdale, John. 1997. Foreign Military Intervention in Somalia: The Root Cause of the Shift from UN Peacekeeping to Peacemaking and Its Consequences. In *Learning from Somalia: The Lessons of Armed Humanitarian Intervention*, edited by W. Clarke and J. Herbst, 118–134. Boulder, CO: Westview Press.

Dryzek, John S. 2001. Legitimacy and Economy in Deliberative Democracy. *Political Theory* 29 (5): 651–669.

Edelstein, David M. 2008. *Occupational Hazards: Success and Failure in Military Occupation.* Ithaca, NY: Cornell University Press.

Eisenstadt, Stuart N. 1966. *Modernization: Protest and Change.* Englewood Cliffs, NJ: Prentice-Hall.

Elmi, Afyare Abdi. 2010. *Understanding the Somalia Conflagration.* London: Pluto Press.

Ertman, Thomas. 1997. *Birth of the Leviathan: Building States and Regimes in Medieval and Early Modern Europe.* New York: Cambridge University Press.

al-Essawi, Rafe, and Atheel al-Nujafi. 2014, July 28. Let Sunnis Defeat Iraq's Militants. *New York Times*, p. A15.

Fahim, Kareen. 2015, January 30. Government Allies Are Said to Have Slaughtered Dozens of Sunnis in Iraq. *New York Times*, p. A10.

Fearon, James D. 1998. Bargaining, Enforcement, and International Cooperation. *International Organization* 52 (2): 269–305.

———. 2007. Iraq's Civil War. *Foreign Affairs* 86 (2): 2–15.

Fearon, James D., and David D. Laitin. 2004. Neotrusteeship and the Problem of Weak States. *International Security* 28 (4): 5–43.

Feith, Douglas J. 2008. *War and Decision: Inside the Pentagon at the Dawn of the War on Terrorism.* New York: Harper.

Ferguson, Niall. 2004. *Colossus: The Price of America's Empire.* New York: Penguin Press.

Fergusson, James. 2013. *The World's Most Dangerous Place: Inside the Outlaw State of Somalia.* Boston: Da Capo Press.

Fertik, Bob. 2007. John Bolton's Astonishing Neo-Neo-con Rewrite of History. http://www.democrats.com/bolton-rewrites-history.

Filippov, Mikhail, Peter C. Ordeshook, and Olga Shvetsova. 2004. *Designing Federalism: A Theory of Self-Sustainable Federal Institutions.* New York: Cambridge University Press.

Filkins, Dexter. 2008. *The Forever War.* New York: Vintage.

Fisman, Raymond. 2001. Estimating the Value of Political Connections. *American Economic Review* 91 (4): 1095–1102.

Flathman, Richard E. 1980. *The Practice of Political Authority: Authority and the Authoritative.* Chicago: University of Chicago Press.

Foote, Christopher, William Block, Keith Crane, and Simon Gray. 2004. Economic Policy and Prospects in Iraq. *Journal of Economic Perspectives* 18 (3): 47–70.

Freedman, Lawrence, and Efraim Karsh. 1993. *The Gulf Conflict, 1990–1991: Diplomacy and War in the New World Order.* Princeton, NJ: Princeton University Press.

Freeman, Waldo D., Robert B. Lambert, and Jason D. Mims. 1993. Operational Restore Hope: A US CENTCOM Perspective. *Military Review* 73 (9): 61–72.

Frieden, Jeffry A. 1999. Actors and Preferences in International Relations. In *Strategic Choice and International Relations,* edited by D. A. Lake and R. Powell, 39–76. Princeton, NJ: Princeton University Press.

Frieden, Jeffry A., and Ronald Rogowski. 1996. The Impact of the International Economy on National Policies: An Analytical Overview. In *Internationalization and Domestic Politics,* edited by R. O. Keohane and H. V. Milner, 25–47. New York: Cambridge University Press.

Friedman, Thomas L. 2014, August 9. Obama on the World. *New York Times,* p. A19.

Fukuyama, Francis. 1992. *The End of History and the Last Man.* New York: Free Press.

———. 2006a. *America at the Crossroads: Democracy, Power, and the Neoconservative Legacy.* New Haven, CT: Yale University Press.

———, ed. 2006b. *Nation-Building: Beyond Afghanistan and Iraq.* Baltimore: Johns Hopkins University Press.

———. 2011. *The Origins of Political Order.* New York: Farrar, Straus and Giroux.

———. 2014. *Political Order and Political Decay.* New York: Farrar, Straus and Giroux.

Galbraith, Peter W. 2006. *The End of Iraq: How American Incompetence Created a War without End.* New York: Simon and Schuster.

Gambetta, Diego. 1993. *The Sicilian Mafia: The Busiess of Private Protection.* Cambridge, MA: Harvard University Press.

Garoweonline. 2011. Somalia President, Parliament Speaker Dispute over TFG Term. http://www.garoweonline.com/artman2/publish/Somalia_27/Somalia_President _Parliament_Speaker_dispute_over_TFG_term_gazette.shtml.

George, John M. 2005. The Politics of Peace: The Challenge of Civil-Military Cooperation in Somalia. *Public Administration and Management* 10 (2): 153–190.

Gerber, Alan S., Gregory A. Huber, David Doherty, and Conor M. Dowling. 2011. The Big Five Personality Traits in the Political Arena. *Annual Review of Political Science* 14, 265–287.

Gerges, Fawaz A. 2009. *The Far Enemy: Why Jihad Went Global.* 2nd ed. New York: Cambridge University Press.

Gettleman, Jeffrey. 2006, September 24. Islamists Calm Somali Capital with Restraint. *New York Times,* pp. A1, 10.

——. 2007a, January 2. After 15 Years, Someone's in Charge in Somalia, if Barely. *New York Times*, p. A6.

——. 2007b, January 8. Islamists out, Somalia Tried to Rise from Chaos. *New York Times*, pp. A1, A10.

——. 2007c, January 22. In Somalia, New Government Faces Age-Old Trouble of Chaos. *New York Times*, pp. A1, A10.

——. 2007d, February 21. The New Somalia: A Grimly Familiar Rerun of Chaos. *New York Times*, p. A3.

——. 2007e, March 7. The Other Somalia: An Island of Stability in a Sea of Armed Chaos. *New York Times*, p. A11.

Ghani, Ashraf, and Clare Lockhart. 2008. *Fixing Failed States: A Framework for Rebuilding a Fractured World*. New York: Oxford University Press.

Girod, Desha M. 2015. *Explaining Post-Conflict Reconstruction*. New York: Oxford University Press.

Glanville, Luke. 2014. *Sovereignty and the Responsibility to Protect: A New History*. Chicago: University of Chicago Press.

Gordon, Michael R., and Alissa J. Rubin. 2014, July 4. Kurdish Officials Seek More Autonomy in Any Deal with a New Government. *New York Times*, p. A9.

Gordon, Michael R., and Bernard E. Trainor. 2006. *Cobra II: The Inside Story of the Invasion and Occupation of Iraq*. New York: Pantheon.

——. 2012. *The Endgame: The Inside Story of the Struggle for Iraq, from George W. Bush to Barack Obama*. New York: Vintage.

Gourevitch, Peter. 1986. *Politics in Hard Times: Comparative Responses to International Economic Crises*. Ithaca, NY: Cornell University Press.

——. 1999. The Governance Problem in International Relations. In *Strategic Choice and International Relations*, edited by D. A. Lake and R. Powell, 137–164. Princeton, NJ: Princeton University Press.

Gravingholt, Jorn, Julia Leininger, and Christian von Haldenwang. 2012. *Effective Statebuilding? A Review of Evaluations of International Statebuilding Support in Fragile Contexts*. Copenhagen: Ministry of Foreign Affairs of Denmark.

Gross, Leo. 1948. The Peace of Westphalia, 1648–1948. *American Journal of International Law* 42 (1): 20–41.

Haggard, Stephan. 1990. *Pathways from the Periphery: The Newly Industrializing Countries in the International System*. Ithaca, NY: Cornell University Press.

Hagmann, Tobias. 2014. *Talking Peace in the Ogaden: The Search for an End to Conflict in the Somali Regional State in Ethiopia*. London: Rift Valley Institute.

Haidt, Jonathan. 2012. *The Righteous Mind: Why Good People Are Divided by Politics and Religion*. New York: Pantheon.

Hamilton, Alexander, John Jay, and James Madison. 1961. *The Federalist Papers (1787–88)*. New York: Penguin.

Hansen, Stig Jarle, and Mark Bradbury. 2007. Somaliland: A New Democracy in the Horn of Africa? *Review of African Political Economy* 34 (113): 461–476.

Hanson, Stephanie, and Eben Kaplan. 2008. Somalia's Transitional Government. *Backgrounder*. http://www.cfr.org/somalia/somalias-transitional-government/p12475.

Harper, Mary. 2012. *Getting Somalia Wrong? Faith, War, and Hope in a Shattered State*. New York: Zed Books.

Harvey, Frank P. 2012. *Explaining the Iraq War: Counterfactual Theory, Logic and Evidence*. New York: Cambridge University Press.

Hatemi, Peter K., and Rose McDermott. 2012. The Genetics of Politics: Discovery, Challenges, and Progress. *Trends in Genetics* 28 (10): 525–533.

Hathaway, Oona. 1998. Positive Feedback: The Impact of Trade Liberalization on Industry Demands for Protection. *International Organization* 52 (3): 575–612.

Havercroft, Jonathan. 2012. Was Westphalia "All That"? Hobbes, Bellarmine, and the Norm of Non-intervention. *Global Constitutionalism* 1 (1): 120–140.

Hawkins, Darren, David A. Lake, Daniel Nielson, and Michael J. Tierney. 2006. Delegation under Anarchy: States, International Organizations, and Principal-Agent Theory. In *Delegation and Agency in International Organizations*, edited by D. Hawkins, D. A. Lake, D. Nielson, and M. J. Tierney, 3–38. New York: Cambridge University Press.

Heathershaw, John, and Daniel Lambach. 2008. Introduction: Post-Conflict Spaces and Approaches to Statebuilding. *Journal of Intervention and Statebuilding* 2 (3): 269–289.

Hegre, Havard, Tanja Ellingsen, Scott Gates, and Nils Petter Gleditsch. 2001. Toward a Democratic Civil Peace? Democracy, Political Change, and Civil War, 1816–1992. *American Political Science Review* 95 (1): 33–48.

Helander, Bernhard. 1998. The Emperor's New Clothes Removed: A Critique of Besteeman's "Violent Politics and the Politics of Violence." *American Ethnologist* 25 (3): 489–491.

Helander, Bernhard, Mohamed H. Mukhtar, and I. M. Lewis. 1995. *Building Peace from Below: A Critical Review of the District Councils in the Bay and Bakool Regions of Southern Somalia*. Uppsala: Life and Peace Insitute.

Henrich, Joseph, Robert Boyd, Samuel Bowles, Colin F. Camerer, Ernst Fehr, and Herbert Gintis, eds. 2004. *Foundations of Human Sociality: Economic Experiments and Ethnographic Evidence from Fifteen Small-Scale Societies*. New York: Oxford University Press.

Herbst, Jeffrey. 2000. *States and Power in Africa: Comparative Lessons in Authority and Control*. Princeton, NJ: Princeton University Press.

Herring, Eric, and Glen Rangwala. 2006. *Iraq in Fragments: The Occupation and Its Legacy*. Ithaca, NY: Cornell University Press.

Hesse, Brian J. 2010a. Introduction: The Myth of "Somalia." *Journal of Contemporary African Studies* 28 (3): 247–259.

———. 2010b. Where Somalia Works. *Journal of Contemporary African Studies* 28 (3): 343–362.

———. 2014. Two Generations, Two Interventions in One of the World's Most-Failed States: The United States, Kenya, and Ethiopia in Somalia. *Journal of Asian and African Studies*. doi:10.1177/0021909614552919.

Hirsch, John L., and Robert B. Oakley. 1995. *Somalia and Operation Restore Hope: Reflections on Peacemaking and Peacekeeping*. Washington, DC: United States Institute for Peace.

Hobbes, Thomas. 1651/1962. *Leviathan*. London: Collier.

Hoddie, Matthew, and Caroline Hartzell. 2005. Power Sharing in Peace Settlements: Initiating the Transition from Civil War. In *Sustainable Peace: Power and Democracy after Civil Wars*, edited by P. G. Roeder and D. Rothchild, 83–106. Ithaca, NY: Cornell University Press.

Hoehne, Markus Virgil. 2013. Limits of Hydrid Political Orders: The Case of Somaliland. *Journal of Eastern African Studies* 7 (2): 199–217.

Holcombe, Randall G. 1989. The Median Voter Model in Public Choice Theory. *Public Choice* 61 (2): 115–125.

Hubbard, Ben. 2014, November 16. Iraq and U.S. Find Some Potential Sunni Allies Have Already Been Lost. *New York Times*, p. 16.

———. 2015, June 17. ISIS Takes Root, Mixing Service with Strictures. *New York Times*, p. A1.

Huliaras, Asteris. 2002. The Viability of Somaliland: Internal Constraints and Regional Geopolitics. *Journal of Contemporary African Studies* 20 (2): 157–182.

Huntington, Samuel P. 1968. *Political Order in Changing Societies*. New Haven, CT: Yale University Press.

Hurd, Ian. 1999. Legitimacy and Authority in International Relations. *International Organization* 53 (2): 379–408.

———. 2007. *After Anarchy: Legitimacy and Power in the United Nations Security Council*. Princeton, NJ: Princeton University Press.

Hyde, Susan. 2011. *The Pseudo-Democrat's Dilemma: Why Election Monitoring Became an International Norm*. Ithaca, NY: Cornell University Press.

Ibrahim, Mohamed. 2010. Somalia and Global Terrorism: A Growing Connection? *Journal of Contemporary African Studies* 28 (3): 283–295.

ICC. 2014. *Somali Pirate Clampdown Caused Drop in Global Piracy, IMB Reveals*. Paris: International Chamber of Commerce.

ICG. 2008. *Somalia: To Move beyond the Failed State*. ICG Africa report, no. 147. Nairobi: International Crisis Group.

——. 2011. *Somalia: The Transitional Government on Life Support*. ICG Africa report, no. 170. Nairobi: International Crisis Group.

——. 2012a. *The Kenyan Military Intervention in Somalia*. ICG Africa report, no. 184. Nairobi: International Crisis Group.

——. 2012b. *Kenyan Somali Islamist Radicalisation*. ICG Africa briefing, no. 85. Nairobi: International Crisis Group.

——. 2014. *Somalia: Al-Shabaab—It Will Be a Long War*. ICG Africa briefing, no. 99. Nairobi: International Crisis Group.

Ikenberry, G. John. 2001. *After Victory: Institutions, Strategic Restraint, and the Rebuilding of Order after Major Wars*. Princeton, NJ: Princeton University Press.

——. 2011. *Liberal Leviathan: The Origins, Crisis, and Transformation of the American World Order*. Princeton, NJ: Princeton University Press.

Inglehart, Ronald. 1997. *Modernization and Postmodernization: Cultural, Economic, and Political Change in 43 Societies*. Princeton, NJ: Princeton University Press.

International Crisis Group. *See* ICG

Isikoff, Michael, and David Corn. 2007. *Hubris: The Inside Story of Spin, Scandal, and the Selling of the Iraq War*. With a new afterword. New York: Three Rivers Press.

Jackson, Robert H. 1990. *Quasi-states: Sovereignty, International Relations and the Third World*. New York: Cambridge University Press.

Jackson, Robert H., and Carl G. Rosberg. 1982. Why Africa's Weak States Persist: The Empirical and Juridical in Statehood. *World Politics* 35 (1): 1–24.

Jamal, Amaney A. 2012. *Of Empires and Citizens: Pro-American Democracy or No Democracy at All?* Princeton, NJ: Princeton University Press.

Jentleson, Bruce. 1998. Preventive Diplomacy and Ethnic Conflict: Possible, Difficult, Necessary. In *The International Spread of Ethnic Conflict: Fear, Diffusion, and Escalation*, edited by D. A. Lake and D. Rothchild, 293–316. Princeton, NJ: Princeton University Press.

Johnston, Harry, and Ted Dagne. 1997. Congress and the Somalia Crisis. In *Learning from Somalia: The Lessons of Armed Intervention*, edited by W. Clarke and J. Herbst, 191–207. Boulder, CO: Westview Press.

Kahler, Miles. 2001. Conclusion: The Causes and Consequences of Legalization. In *Legalization and World Politics*, edited by J. Goldstein, M. Kahler, R. O. Keohane, and A.-M. Slaughter, 277–299. Cambridge, MA: MIT Press.

Kaplan, Fred. 2013. *The Insurgents: David Petraeus and the Plot to Change the American Way of War*. New York: Simon and Schuster.

Kaplan, S. 2008. The Remarkable Story of Somaliland. *Journal of Democracy* 19 (3): 143–157.

Kapstein, Ethan B. 2014. How to Do Intervention without Blowing Stuff Up. http://www.foreignpolicy.com/articles/2014/05/27/how_to_do_intervention_without_blowing_stuff_up_cold_war.

Katzenstein, Peter J. 1985. *Small States in World Markets: Industrial Policy in Europe*. Ithaca, NY: Cornell University Press.

Keene, Edward. 2002. *Beyond the Anarchical Society: Grotius, Colonialism and Order in World Politics*. New York: Cambridge University Press.

Keister, Jennifer. 2011. States within States: How Rebels Rule. PhD diss., University of California–San Diego, La Jolla, CA.

Kennedy, Kevin M. 1997. The Relationship between the Military and Humanitarian Organizations in Operation Restore Hope. In *Learning from Somalia: The Lessons of Armed Humanitarian Intervention*, edited by W. Clarke and J. Herbst, 99–117. Boulder, CO: Westview Press.

Kinzer, Stephen. 2006. *Overthrow: America's Century of Regime Change from Hawaii to Iraq.* New York: Times Books.

Kirkpatrick, David D. 2014, November 24. Graft Hobbles Iraq's Military in Fighting ISIS. *New York Times*, pp. A1, A3.

Kramer, Gerald H. 1977. A Dynamical Model of Political Equilbrium. *Journal of Economic Theory* 16 (2): 310–334.

Krasner, Stephen D. 1999. *Sovereignty: Organized Hypocrisy.* Princeton, NJ: Princeton University Press.

——. 2004. Sharing Sovereignty: New Institutions for Collapsed and Failing States. *International Security* 29 (2): 85–120.

——. (Producer). 2013, December 30. Seeking "Good-Enough-Governance"—Not Democracy. http://blogs.reuters.com/great-debate/2013/09/22/seeking-good-enough-governance-not-democracy/.

Kruzel, John J. 2009, January 2. U.S. Deaths in Iraq Decrease in 2008. *DoD News.* http://www.defense.gov/news/newsarticle.aspx?id=52539.

Kuran, Timur. 1991. Now out of Never: The Element of Surprise in the East European Revolution of 1989. *World Politics* 44 (1): 7–48.

——. 1995. *Private Truths, Public Lies: The Social Consequences of Preference Falsification.* Cambridge, MA: Harvard University Press.

LaFeber, Walter. 1983. *Inevitable Revolutions: The United States in Central America.* New York: W. W. Norton.

——. 1994. *The American Age: U.S. Foreign Policy at Home and Abroad, 1750 to the Present.* 2nd ed. New York: W. W. Norton.

Laitin, David D. 1976. The Political Economy of Military Rule in Somalia. *Journal of Modern African Studies* 14 (3): 449–468.

Laitin, David D., and Said S. Samatar. 1987. *Somalia: Nation in Search of a State.* Boulder, CO: Westview Press.

Lake, David A. 1999. *Entangling Relations: American Foreign Policy in Its Century.* Princeton, NJ: Princeton University Press.

——. 2009. *Hierarchy in International Relations.* Ithaca, NY: Cornell University Press.

——. 2010a. The Practice and Theory of U.S. Statebuilding. *Journal of Intervention and Statebuilding* 4 (3): 257–284.

——. 2010b. Rightful Rules: Authority, Order, and the Foundations of Global Governance. *International Studies Quarterly* 54 (3): 587–613.

——. 2010–11. Two Cheers for Bargaining Theory: Rationalist Explanations of the Iraq War. *International Security* 35 (3): 7–52.

——. 2013a. Iraq: U.S. Approaches to Statebuilding in the Twenty-First Century. In *The Routledge Handbook of International Statebuilding*, edited by D. Chandler and T. D. Sisk, 293–303. New York: Routledge.

——. 2013b. Legitimating Power: The Domestic Politics of U.S. International Hierarchy. *International Security* 38 (2): 74–111.

——. 2014. Crises of Authority: Domestic Structures and the Changing American Imperium. In *Power in a Complex Global System*, edited by L. W. Pauly and B. Jentleson, 115–130. New York: Routledge.

——. 2015. *Origins of Hierarchies: Laws, Norms, and Sovereignty.* Prepared for the workshop on Hierarchies in World Politics, University of Cambridge, June 21–22, 2015.

Lake, David A., and Matthew A. Baum. 2001. The Invisible Hand of Democracy: Political Control and the Provision of Public Services. *Comparative Political Studies* 34 (6): 587–621.

Lake, David A., and Christopher Fariss. 2014. International Trusteeship: External Authority in Areas of Limited Statehood. *Governance* 27 (4): 569–587.

Lake, David A., and Donald Rothchild. 1996. Containing Fear: The Origins and Management of Ethnic Conflict. *International Security* 21 (2): 41–75.

Lake, David A., and Donald Rothchild, eds. 1998. *The International Spread of Ethnic Conflict: Fear, Diffusion, and Escalation*. Princeton, NJ: Princeton University Press.

Lake, David A., and Donald Rothchild. 2005. Territorial Decentralization and Civil War Settlements. In *Sustainable Peace: Power and Democracy after Civil Wars*, edited by P. G. Roeder and D. Rothchild, 109–132. Ithaca, NY: Cornell University Press.

Lansing, J. Stephen. 2006. *Perfect Order: Recognizing Complexity in Bali*. Princeton, NJ: Princeton University Press.

Lasswell, Harold D., and Abraham Kaplan. 1950. *Power and Society: A Framework for Analysis*. New Haven, CT: Yale University Press.

Leeson, Peter T. 2007. Better off Stateless: Somalia before and after Government Collapse. *Journal of Comparative Economics* 35 (4): 689–710.

Levi, Margaret. 1988. *Of Rule and Revenue*. Berkeley: University of California Press.

Levi, Margaret, Audrey Sacks, and Tom R. Tyler. 2009. Conceptualizing Legitimacy, Measuring Legitimate Beliefs. *American Behavioral Scientist* 53 (3): 354–375.

Lewis, I. M. 2002. *A Modern History of the Somali*. Revised, updated, and expanded ed. Oxford: James Currey.

———. 2004. Visible and Indivisible Differences: The Somali Paradox. *Africa: Journal of the International African Institute* 74 (4): 489–515.

———. 2008. *Understanding Somalia and Somaliland*. New York: Columbia University Press.

———. 2010. *Making and Breaking States in Africa: The Somali Experience*. Trenton, NJ: Red Sea Press.

Lijphart, Arend. 1968. *The Politics of Accommodation: Pluralism and Democracy in the Netherlands*. Berkeley: University of California Press.

Lohmann, Susanne. 1994. The Dynamics of Informational Cascades: The Monday Demonstrations in Leipzig, East Germany, 1989–1991. *World Politics* 47 (1): 42–101.

Loveman, Brian. 2010. *No Higher Law: American Foreign Policy and the Western Hemisphere since 1776*. Chapel Hill: University of North Carolina Press.

Lowenthal, Abraham F. 1995. *The Dominican Intervention*. Baltimore: Johns Hopkins University Press.

MacDonald, Paul K. 2014. *Networks of Domination: The Social Foundations of Peripheral Conquest in International Politics*. New York: Oxford University Press.

Mackie, Gerry. 2003. *Democracy Defended*. New York: Cambridge University Press.

Mansfield, Edward, and Jack Snyder. 2007. The Sequencing "Fallacy." *Journal of Democracy* 18 (3): 5–9.

Markey, Daniel. 2008. Securing Pakistan's Tribal Belt. *Center for Preventive Action*. Council Special Report No. 36. New York: Council on Foreign Relations.

Marquette, Heather, and Danielle Beswick. 2011. State Building, Security and Development: State Building as a New Development Paradigm. *Third World Quarterly* 32 (10): 1703–1714.

Marr, Phebe. 2006. *Who Are Iraq's New Leaders? What Do They Want?* Special report, no. 160. Washington, DC: United States Institute of Peace.

Matanock, Aila. 2013. Bullets for Ballots: Examining the Effect of Electoral Participation on Conflict Recurrence. Working paper, University of California–Berkeley.

Mazarr, Michael J. 2014. The Rise and Fall of the Failed-State Paradigm: Requiem for a Decade of Distraction. *Foreign Affairs* 93 (1): 113–121.

McGarry, Stephen. 2013. *Irish Brigades Abroad*. Dublin: History Press Ireland.

McKelvey, Richard D. 1976. Intransitivities in Multi-dimensional Voting Models and Some Implications for Agenda Control. *Journal of Economic Theory* 12 (3): 472–482.

———. 1979. General Conditions for Global Intransitivities in Formal Voting Models. *Econometrica* 47 (5): 1085–1112.

McLoughlin, Claire. 2015. When Does Service Delivery Improve the Legitimacy of a Fragile or Conflict-Affected State? *Governance* 28 (3): 341–356.

McMahon, R. Blake, and Branislav Slantchev. 2015. The Guardianship Dilemma: Regime Security through and from the Armed Forces. *American Political Science Review* 109 (2): 297–313.

Menkhaus, Ken. 2003. State Collapse in Somalia: Second Thoughts. *Review of African Political Economy* 30 (97): 405–422.

———. 2009. Somalia: "They Created a Desert and Called It Peace(building)." *Review of African Political Economy* 36 (120): 223–233.

Miller, John. 1999. Greetings America, My Name Is Osama Bin Laden. http://www.pbs.org/wgbh/pages/frontline/shows/binladen/who/miller.html.

Miller, Paul D. 2013. *Armed State Building: Confronting State Falure, 1898–2013*. Ithaca, NY: Cornell University Press.

Mills, Greg, J. Peter Pham, and David Kilcullen. 2013. *Somalia: Fixing Africa's Most Failed State*. Cape Town: Tafelberg (Kindle Edition).

Moller, Bjorn. 2009. *The Somali Conflict: The Role of External Actors*. DIIS report. Copenhagen: Danish Institute for International Studies.

Monroe, Burt L. 1994. Disproportionality and Malapportionment: Measuring Electoral Inequity. *Electoral Studies* 13 (2): 132–149.

Monten, Jonathan. 2014. Intervention and State-Building: Comparative Lessons from Japan, Iraq, and Afghanistan. *Annals of the American Academy of Political and Social Science* 656 (November): 173–191.

Moore, Jack. 2015, February 9. ISIS Grows "International Footprint" as Affiliate Jihadist Groups Spring Up. *Newsweek*.

Myerson, Roger B. 2006. Federalism and Incentives for Success of Democracy. *Quarterly Journal of Political Science* 1 (1): 3–23.

North, Douglass C. 1981. *Structure and Change in Economic History*. New York: W. W. Norton.

North, Douglass C., John Joseph Wallis, and Barry R. Weingast. 2009. *Violence and Social Orders: A Conceptual Framework for Interpreting Recorded Human History*. New York: Cambridge University Press.

North, Douglass C., and Barry R. Weingast. 1989. Constitutions and Commitment: The Evolution of the Institutions of Public Choice in 17th Century England. *Journal of Economic History* 49 (4): 803–832.

Olson, Mancur. 1982. *The Rise and Decline of Nations: Economic Growth, Stagflation, and Social Rigidities*. New Haven, CT: Yale University Press.

———. 2000. *Power and Prosperity: Outgrowing Communist and Capitalist Dictatorships*. New York: Basic Books.

Onuf, Nicholas Greenwood. 1998. *The Republican Legacy in International Thought*. New York: Cambridge University Press.

Osiander, Andreas. 2001. Sovereignty, International Relations, and the Westphalian Myth. *International Organization* 55 (2): 251–287.

Ostrom, Elinor. 1990. *Governing the Commons*. New York: Cambridge University Press.

Owen, John M., IV. 2002. The Foreign Imposition of Domestic Institutions. *International Organization* 56 (2): 375–409.

Packer, George. 2005. *The Assassins' Gate: America in Iraq*. New York: Farrar, Straus and Giroux.

Pan, Jennifer, and Yiqing Xu. 2015. *China's Ideological Spectrum*. MIT Political Science Department Research Paper No. 2015-6.

Papagianni, Katia. 2007. State Building and Transitional Politics in Iraq: The Perils of a Top-Down Transition. *International Studies Perspectives* 8 (3): 253–271.

Paris, Roland. 2004. *At War's End: Building Peace after Civil Conflict*. New York: Cambridge University Press.

Parker, Tom. 2003. *The Ultimate Intervention: Revitalizing the UN Trusteeship Council for the 21st Century*. Sandvika: Center for European and Asian Studies, Norwegian School of Management.

Patman, Robert G. 1997. Disarming Somalia: The Contrasting Fortunes of United States and Australian Peacekeepers during United Nations Intervention, 1992–1993. *African Affairs* 96 (385): 509–533.

Patrick, Stewart. 2006. Weak States and Global Threats: Fact or Faction? *Washington Quarterly* 29 (2): 27–53.

———. 2007. "Failed" States and Global Security: Empirical Questions and Policy Dilemmas. *International Studies Review* 9 (4): 644–662.

Patty, John W., and Elizabeth Maggie Penn. 2014. *Social Choice and Legitimacy: The Possibilities of Impossibility*. New York: Cambridge University Press.

Peace Corps. n.d. Peace Corps, History, Decades of Service, 1960s. http://www.peacecorps.gov/about/history/decades/1960/.

Pedersen, Jon. 2007. Three Wars Later . . . Iraqi Living Conditions. In *Iraq: Preventing a New Generation of Conflict*, edited by M. E. Bouillon, D. M. Malone, and B. Rowswell, 55–70. Boulder, CO: Lynne Rienner.

Pei, Minxin, Samia Amin, and Seth Garz. 2006 Building Nations: The American Experience. In *Nation-Building: Beyond Afghanistan and Iraq*, edited by Francis Fukuyama, 64–85. Baltimore: Johns Hopkins University Press.

Peterson, Scott. 2000. *Me against My Brother: At War in Somalia, Sudan, and Rwanda*. New York: Routledge.

Pevehouse, Jon C. 2005. *Democracy from Above? Regional Organizations and Democratization*. New York: Cambridge University Press.

Pham, J. Peter. 2010. Putting Somali Piracy in Context. *Journal of Contemporary African Studies* 28 (3): 325–341.

———. 2011. Somalia: Where a State Isn't a State. *Fletcher Forum of World Affairs* 35 (2): 133–151.

———, ed. 2013. *State Collapse, Insurgency, and Counterinsurgency: Lessons from Somalia*. Carlisle, PA: U.S. Army War College Press.

Phillips, Andrew, and J. C. Sharman. 2015. *International Order in Diversity: War, Trade, and Rule in the Indian Ocean*. New York: Cambridge University Press.

Pickering, Jeffrey, and Emizet F. Kisangani. 2014. Foreign Military Intervention and Post-Colonial State-Building: An Actor-centric Analysis. *Conflict Management and Peace Science* 3 (3): 244–264.

Pollack, Kenneth M. 2015, February 4. ISIS Is Losing Iraq. But What Happens Next? *New York Times*, p. A23.

Porch, Douglas. 2013. *Counterinsurgency: Exposing the Myths of the New Way of War*. New York: Cambridge University Press.

Posen, Barry R. 1993. The Security Dilemma and Ethnic Conflict. *Survival* 35 (1): 27–47.

Pouligny, Beatrice. 2006. *Peace Operations Seen from Below: UN Missions and Local People*. Bloomfield, CT: Kumarian Press.

Przeworski, Adam, Michael E. Alvarez, Jose Antonio Cheibub, and Fernando Limongi. 2000. *Democracy and Development: Political Institutions and Well-Being in the World, 1950–2000*. New York: Cambridge University Press.

Rawls, John. 1999. *A Theory of Justice*. Cambridge, MA: Harvard University Press.

Reilly, Benjamin. 2002. Post-Conflict Elections: Constraints and Dangers. *International Peacekeeping* 9 (2): 118–139.

———. 2008. Post-Conflict Elections: Uncertain Turning Points of Transition. In *From War to Democracy: Dilemmas of Peacebuilding*, edited by A. Jarstad and T. D. Sisk, 157–181. New York: Cambridge University Press.

Renders, Marleen. 2007. Appropriate "Governance-Technology"? Somali Clan Elders and Institutions in the Making of the "Republic of Somaliland." *Afrika Specturm* 42 (3): 439–459.

Reus-Smit, Christian. 1999. *The Moral Purpose of the State: Culture, Social Identity, and Institutional Rationality in International Relations.* Princeton, NJ: Princeton University Press.

Rice, Condoleezza. 2011. *No Higher Honor: A Memoir of My Years in Washington.* New York: Crown.

Richmond, Oliver P. 2014. Jekyll or Hyde: What Is Statebuilding Creating? Evidence from the "Field." *Cambridge Review of International Affairs* 27 (1): 1–20.

Richmond, Oliver P., and Audra Mitchell, eds. 2012. *Hybrid Forms of Peace: From Everyday Agency to Post-Liberalism.* New York: Palgrave Macmillan.

Ricks, Thomas E. 2006. *Fiasco: The American Military Adventure in Iraq.* New York: Penguin Press.

———. 2009. *The Gamble: General David Petraeus and the American Military Adventure in Iraq, 2006–2008.* New York: Penguin.

Riker, William H. 1980. Implications from the Disequilibrium of Majority Rule for the Study of Institutions. *American Political Science Review* 74 (2): 432–446.

———. 1984. The Heresthetics of Constitution-Making: The Presidency in 1787, with Comments on Determinism and Rational Choice. *American Political Science Review* 78 (1): 1–16.

Risse, Thomas, ed. 2011. *Governance without A State? Politics and Politics in Areas of Limited Statehood.* New York: Columbia University Press.

Roberts, J. Timmons, and Any Hite. 1999. *From Modernization to Globalization: Social Perspectives on International Development.* Malden, MA: Blackwell.

Robinson, Linda. 2008. *Tell Me How This Ends: General David Patraeus and the Search for a Way out of Iraq.* New York: PublicAffairs.

Roeder, Philip G. 2005. Power Dividing as an Alternative to Ethnic Power Sharing. In *Sustainable Peace: Power and Democracy after Civil Wars,* edited by Philip G. Roeder and Donald Rothchild, 51–82. Ithaca, NY: Cornell University Press.

Roeder, Philip G., and Donald Rothchild, eds. 2005. *Sustainable Peace: Power and Democracy after Civil Wars.* Ithaca, NY: Cornell University Press.

Rogowski, Ronald. 1989. *Commerce and Coalitions: How Trade Affects Domestic Political Alignments.* Princeton, NJ: Princeton University Press.

Romer, Thomas, and Howard L. Rosenthal. 1978. Political Resource Allocation, Controlled Agendas, and the Status Quo. *Public Choice* 33 (4), 27–43.

Rostow, Walt W. 1960. *The Stages of Economic Growth: A Non-communist Manifesto.* New York: Cambridge University Press.

Rotberg, Robert I., ed. 2004. *When States Fail: Causes and Consequences.* Princeton, NJ: Princeton University Press.

Rowswell, Ben, Markus E. Bouillon, and David M. Malone. 2007. Looking Back: State Fragility and a Generation of Conflict. In *Iraq: Preventing a New Generation of Conflict,* edited by M. E. Bouillon, D. M. Malone, and B. Rowswell, 1–19. Boulder, CO: Lynne Rienner.

Roy, Olivier. 2004. Development and Political Legitimacy: The Cases of Iraq and Afghanistan. *Conflict, Security and Development* 4 (2): 167–179.

Sabl, Andrew. 2015. The Two Cultures of Democratic Theory: Responsiveness, Democratic Quality, and the Empirical-Normative Divide. *Perspectives on Politics* 13 (2): 345–365.

Sahnoun, Mohamed. 1994. *Somalia: The Missed Opportunities.* Washington, DC: United States Institute of Peace Press.

Salehyan, Idean. 2009. *Rebels without Borders: Transnational Insurgencies in World Politics.* Ithaca, NY: Cornell University Press.

Samatar, Said S. 2010. An Open Letter to Uncle Sam: America, Pray Leave Somalia to Its Own Devices. *Journal of Contemporary African Studies* 28 (3): 313–323.

Samuels, David, and Richard Snyder. 2001. The Value of a Vote: Malapportionment in Comparative Perspective. *British Journal of Political Science* 31 (1): 651–671.

Schelling, Thomas C. 1966. *Arms and Influence.* New Haven, CT: Yale University Press.

Schmidt, Michael S., and Jack Healy. 2011, December 27. Powerful Iraqi Bloc Calls for New Elections in Blow to Government. *New York Times*, p. A8.

Schmitt, Eric, and Michael R. Gordon. 2014, July 14. U.S. Sees Risks in Assisting a Compromised Iraq Force. *New York Times*, pp. A1, A8.

Schmitter, Philippe C. 1974. Still the Century of Corporatism? *Review of Politics* 36 (1): 85–131.

Schumpeter, Joseph A. 1942/1994. *Capitalism, Socialism, and Democracy.* London: Routledge.

Schwartz, Thomas. 1987. Votes, Strategies, and Institutions: An Introduction to the Theory of Collective Choice. In *Congress: Structure and Policy*, edited by M. D. McCubbins and T. Sullivan, 318–345. New York: Cambridge University Press.

Scott, James. 1999. *Seeing Like a State: How Certain Schemes to Improve the Human Condition Have Failed.* New Haven, CT: Yale University Press.

Semple, Kirk. 2014, October 16. At War against Islamic State, Iraqi Premier Is Facing Battles Closer to Home. *New York Times*, p. A12.

Sen, Amartya. 1981. *Poverty and Famines: An Essay on Entitlement and Deprivation.* New York: Oxford University Press.

Shabazz, Saeed. 2006. Annan: U.S. Wrong to Support Warlords in Somalia. The Final Call. http://www.finalcall.com/artman/publish/World_News_3/article_2716.shtml.

Shepsle, Kenneth A. 1979. Institutional Arrangements and Equilibrium in Multidimensional Voting Models. *American Journal of Political Science* 23 (1): 27–59.

Shinn, David. 2011. Al Shabaab's Foreign Threat to Somalia. *Orbis* 55 (2): 203–215.

Shleifer, Andrei, and Robert W. Vishny. 1998. *The Grabbing Hand: Government Pathologies and Their Cures.* Cambridge, MA: Harvard University Press.

Simons, Anna, Joe McGraw, and Duane Lauchengco. 2011. *The Sovereignty Solution: A Commonsense Approach to Global Security.* Annapolis, MD: Naval Institute Press.

Sisk, Timothy D. 1992. *Islam and Democracy: Religion, Politics, and Power in the Middle East.* Washington, DC: USIP Press.

——. 2013. *Statebuilding: Consolidating Peace after Civil War.* Malden, MA: Polity Press.

Skocpol, Theda. 1979. *States and Social Revolutions: A Comparative Analysis of France, Russia, and China.* New York: Cambridge University Press.

Smelser, Neil J. 1966. The Modernization of Social Relations. In *Modernization: The Dynamics of Growth*, edited by M. Weiner, 119–148. New York: Basic Books.

Smith, Peter H. 1996. *Talons of the Eagle: Dynamics of U.S.–Latin American Relations.* New York: Oxford University Press.

Snyder, Jack. 2000. *From Voting to Violence: Democratization and Nationalist Violence.* New York: W. W. Norton.

So, Alvin. 1990. *Social Change and Development: Modernization, Dependency and World-Systems Theories.* Newbury Park, CA: Sage.

Sokoloff, Kenneth L., and Stanley L. Engerman. 2000. History Lessons: Institutions, Factor Endowments, and Paths of Development in the New World. *Journal of Economic Perspectives* 14 (3): 217–232.

Spruyt, Hendrik. 1994. *The Sovereign State and Its Competitors: An Analysis of Systems Change.* Princeton, NJ: Princeton University Press.

Stevenson, Jonathan. 1993. Hope Restored in Somalia? *Foreign Policy* (91), 138–154.

Tansey, Oisin. 2013. Evaluating the Legacies of State-Building: Success, Failure, and the Role of Responsibility. *International Studies Quarterly* 58 (1): 174–186.

Thompson, Alexander. 2009. *Channels of Power: The UN Security Council and U.S. Statecraft in Iraq*. Ithaca, NY: Cornell University Press.

Thomson, Janice E. 1994. *Mercenaries, Pirates, and Sovereigns: State-Building and Extraterritorial Violence in Early Modern Europe*. Princeton, NJ: Princeton University Press.

Tilly, Charles. 1990. *Coercion, Capital, and European States, AD 990–1990*. Cambridge, MA: Basil Blackwell.

Tschirgi, Necla. 2010. The Security-Politics-Development Nexus: The Lessons on State-Building in Sub-Saharan Africa. Florence: Robert Schuman Centre for Advanced Studies, European University Institute.

Tyler, Tom R. 1990. *Why People Obey the Law*. New Haven, CT: Yale University Press.

——. 2001. A Psychological Perspective on the Legitimacy of Institutions and Authorities. In *The Psychology of Legitimacy: Emerging Perspectives on Ideology, Justice, and Intergroup Relations*, edited by J. T. Jost and B. Major, 416–435. New York: Cambridge University Press.

United Nations. n.d. Somalia—UNOSOM II Background. http://www.un.org/en/peacekeeping/missions/past/unosom2backgr2.html.

——. 1996. *The United Nations and Somalia, 1992–1996*. Blue Book Series, vol. 8. New York: United Nations.

United States, Department of the Army. 2007. *The U.S. Army/Marine Corps Counterinsurgency Field Manual: U.S. Army Field Manual No. 3-24. Marine Corps Warfighting Publication No. 3-33.5*. Chicago: University of Chicago Press.

United States, Senate, 103rd Congress, 1st Sess. 1993. *Hearings on Current Military Operations in Somalia*. Washington, DC: Government Printing Office.

Vattel, Emmerich de. 1758/2008. *The Law of Nations*. Indianapolis, IN: Liberty Fund.

Verhoeven, Harry. 2009. The Self-Fulfilling Prophecy of Failed States: Somalia, State Collapse, and the Global War on Terror. *Journal of East African Studies* 3 (3): 405–425.

von Einsiedel, Sebastian. 2005. Policy Responses to State Failure. In *Making States Work: State Failure and the Crisis of Governance*, edited by S. Chesterman, M. Ignatieff, and R. Thakur, 13–35. New York: United Nations University Press.

von Hippel, Karin. 2000. *Democracy by Force: US Military Intervention in the Post–Cold War World*. New York: Cambridge University Press.

Walter, Barbara F. 1997. The Critical Barrier to Civil War Settlement. *International Organization* 51 (3): 335–364.

——. 2002. *Committing to Peace: The Successful Settlement of Civil Wars*. Princeton, NJ: Princeton University Press.

War-torn Societies Project. *See* WSP.

Washington, Wayne. 2004, March 2. Once against Nation-Building, Bush Now Involved. *Boston Globe*, p. A11.

Weber, Max. 1978. *Economy and Society*. Berkeley: University of California Press.

Weiner, Mark S. 2013. *The Rule of the Clan: What an Ancient Form of Social Organization Reveals about the Future of Individual Freedom*. New York: Farrar, Straus and Giroux.

Weingast, Barry R. 1995. The Economic Role of Political Institutions: Market-Preserving Federalism and Economic Development. *Journal of Law, Economics, and Organization* 11 (1): 1–31.

——. 1997. The Political Foundations of Democracy and the Rule of Law. *American Political Science Review* 91 (2): 245–263.

Whaites, Alan. 2008. *States in Development: Understanding State-Building*. London: Governance and Social Development Group, Policy and Research Division, Department for International Development.

Williams, Michael C. 2006. The Hobbesian Theory of International Relations: Three Traditions. In *Classical Theory in International Relations*, edited by B. Jahn, 253–276. New York: Cambridge University Press.

Williamson, Oliver E. 1975. *Markets and Hierarchies: Analysis and Antitrust Implications.* New York: Free Press.

——. 1985. *The Economic Institutions of Capitalism: Firms, Markets, and Relational Contracting.* New York: Free Press.

Woods, James L. 1997. U.S. Government Decisionmaking Processes during Humanitarian Operations in Somalia. In *Learning from Somalia: The Lessons of Armed Humanitarian Intervention*, edited by W. Clarke and J. Herbst, 151–172. Boulder, CO: Westview Press.

Woodward, Susan L. 1995. *Balkan Tragedy: Chaos and Dissolution after the Cold War.* Washington, DC: Brookings Institution.

World Bank. 1997. *World Development Report 1997: The State in a Changing World.* New York: Oxford University Press.

Worth, Robert F. 2014, June 27. Redrawn Lines Seen as No Cure in Iraq Conflict. *New York Times*, pp. A1, A8.

WSP. 2005. *Rebuilding Somaliland: Issues and Possibilities.* Lawrenceville, NJ: Red Sea Press.

Yourish, Karen, Tom Giratikanon, and Derek Watkins. 2015, July 18. Where ISIS Has Directed and Inspired Attacks around the World. *New York Times*, p. A8.

Zacher, Mark W. 2001. The Territorial Integrity Norm: International Boundaries and the Use of Force. *International Organization* 55 (2): 215–250.

Zelditch, Morris, Jr. 2001. Theories of Legitimacy. In *The Psychology of Legitimacy: Emerging Perspectives on Ideology, Justice, and Intergroup Relations*, edited by J. T. Jost and B. Major, 33–53. New York: Cambridge University Press.

Acknowledgments

Many friends and colleagues have contributed to the ideas in this book. The late Donald Rothchild taught me much about ethnic conflict and, by extension, failed states. I would have never ventured down this road were it not for his wisdom and initial guidance. Miles Kahler provoked my interest in international trusteeship and helped arrange funding to pursue this line of inquiry through a Carnegie Corporation grant in 2005–2007. In this context, I would like to thank Steve Del Rosso and the Carnegie Corporation for their support; this is a long-delayed payment on that initial investment, and suggests that grants may have unanticipated consequences long after they have ended. Conversations with Miles, our co-taught course on political authority in the international system, and his comments on various papers and especially the penultimate draft of this book have had a profound impact on my thinking. Peter Gourevitch, as ever, has been a friendly critic and interlocutor; the focus on social formations and the need for legitimacy in statebuilding originated in early conversations with Peter, and he has pressed me over the years to refine and extend that line of inquiry in failed states and—though it is not adequately represented here—in statebuilders as well. Peter Halden listened sympathetically as I tried to work through the argument at a particularly important formative stage, and then provided detailed and extensive comments on the manuscript. An anonymous reviewer, Michael Barnett, Desha Girod, and Stephen Krasner also read the penultimate draft and provided helpful comments. Many others—too numerous to thank for fear of slighting someone—read chapters over many different drafts, though Eli Berman, Susan Hyde, and Jason Lyall deserve special thanks.

I have benefited from many opportunities to present this manuscript as a work in progress to diverse audiences. I am especially grateful to the East Asian Peace Program at the Department of Peace and Conflict Research at Uppsala University, which hosted me for an extended visit in fall 2013. It was at this scholarly haven that the main argument of this book took form. Questions and feedback from workshop participants at the University of California–Berkeley; the Peace Research Institute, Frankfurt; the University of California–San Diego; Cornell University; the University of Michigan; Yale University; Emory University; and the Juan March Institute in Madrid were critical in refining the argument and its presentation.

Jennifer Keister did the first research on Somalia in the 1990s; Marissa Cohen updated sources and provided invaluable assistance on the post-2002 period. Christopher Fariss contributed essential empirical research to a paper in which many of the themes in this book were first articulated (eventually appearing as Lake and Fariss 2014). Responsibility for all errors, large and small, remains mine alone.

As always, I am indebted to Wendy, my wife of nearly thirty-seven years and best friend for even longer. From the day we met, she has encouraged my intellectual pursuits without reservation and, indeed, with great forbearance. Her continuing love provides the confidence, freedom, and support necessary to chase ideas for days, weeks, or even years until they are finally corralled, however imperfectly, on paper. For this, and so much more, I am forever grateful.

Index

Page numbers in *italics* refer to figures, tables, or material contained in their captions.